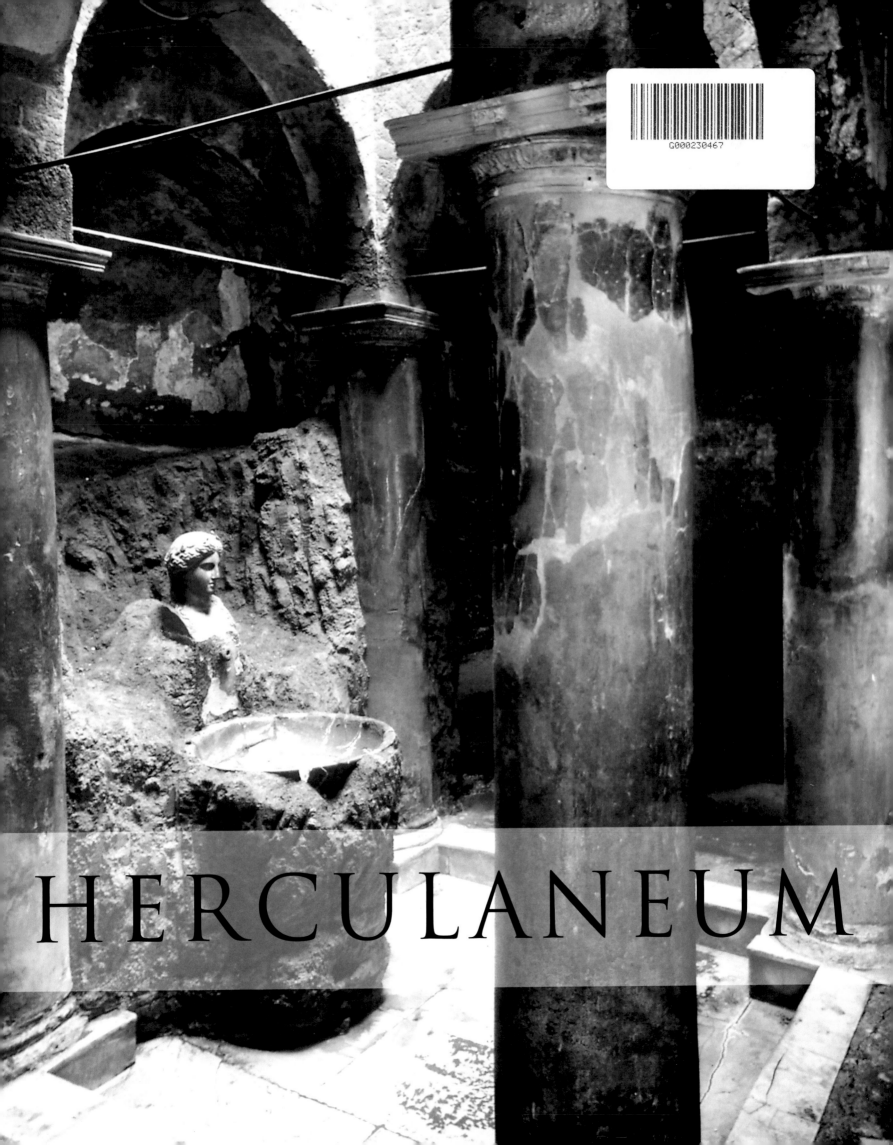

# HERCULANEUM

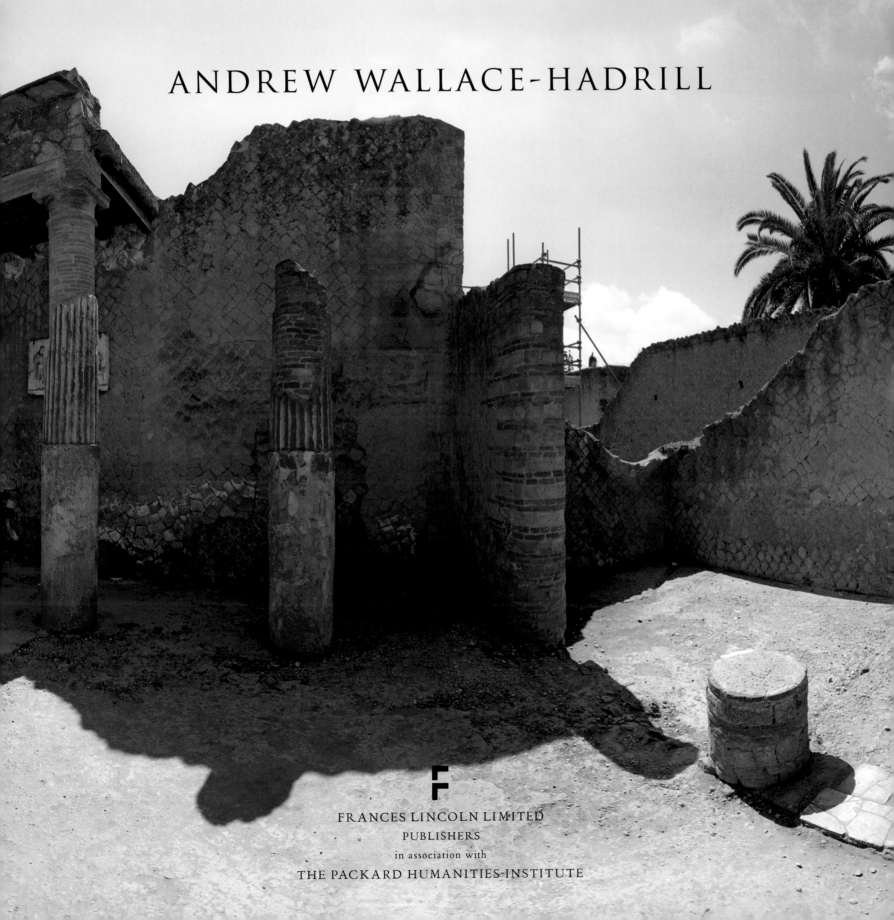

# HERCULANEUM
## PAST AND FUTURE

### ANDREW WALLACE-HADRILL

**F**

FRANCES LINCOLN LIMITED

PUBLISHERS

in association with

THE PACKARD HUMANITIES INSTITUTE

*For Jo*

Frances Lincoln Ltd
4 Torriano Mews
Torriano Avenue
London NW5 2RZ
www.franceslincoln.com

Published in collaboration with
The Packard Humanities Institute
Los Altos, California

First Frances Lincoln edition: 2011
Paperback edition: 2012

Hardback ISBN: 978-0-7112-3142-9
Paperback ISBN: 978-0-7112-3389-8

Printed and bound in China

9 8 7 6 5 4 3 2 1

THE PACKARD HUMANITIES INSTITUTE

THE BRITISH SCHOOL AT ROME

Soprintendenza
Archeologica
Napoli e Pompei

Herculaneum Conservation Project

# CONTENTS

# PREFACE

Pompeii has been the subject of a flood of books, one that grows every year. The site, now attracting not far short of 3 million visitors a year, has become one of our principal, perhaps *the* principal window on the Roman world and on everyday life in antiquity. It is studied in schools and universities all over the world, and is the focus of a steady stream of television documentaries. Novels like Robert Harris's excellent *Pompeii* only increase the appeal. But the focus on Pompeii is not limited to 'popularizing' works: over the last decade, several dozen teams from universities in at least ten countries have undertaken projects of archaeological investigation in Pompeii. It has benefited from publication, house by house, in a ten-volume encyclopaedia, and the aim to provide scholarly publication block by block of houses is rapidly progressing.

In all this, Herculaneum has progressively been left behind. There are at most three books in English devoted to the site, one by a passionate but frustrated Cambridge professor, Sir Charles Waldstein, who at the beginning of the twentieth century led an unsuccessful campaign to relaunch the excavation of the site, another by a young English lady, Ethel Barker, who had the misfortune to publish in the same year as Waldstein and has been overlooked ever since, and one by an American amateur (in the best sense of the word) with a passion for things Italian, Joseph Jay Deiss. There are still only a handful of books devoted to the site in any language, mostly guidebooks and exhibition catalogues, though, as the Further Reading list shows, there are interminable scholarly articles. The site has, until recently, had few foreign projects, no encyclopaedia, and a tenth the number of visitors that Pompeii boasts. It was also, by the end of the twentieth century, entering a precipitous state of decay. The Villa of the Papyri was the only aspect of Herculaneum that seemed to capture the popular imagination, and even this because of the

*View across Cardo IV from the upper balcony of the House of Wattlework (a Graticcio).*

prospect it seemed to dangle of the rediscovery of a lost library of antiquity, something like the lost library of Alexandria, rather than anything visible on the ground (let alone readable in a library).

Herculaneum has not merited this neglect. Even this is to put it too negatively. Herculaneum is an extraordinary site, of the very highest world class. Small it may be, at least compared to the rolling acres of Pompeii, but in quality it has no match. The freak of chance that meant Pompeii was blanketed in ash and pumice pebbles, while Herculaneum was covered in the fine, hot dust of pyroclastic surges and flows, resulted in the extensive preservation at Herculaneum of organic material – principally wood, but also foodstuffs, papyrus and cloth. At the same time, the depth of cover in Herculaneum, much closer to the crater of Vesuvius than Pompeii, is three or four times greater, resulting in the extensive preservation of upper floors. Measured from the ancient seashore to the highest level preserved, Herculaneum can account for no less than six storeys. Only in Herculaneum is it possible to examine a latrine two floors above the street level; only in Herculaneum is it possible to examine a sewer 50 metres long, full to a depth of up to half a metre with the contents of ancient kitchens and human bowels. Only in Herculaneum is it possible to put names to nearly half the free, adult, male inhabitants of the final years, and through its documents enter into the intimate detail of their legal and commercial lives.

I would not suggest for a moment that Herculaneum can be a substitute for Pompeii. There are several things in which Pompeii is much richer (more sex, more violence). These do much to explain Pompeii's popular appeal. But at the very least, we need to look at both sites together. They are complementary, and each offers its own angle. Nobody would want to suggest that the 2.5 million visitors to Pompeii should

*Detail from the marble funerary altar of Marcus Nonius Balbus.*

transfer their affections to Herculaneum: much of the appeal of Herculaneum lies in being smaller and quieter. Any visitor to Herculaneum is struck by its intimacy and immediacy. A higher proportion of the visitors to Herculaneum are schoolchildren. The appeal is instant, and the stimulus to the imagination effective at almost any age.

The intimacy which attracts the visitor is also what makes the site so important for understanding the ancient world. We know plenty about the cities of the Roman empire, their urban form, their administration and economy, and about Roman law and society and politics. What makes Herculaneum special is not any addition to our knowledge on the grand scale, but the chance to look in intimate detail at the workings of one particular city at one moment in time. We can look at this society under the microscope: whether the contents of their bowels or the legal and economic transactions that made

up their daily lives. What emerges is in many ways surprising. We knew for instance that this was a slave society, and that slaves could be freed and flourish. But the evidence, as we will see, suggests that freed slaves outnumbered the freeborn (which necessarily means that slaves outnumbered them both). Trying to understand such a society stretches our imagination, and requires patient attention to minute detail.

This is no guidebook, though I hope that visitors to the site will find it helpful both before and after a visit. A guidebook needs to be descriptive and thorough; and though there are few corners of the site I do not discuss, there is no itinerary. Several adequate guidebooks already exist. Nor does this book attempt to offer a definitive account. It is too early for any account to be definitive, and both new evidence and new questions are constantly emerging. Instead, this book attempts an overview of what we do and, equally interesting, what we *do not* know or understand about Herculaneum; about what has attracted interest in the past, and why, and what the potential is for future insights. The game is certainly not over until the analysis of the skeletal remains, the new publication of the waxed wooden tablets, the study of the finds, including the organic remains from the sewers, are all complete, not until new excavations and investigations have cast light on the frustrating question of where the forum and heart of the city was, and the basic question of where the town walls ran, especially to the north, all areas in which we can expect to see progress in the next decade. Nor will the visitor experience have achieved its full potential until the museum containing the site's rich harvest of finds is open, and until the two great excavations of the eighteenth century – the theatre and the Villa of the Papyri – are reconnected to the main site.

That I have been able to write this book is wholly due to my participation in an exceptional project. In 2001, the Packard Humanities Institute of California launched the extraordinary initiative of a collaborative project with the local heritage agency, the Archaeological Superintendency of Pompeii (now Naples and Pompeii), with the aim of addressing some of the root causes of decay on the site. Invited by Dr David Woodley Packard to set up the project, I have had the privilege of working closely since 2001 with a talented team of (mostly Italian) specialists drawn from a wide range of disciplines. There is no point at which my understanding of the site, and consequently my framing of this book, has not benefited from their insight and enthusiasm, and the numerous new results they have generated. It is only too rare for archaeologists and historians to work hand in hand with conservationists, architects, engineers, surveyors, materials scientists and geologists. Our experience, from the beginning of the project, has been that, through collaboration in a multidisciplinary team, addressing seemingly banal issues of conservation can deliver a stream of exciting results.

I am deeply grateful to the members of the Herculaneum Conservation Project team, both individually and as a group. I owe a particular debt to Domenico (Mimmo) Camardo, our lead archaeologist, and his collaborators from Sosandra, especially Domenico (Mimmo) Esposito, and to the geological team of Aldo Cinque, Professor of Geology at the University of Naples Federico II, and Linda Irollo, whose work on the ancient seashore has produced vital new evidence of the changing morphology of the town; likewise to Mark Robinson, Professor of Environmental Archaeology at the University of Oxford, and Erica Rowan, for their analysis of the contents of the great sewer, and to our lead architect, Paola Pesaresi, for showing what can be learnt from reopening Bourbon tunnels. Gionata Rizzi, conservation architect, introduced me to some of the great debates about restoration, and taught me that restoration is open to as many interpretations as a musical score. From Monica Martelli Castaldi I have learned that the key to conservation lies in a constant and thorough programme of maintenance, and that it is indeed possible if not to stop then at least to slow down decay. From engineer Ippolito Massari I have learned how the acute problems of damage caused by water can be managed, and an ancient drainage system reactivated. From the late Giorgio Torraca, Professor Emeritus of Chemistry at the University of Rome, and his numerous collaborators in the Getty Conservation Institute and universities all round the world co-ordinated by Alessandra De Vita, I have learned that we cannot expect ancient frescoes, surface and wooden elements to survive without the support of research chemists. To Massimo Brizzi and his patient team of archaeological surveyors I owe a new set of plans of a degree of accuracy that was previously lacking. To Ascanio D'Andrea I owe the use of a database that makes possible the co-ordination of vast amounts of information, archival and new. To Sarah Court I owe the co-ordination of the multiple lines of communication with the scholarly and scientific and educational world – the constant stream of researchers, interns, student and teacher groups that visit the site – and the local community, of schools, local residents and members of the local administration, from whose interest and appreciation the site can only benefit. To our Project Manager, Jane Thompson, I owe the vision and the reality of a team that works together effectively through the regular exchange of information, and which allows the constant evolution in the light of experience of the aims and priorities of the project.

Beyond the conservation team, I have enjoyed the support of many allies. Professor Pietro Giovanni Guzzo, Archaeological Superintendent of Pompeii from 1995 to 2009, and latterly also of Naples, was the key figure without whose courageous openness to experiment the project could not have happened: he has supported it throughout with his wisdom, determination and friendship. He made an inspired choice in appointing Maria Paola Guidobaldi as Director of the site when the project started; she, supported by a fine team on site, especially architects Valerio Papaccio, Maria Pirozzi and Giuseppe Zolfo, has been the staunch ally of the project, and the Further Reading shows how much I owe to her in writing this book. The project has been overseen by a scientific committee whose distinction is equalled by their passion for the site. Professor Stefano De Caro has helped us through the labyrinthine bureaucracy of the Italian State, first as Superintendent at Naples, then as Regional Director for Campania, finally as Director General of Archaeology. Professor Fausto Zevi has brought us the fruit of decades of knowledge and experience of Campanian archaeology. My former colleagues as Directors of Foreign Institutes at Rome, Professor Herman Geertman at the Dutch Institute and Professor Paul Zanker at the German Archaeological Institute, have shown that archaeologists can care about conservation. Rome is the seat of ICCROM, the international body dedicated to the conservation and management of heritage across the world; we are

especially lucky to enjoy the support and advice of its former Director General, Dr Nicholas Stanley-Price, and his colleague Dr Valerie Magar, helping us to see the problems of Herculaneum in a broader international context, and to recruit the advice and comments of many participants in ICCROM courses.

We have also been fortunate in the support of the municipal authority, the Comune di Ercolano. Three city mayors in succession, Luisa Bossa and Gaetano (Nino) Daniele and Vincenzo Strazzullo, have proved enthusiastic allies, and helped us to set up together an Association and an International Centre for the Study of Herculaneum. Massimo Iovino, the architect responsible for Ercolano's ambitious plan of urban regeneration ('Urban Herculaneum'), worked with Jane Thompson and Sarah Court to see through all the practicalities of a collaboration between local authority, the Italian State, represented by the Superintendency, and the Herculaneum Conservation Project and the international community, represented by the British School at Rome. The first Centre Manager, Christian Biggi, has successfully brought together these diverse interests, and launched a programme of seminars, initiatives with local schools, and research into local oral history. The President of the Association, Professor Dieter Mertens, has brought us the great benefit of his long experience with similar challenges in Sicily.

Without the Herculaneum Conservation Project and the contributions of all those named, and many more, I would not have dreamed of writing this book. But though it comes out of and has been inspired by the project, and reflects many of its new findings, this is not a publication of the results of the project. Several volumes are planned and under way. This is a completely personal interpretation of Herculaneum, and none of the others should be blamed for my views or errors. John Nicoll persuaded me of the need to write a book on Herculaneum: his tenacity and enthusiasm brought it to fruition, and in a more lavish format than I had ever dreamed possible. Further stimulus came from an invitation to deliver the Gray lectures in Cambridge in 2008; to my friends in the Faculty of Classics, especially Mary Beard, Henry Hurst and Martin Millett I owe much stimulating discussion. Mary did the further favour of reading the text of this book and helping removing errors and stumbling blocks, as did Kenneth Lapatin, Alex Hall repeatedly combed through the text, always improving it, and made the index. Michael Brunström, as editor, lavished equal care on text and illustrations. To all both I and the reader are deeply indebted. Amy Richardson came to my rescue for a second time in sorting out the endless mass of illustrations. Brian Donovan, to whose skill as a photographer this book owes much of its appeal, was generous as ever with his time in making attractive house plans. To two institutions I owe the gift of time: to the British School at Rome for enabling me to continue to work on Herculaneum despite leaving them, to Sidney Sussex College, Cambridge for enabling me to continue to work despite joining them. To David Packard I owe not only the chance to work on this magical site, but the encouragement and financial support to write the book. My greatest debt, as ever, is personal: Jo encouraged me to write when I should have been sorting out a move, read each chapter as it came out and helped ensure that it would be readable. To her this book is dedicated.

AWH

*Below: Detail of a theatrical mask from the so-called College of the Augustales.*

*Overleaf: View of the site from the north-east towards the west.*

# 1
# GEOLOGY

Let us stop listening to people who have abandoned Campania and who have moved out after this catastrophe, saying they will never again return to the region. . . . For we are wrong if we think that any part of the earth's surface is safe and immune from this risk [earthquakes]. Everywhere is subject to the same laws: nature conceived nothing to be unmoveable. Things collapse at different times: just as in cities different houses collapse at different moments, so on the earth's surface flaws make themselves apparent at different times.

(Seneca, *Natural Questions* 6.1.10–12)

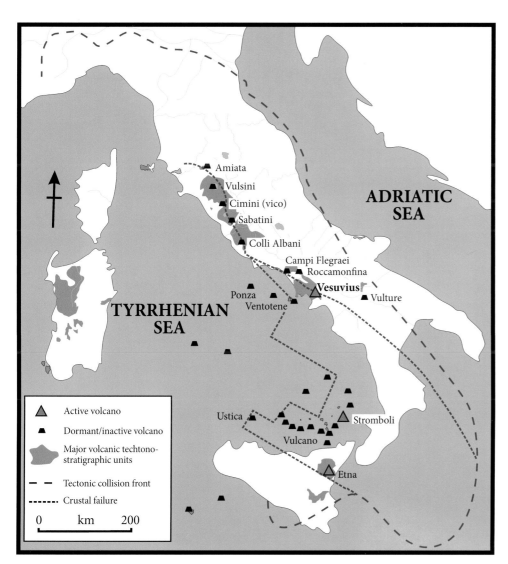

Map of Italy showing principal volcanic areas.

**Active volcano**

**Dormant/inactive volcano**

**Major volcanic techtono-stratigraphic units**

**Tectonic collision front**

**Crustal failure**

0    km    200

Writing in the immediate aftermath of the major earthquake in Campania that shook the cities of Pompeii and Herculaneum to their foundations, on a date he gives very precisely as 5 February AD 63, Seneca, one of the major figures of Latin literature – dramatist, letter writer, philosopher and, until shortly before, adviser to the Emperor Nero – considers the implications of this natural event with Stoic detachment. He wishes to account for natural phenomena, winds, thunder and lightning, snow, comets, as well as earthquakes, in the purely scientific terms established by Greek science. There is no room here for the gods, for natural phenomena as a manifestation of divine anger and retribution. For him, there is no predicting earthquakes or natural disasters, let alone propitiating the gods. Humans just have to realize that the laws of nature allow no risk-free life. The earth's crust, the very element which humans count on to be stable, is in fact fluid, subject to constant and unpredictable movement.

The science of geology has been transformed in the intervening two millennia, yet his fundamental point remains true. Italy, itself the product of the slow shifting of plates over tens of millions of years, the African plate pushing against and sliding beneath the Eurasian plate to create the ridge of the Apennines and Alps, remains a zone of persistent seismic and volcanic activity. The western coast of

*Opposite: View of the seafront of the town from the west.*

*Left: Map of Italy showing principal volcanic areas.*

Italy is characterized by a long string of volcanoes, some live, some dead, from the Tuscan lakes to the Aeolian islands and Etna. To the north, it is so long since these volcanic formations have seen activity that human life has long flourished on the mineral-rich soils, in Tuscany, northern Lazio and the Alban hills, and as far south as Roccamonfina on the north of the Campanian plain. To the south, the spectacular activity is visible on a daily basis, on Stromboli with its constant fountains of magma, and Etna, with lava flows that cause regular problems. The Campanian volcanoes are more intermittent. West of Naples, the Campi Flegraei offer ongoing reminders of the danger beneath with their sulphurous geysers. There has been no major eruption since 1538, when the mound of Montenuovo appeared overnight, deleting the village of Tripergole and causing great destruction to nearby Pozzuoli. But Pozzuoli remains today a highly unstable area. Its historic centre, Rione Terra, has been abandoned, officially evacuated after the catastrophic earthquake of 1980, and the area today shows the clear signs of the 'slow quaking', the bradyseism which makes the earth's crust expand and contract, creating the false impression that the sea is rising and falling.

Vesuvius itself is evidently still active, though on the slow and unpredictable rhythms of geology it is impossible and absurd to suggest we can predict when the next eruption is 'due'. A major eruption in 1631 initiated a phase in which low-level activity was regular for 150 years. It was in this phase that the Grand Tourists gathered to admire the spectacle, and commissioned or bought paintings, whether by major artists like Hackert or Volaire or Joseph Wright of Derby, or by the hundreds of local craftsmen who churned out charming gouaches. The phase of activity also coincided with the long stay in Naples of Sir William Hamilton, a volcano lover, and his reports to the Royal Society and his beautifully produced *Campi Phlegraei* (1776) are among the first significant contributions to the emergent science of volcanology.

*Left: Day and night views of Vesuvius from Naples by an anonymous local artist in gouache, c.1815 (British School at Rome collection).*

Vesuvius has been dormant since the eruption of 1944, strangely coincident with the Allied advance through Italy, and that means that modern tourists are deprived of the frisson of this spectacle, and can only imagine the likely impact of a new earthquake or eruption on the hundreds of thousands of modern dwellings in the immediate shadow of the mountain. Civil defence would love the volcanologists to be able to make a prediction. Yet, short of this, they collaborate with archaeologists in trying to understand the anatomy of past eruptions. It is a rich field for inter-disciplinary collaboration.

Seneca quite evidently could not predict. In scoffing at the Campanian landowners who fled the area, swearing never to return, quite rightly as it turned out, he did not even succeed in associating earthquakes with volcanic activity. Indeed, he does not discuss volcanoes at all in his *Natural History*. Earthquakes were a far more frequent phenomenon, and only rarely are they in fact associated with volcanoes, though it is the same deep shifting of plates that generates both phenomena. By quirk of fate, neither Seneca nor any other Greek or Roman author witnessed a volcanic eruption until of course the young Gaius Plinius Secundus, and his uncle, the distinguished naturalist and admiral of the imperial fleet, witnessed the eruption of 79. It is significant that the uncle's first reaction was to go to study it closer: as author of thirty-six volumes of *Natural History*, he shared Seneca's scientific interests and approach, and wanted to find out more.

This innocence about volcanoes meant of course that the inhabitants of the area had little idea, even after the earthquake dated by Seneca to 63, but by the historian Tacitus to 62, of the imminent danger in which they stood. But even if they had done so, there is little probability, especially to judge by the behaviour of the contemporary population, that they would have abandoned their lands and houses. Then, as now, there was too much profit to be made, whether from the fields with their boosted fertility, or from the flourishing trade that spread its tentacles around the Bay of Naples, the best natural harbour in Italy, and the focus, over the preceding three centuries, of the massive trade and importations that sustained Rome as the capital of a new global power. To understand the degree and urgency of the danger, you have to speed up the passage of time beyond the rhythm of human generations. It is only archaeology, a science intimately linked in its methods to geology, which allows us to say how frequently the Vesuvian region is devastated by eruptions. Preparations for the construction of a new NATO base at Gricignano showed three successive episodes in which human cultivation was covered under a blanket of ashes, on top of which later cultivation began. Over the course of 20,000 years, there have been no less than five 'Plinian' eruptions, of the magnitude of that of 79, each of which will have impacted on human inhabitants. The one most clearly visible today is that called 'the pumice of Avellino', which took place around 1700 BC, destroying, and thereby preserving the traces of, early Bronze Age settlements. The remains of oval huts near Nola, preserving timbers, pottery wares, and even the bodies of goats and livestock tethered in their pens, is a vivid reminder of what was absolutely invisible 2,000 years later to the inhabitants of Pompeii and Herculaneum, separated from this catastrophe by an interval very nearly as long as that which separates us from them.

It would be wrong to suggest that the Romans had no inkling that Vesuvius was a volcano. The Greek geographer, Strabo, writing at the end of the first century BC, describes how the summit of Vesuvius is ash-coloured and entirely unfruitful:

> It shows pore-like cavities in masses of rock
> looking as though they had been eaten out by fire:
> one might infer from this evidence that the area
> was previously burning and had craters of fire,
> which were extinguished when the fuel ran out.
>
> (*Geography* 5.4.8)

Not only could they see the evidence of previous activity, but in their mythology they associated the area with the gateway to the underworld (Aeneas descends there at Lake Avernus), with the titanic battle of the gods and giants, whose bodies lay beneath, smitten by the thunderbolts of Jupiter ('it is the wounds of the fallen giants, inflicted by the thunderbolts, that pour forth those streams of fire and water', says Strabo of the fumaroles of the Campi Phlegraei), and with Vulcan, god of blacksmiths, in whose furnaces beneath the ground the magic armour of Aeneas was forged. It is not that the ancients were completely innocent, merely that they lacked the experience over two millennia to foresee what might happen.

In fact, the signs of big trouble brewing are clear, if only in retrospect. Recent work down by the ancient seashore of Herculaneum in the context of the Herculaneum Conservation Project has revealed a dramatic sequence of seismic activities, stretching over a century. At the south-eastern corner of the city, an impressive tower-like building juts out over the edge of the shore, providing the House of the Telephus Relief with a series of rooms with wonderful views out to sea. As it survives today, this structure stands on three levels. But a test trench has revealed that beneath the ground level was originally an entire additional floor, built with the same style of arches and columns as the floors above. Plaster survives on the outer face, but also on the inside edge of the arch. Yet this arch was blocked up in antiquity, implying the abandonment of the floor. Not only that, but the masonry that blocks the arch shows clear signs of erosion by water. The sea had invaded, not only forcing them to abandon the ground floor, but even causing damage to their new defences. The final response was to build an enormous containing wall, between the sea and the building, and to backfill the area, raising it with 3 metres of Roman rubble. The black, volcanic sand of the ancient beach could be seen at the foot of the containing wall.

*Left: Clearance of the seafront with remains of quarrying outside the Suburban Baths (2008).*

*Right: The tower of the House of the Telephus Relief before (above) and after (below) conservation work.*

*Left: Excavation beneath ground level at the base of the House of the Telephus Relief reveals signs of an abandoned lower floor.*

*Below: 3D model of the House of the Gem (Akhet).*

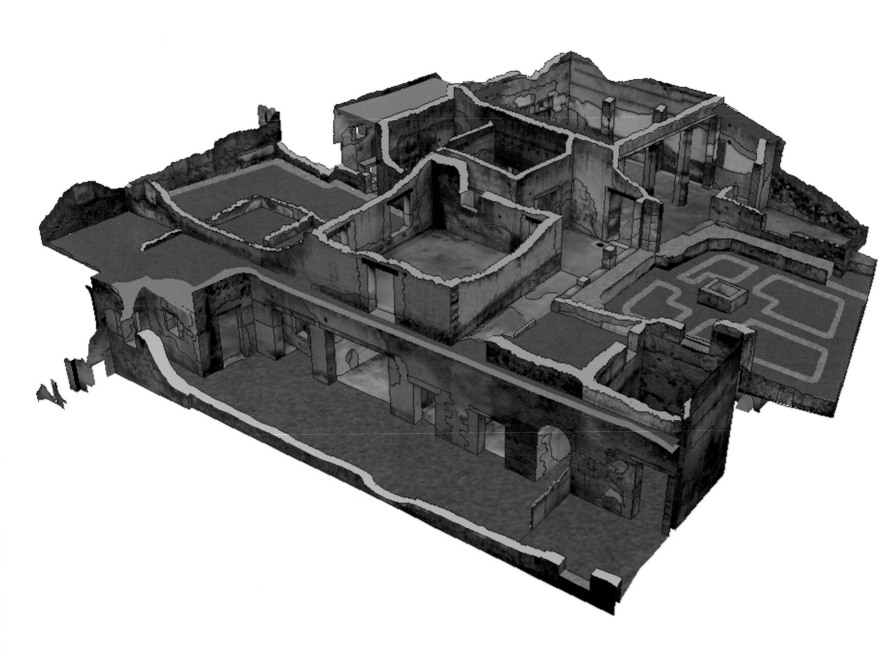

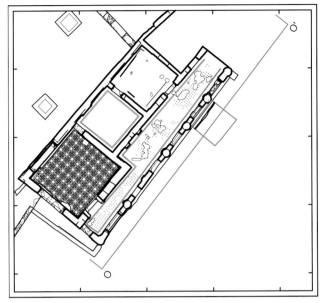

*Far left: Plan of the tower of the House of the Telephus Relief.*

*Left: Black volcanic sand of the ancient beach.*

*Below: Elevation of the east façade of the House of the Telephus Relief.*

Such a dramatic change of sea level is compatible with the phenomenon of bradyseism, still visible at Pozzuoli. As activity in the magma chamber, many kilometres below the earth's surface, builds up, the ground above expands and rises, and the sea level apparently falls; as the activity in the magma chamber recedes, so the ground falls again, and the sea invades. The Telephus tower was built somewhere around the beginning of the first century AD, in one of the phases when the ground was high and dry; the floor was abandoned as it progressively sank. The great earthquake of 62/63 probably belongs to a turning point in this slow process.

Further evidence is visible a little further round the seafront in the walls of the Suburban Baths, built, as was the fashion of the first century AD, right down by the sea (bathing *in* the sea was not yet a fashion; bathing *close to it* was). Under the foundations of the baths, caught in the cracks in the tufo bank (see page 25) on which it stands, there are grains of sand, mixed with fragments of Roman pottery. The baths were built on what evidently had been a beach, though the sea must have by now been far enough away as to constitute no imminent threat. Yet the walls of the baths show that the sea came back, with a vengeance. Sand was piled up to a metre high against the walls, where it formed a solid crust. The walls were extensively repaired, adding a whole extra skin of construction in the contemporary 'network' style known as *opus reticulatum* (see image, right). Windows on the first floor were blocked up to waist level on the side closest to the sea; and the old back door that led down a ramp to the beach had also been blocked up. The baths, like the tower, had suffered badly from 'marine ingression', not that long before the eruption.

But this episode was almost certainly the second time in the course of a century that the sea had invaded and retreated. The 'shore', on which ancient sand can be seen, is in fact an abandoned quarry. Numerous rectilinear edges show where blocks of

*The Suburban Baths viewed from above (top) and below (middle).*

*Right: Detail of the wall of the Suburban Baths, showing second skin in opus reticulatum added after damage by the sea.*

*Façade of the Suburban Baths, showing masonry blocking above original wooden sills to protect from damage by the sea.*

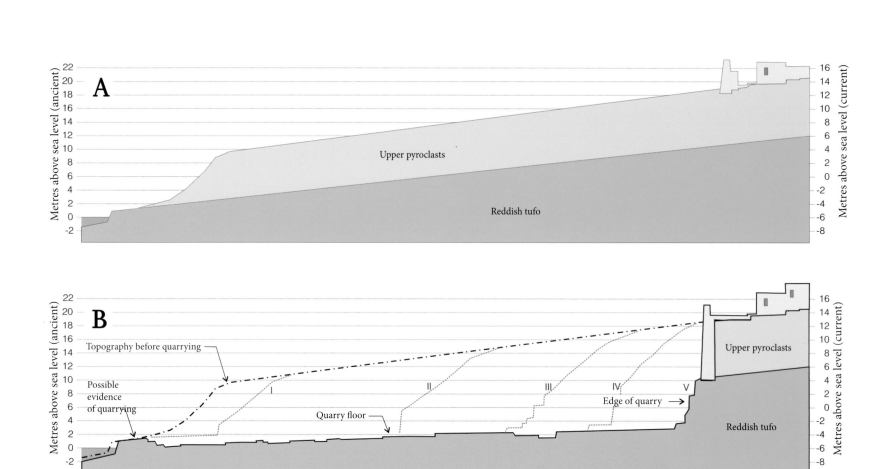

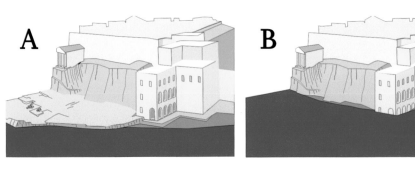

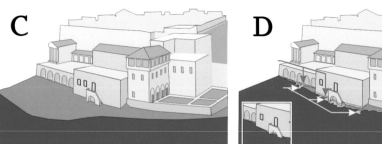

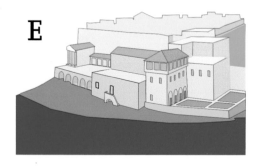

*Above: North–south section of seafront of Herculaneum showing situation before (above) and after (below) quarrying.*

*Left: Phases of the marine invasions of Herculaneum. A (early first century BC): lower floor of the House of the Telephus Relief accessible and quarry still visible. B (late first century BC): the sea rises, covering quarry and lower floor. C (early first century AD): the sea retreats and Suburban Baths constructed on the shore. D (mid-first century AD): the sea rises, damaging the baths. E (AD 79): the sea has retreated again as the earth rises in preparation for the eruption.*

tufo had been cut out and removed. It cannot have been a shore when it was a quarry, so the sand represents a first phase of marine ingression, followed by retreat and the building of baths and tower, followed by the second ingression and the abandonment of the bottom level. If Seneca had been able to place this evidence in the context of the great earthquake, and if only he had known what the modern geologist knows, he would have been a good deal less sanguine about whether to flee Campania or not.

The catastrophe of 79 thus had long precursors, stretching over at least a century. A generation ago, scholars still assumed that there were only two events that disturbed the calm of the Bay of Naples: the earthquake and the eruption. Increasingly, signs have emerged of repeated seismic activity doing repeated damage to buildings, even if not on the dramatic scale of 62/63. One of the telltale signs is the frequency of new construction work, typically repairs, and new decoration going on in the houses, right up to the moment of the eruption. In some cases, as most clearly in the House of the Painters at Pompeii, we find all the traces of redecoration underway on the very day of the eruption, with walls half-plastered, decorations half-complete, and ceramic pots of pigment, plumb-bobs and compasses close to the paintings. Geologists confirm that we should predict a continuum of seismic activity in the build-up to a major eruption, and the signs of major changes in ground level, in both directions, in the decades preceding the eruption, offer strong confirmation. What is most impressive is how, in the face of what in retrospect can be read as signals of the disaster to come, the inhabitants continued to make good the damage and rebuild their lives.

In any case, the scale of the catastrophe of the eruption itself was beyond human imagination. The pyrotechnic displays that Sir William Hamilton and his friends watched with such morbid fascination, knowing the damage done in the past, were completely trivial compared to what the younger

Pliny watched from the safety of his uncle's house on the far side of the bay. It is only over the last twenty years or so that the mechanics of the eruption have been fully understood by scientists. It used to be normal to speak of Herculaneum as having been buried in an avalanche of mud. So in 1908 Charles Waldstein accounted for the unique preservation of Herculaneum in these words:

> . . . suddenly there appeared the torrent of liquid mud, of ashes mixed with water from torrential rains or from the lakes and rivulets, along the courses of which it moved down the slope, and this swept all before it. . . . Gradually it penetrated the houses, and in these, gently, without violent breakage, it filled up the interior, preserving the articles of furniture and decoration from undue pressure and from the corroding influence of moisture and chemical disintegration, except for the carbonization of wood . . .

Waldstein could not have been more wrong, and strangely enough, he did not even heed the advice of the geologist he consulted, Professor McKenny Hughes, whom he cites as saying: 'Nor can tuff like that seen in Herculaneum be due to a flow of mud from the volcano.' Hughes rightly identifies the material as tuff or tufo formed by consolidated ash (rejecting the older idea of a lava flow), casting strong doubt on the presence of water. Later volcanology was to prove him right, but the Waldstein interpretation of a mud flow persisted, and even today, the word 'fango' is used to describe the deep wall of tufo that covers the site.

As Haraldur Sigurdsson and his colleagues have worked out the sequence, we must distinguish two separate major phases of the eruption. The first phase was described by Pliny, watching from his vantage point in the admiral's villa at Misenum, 30 kilometres away from the cone:

A cloud rose, from which mountain one could not make out (later we learned it was Vesuvius), the shape and form of which could best be compared to a pine tree. It rose up on high with an extremely long trunk, then spread out into branches, I imagine because it was carried out by the fresh breath, then as the breath grew older, it was let down or even spread laterally and vanished under its own weight.

(*Letters* 6.16.6)

The observation, according to volcanologists, is accurate. The initial eruption produces a tall eruptive column, progressively rising higher into the atmosphere under the force of a series of explosions equivalent to a nuclear bomb exploding every few seconds. On reaching an altitude of about 27 kilometres, and penetrating the thin air of the stratosphere, it spreads laterally, producing the rain of tiny pellets of pumice called *lapilli*, which we find blanketing Pompeii to the depth of several metres. The eruptive column continues to rise, to a maximum of about 33 kilometres. The winds in the stratosphere were southwards that day, so that Pompeii, Stabiae, the Sarno valley and even as far as the ridge of the Sorrentine peninsula received this cover (*lapilli* have

*Below: Skeletons in the vaults by the seashore.*

*Inside: Panoramic view of the seafront and vaults.*

been found in excavations beneath the cathedral of Positano, 20 kilometres south of the cone), whereas Herculaneum was wholly unscathed by this phase of the eruption.

The second phase, as Pliny hints, is when, with the progress of time, the force of the eruption slackens and the column can no longer sustain its own very considerable weight. At this point, when the eruption itself is reaching its end, it enters its most destructive form. The billowing hot gases, mixed with a dense cloud of extremely fine ash, begin to collapse down the side of the mountain in great swirling clouds. Their heat is intense; by the time they reach Herculaneum, where the volcano meets the sea, they are still at a range of 400–500°C, not hot enough for a ceramic furnace, but hot enough to ensure instant death to any living being in its path, and the consequent carbonization of wood. It was a joint team of a volcanologist and a physical anthropologist who were able to make sense of the skeletons at Herculaneum, and detect from their 'pugilistic' poses, the muscles involuntarily contracted like those of boxers in the

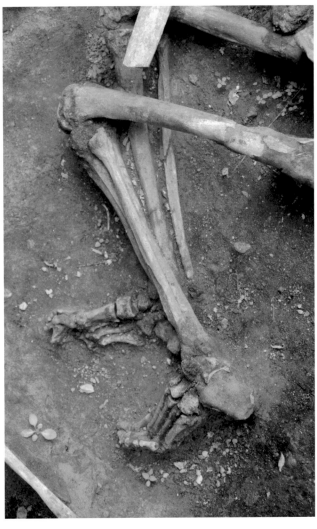

*Right: Detail of skeleton showing 'pugilist' pose cause by muscle contractions.*

*Below: Plan of positions of the skeletons excavated in 1981 by the seashore (Amy Richardson).*

*Overleaf: View of the site from the seafront towards Vesuvius.*

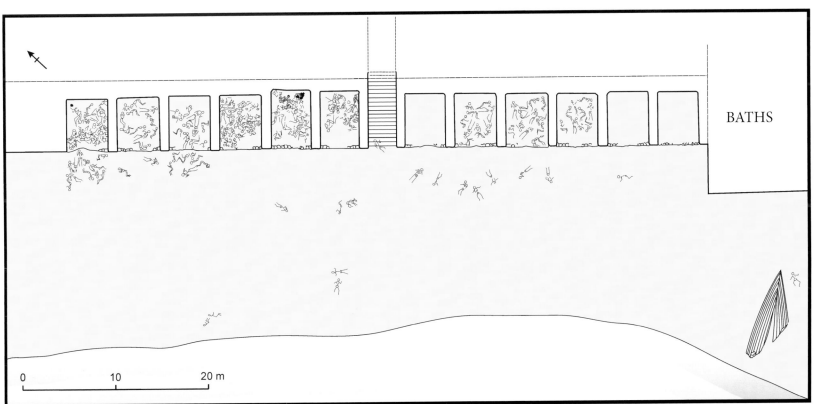

BATHS

0    10    20 m

final spasm, and the signs of crania that exploded under the force of the instant vaporization of the brains, that their end was quite different from that of the corpses at Pompeii.

For long, it was one of the curious contrasts between Pompeii and Herculaneum that corpses were found in the former but not the latter. (We will see in a later chapter that there are many contrasts between the sites, and the importance of Herculaneum is to offer an alternative perspective on similar issues.) Hence it was in Pompeii that the archaeologist Giuseppe Fiorelli in the second half of the nineteenth century developed his technique of making 'casts' of corpses, by filling with cement the voids left by the rotted organic matter of the bodies. Such casts were never possible at Herculaneum, because the more intense heat stripped the bodies of their organic matter, and left only the skeletons encased in rock. But even skeletons were rare on site, not more than a dozen or two, until the new phase of excavations in the 1980s down by the ancient seashore revealed where the victims were concentrated.

The lowest level of the seafront of the city consists of a series of arches or vaults. They are sometimes referred to as 'boat sheds', but there is no trace of marine equipment, and they seem simply to have served the function of substructures to the terraces above them. Nevertheless, they offered the inhabitants the equivalent of a dozen or so 'bomb shelters', where people could take refuge from the blast. Several dozen bodies, of people young and old, male and female, rich and poor, master and slave, have been found crowded into each of these arches, giving a total of more than 300 victims. Almost certainly there were others, and if one day the location of the ancient harbour is excavated, perhaps immediately to the east of the town, many hundreds more might emerge.

Why did they take shelter here? Their virtual absence from the houses of the town, in contrast to Pompeii, suggests that they had good warning of an impending event so catastrophic that it was no longer safe to wait in their houses. Pliny's second letter evokes the context of midnight on the day of the eruption. He confirms that 'for many days before [the eruption] there had been earth tremors, less frightening because it was so common in Campania, but that night [i.e. of the eruption] it became so strong that everything seemed not simply moving, but turned upside down' (*Letters* 6.20.4). His mother insisted on flight, and they found themselves on the road amid crowds of terrified refugees. They looked in astonishment to see the sea had retreated, leaving marine life high and dry on the shore: another observation of the movement of the crust that had affected Herculaneum over the years before.

If that is what it felt like at distant Misenum, the effect in Herculaneum must have been truly terrifying, and it is interesting that the places they chose to take refuge, deep concrete vaults, were indeed ideal in the case of an earthquake rather than an eruption. They could not imagine what was about to descend. Even from

the other side of the bay, Pliny could watch: great flashes of fire, then the cloud descending to the land, covering the sea, and removing Capri from his sight. He was observing what we now know as pyroclastic surges and flows, the descent of the clouds of hot gas. At Herculaneum, we can observe the long and remorseless sequence. The first or second surge to reach the city will have killed all those left. They advanced through the streets like a firestorm, ripping off roofs, and smashing down walls. Heavy material was carried for considerable distances. Down by the seashore, we have found an entire roof, beams, rafters and roof-tiles hurled down. The lowest levels of the wall of rock that blankets the site are full of building materials: a column, inverted like a projectile, tossed down from a terrace above, and beams

and tiles everywhere. The body of the marble statue of Nonius Balbus was found down by the sea, many metres away from his head, which had rolled off to the base of his tomb on the terrace above.

The site witnessed by the modern visitor has been carefully recomposed. It creates the impression of a city 'frozen in time', preserved intact by the disaster that overwhelmed it. But if you look attentively at the excavation reports, you discover that the state of what was excavated was far different. The destruction was so widespread and chaotic, with vast chunks of masonry tossed sideways, that the archaeologists could not excavate before restoring, but had literally to put buildings back together again as they were exposed. There were even situations where a wall initially exposed seemed intact, yet below it emerged that the lower levels of the wall had been swept away, so that the portion above was suspended in mid-air.

The pyroclastic surges and flows were not merely hot and destructive; they also came under high pressure. The dense ash did not simply settle on surfaces: it penetrated cavities, with all the force of injection moulding. A sewer, deep beneath a block of flats, was filled floor to ceiling with dense rock throughout its entire length. Even the pottery tubes stacked in the Suburban Baths, and still awaiting installation as heating flues, are completely filled with the material. It found every void, penetrated every crevice, and gradually entombed the town in a total shroud of stone. The pyroclastic surges probably started, to judge from Pliny's description, around midnight. They continued for at least twelve hours, covering Herculaneum in layer after layer of solid material. The deepest point is down by the shore. When a surge hits the sea, it starts to cool, and back up, so that the depth of cover increases to some 25 metres. But the surge continued to advance, and the modern shoreline is a full 400 metres further out than the ancient. The sheer quantity of solid material moved in the course of twenty-four hours – calculated at 4 cubic kilometres of material devastating an area of 300 square kilometres – is scarcely imaginable in ordinary human terms.

This is the 'avalanche of mud' which was the standard description in the mid-twentieth century. A natural event had moved mountains. It is the ideal material for tunnelling. Such 'tufo' is soft enough to hack through with a pickaxe, yet rapidly sets hard enough not to collapse on your head. And it was by tunnelling that the site was first explored.

*Stack of terracotta heating flues awating installation in the Suburban Baths: every flue is full of ash from the pyroclastic flow.*

Villa of the
Papyri

Theatre

# SITE PLAN OF HERCULANEUM

Structures known only from Bourbon plans

Visible excavated structures

Plan of modern city

Edges of excavation

Cardo I

Cardo II

Cardo III

Cardo IV

Cardo V

Decumanus Maximus

Decumanus Inferior

*Surveyed and drawn for HCP by Massimo Brizzi and Lieven Loots*

# 2
# THE POLITICS
# OF ARCHAEOLOGY

Why dig up the past? Archaeology is a recent science, one which depends on geology for its 'stratigraphic method', of looking at the build-up of layers of human activity over the course of time. Though we use it to study antiquity, it did not exist in antiquity, even if the word (literally 'the study of the ancient') is Greek. Had Seneca and his contemporaries studied the ground they excavated to build their great villas, they would have been driven to ask questions about the previous volcanic catastrophes of the area. The emperor Augustus had a collection of 'giants' bones', perhaps dinosaur fossils, but these were a curiosity. Cicero explored the cemetery of Syracuse to rediscover the abandoned and overgrown tomb of Archimedes. When they talked about the 'heroic ages' that preceded recorded history, they doubtless had in mind the traces of the past they necessarily

*Left: The eighteenth-century access shaft to the Theatre.*

*Below: The Peutinger map of the Roman empire, still marking Pompeii and Herculaneum in the fourth century AD.*

*Overleaf: Panoramic view of a reopened Bourbon tunnel to the north of the Basilica.*

came across. Nevertheless, the idea of digging systematically in order to study the past was foreign to them.

Why then do *we* dig up *our* past? After centuries of modern excavation, and after discoveries that make as big an impact on the public imagination as Pompeii and Herculaneum – Troy and Mycenae, or the Valley of the Kings – the question of why we dig seems too obvious to ask. Yet to understand the rediscovery of Herculaneum, we have to project ourselves backwards to a time when such activity, and the considerable strain on resource that it implies, was anything but obvious. The question usually posed is why and how the excavation of the Vesuvian sites started in the early eighteenth century. The answer reads like, and indeed is, propaganda for the the Spanish regime of Charles Bourbon and his heirs, so heroically responsible for initiating the

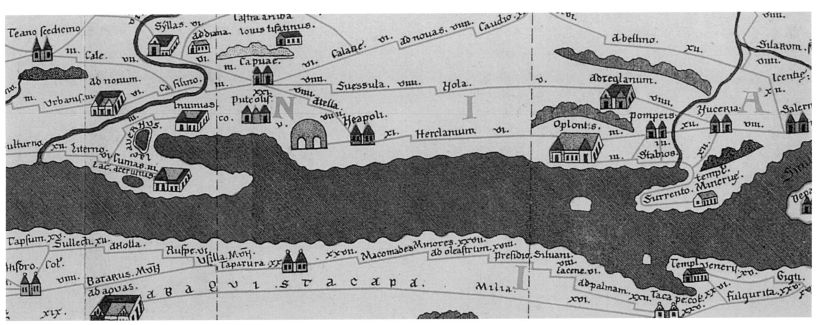

excavations, though this in turn is undercut by the rejection of Bourbon propaganda by the nationalist Italian regime that replaced it in the mid-nineteenth century. It is more revealing to start from the opposite question: why did nobody think of digging up these cities before?

The implicit answer in the standard version is that the cities were lost, and had to be rediscovered by happy chance under an enlightened regime. But the truth is that the cities were never completely lost. Even in antiquity, their position was clearly marked on the fourth-century AD road map known as the Peutinger Table, along with Oplontis, where a cluster of villas was to be found in the 1970s. Knowledge of the position of the cities must have persisted long in antiquity. Indeed, Roman treasure-hunters did their own explorations, and the numerous tunnels crisscrossing Pompeii, long taken to be the result of Bourbon exploration, can be nothing of the sort, and must represent treasure-hunting in antiquity. The Forum of Pompeii, so much easier than Herculaneum to explore beneath its soft blanket of *lapilli*, was stripped of marble and bronze by the time that modern excavators reached it.

Some knowledge of the position of Pompeii certainly survived into the Middle Ages. A ninth-century chronicler, Martin of Monaco, spoke of a 'Pompeio campo' which he thought was named after 'Pompeii, the ancient city of Campania'. In the Renaissance, the location of Pompeii was frequently, and correctly, identified with the area by then called 'La Città'. To call a patch of farmland 'the City' already implies knowledge. By 1689 an inscription had been found there mentioning Pompeii, and confirming the identification. But it suited Bourbon propaganda to play down this background, and to emphasize its own 'discovery'.

More significantly, the first modern excavations of Pompeii belong to the late sixteenth century, in the years 1592–1600, when the architect Domenico Fontana cut a canal to bring water from Sarno to

*Above: Mimmo Camardo and Maria Paola Guidobaldi inspect a Bourbon tunnel.*

*Opposite above: Renaissance and medieval pottery from the back-filled tunnels.*

*Opposite below: Fragments of a Harlequin plate dated to the seventeenth century.*

the mills of Torre Annunziata. The canal cuts across the entire breadth of the ancient city, so that there is no way he and his engineers missed it. And yet there were no dramatic announcements of the redis-covery of an ancient city. It has been suggested, quite plausibly, that the silence was in order to avoid the attention of the Office of the Inquisition, established in Naples in the sixteenth century. The rediscovery of antiquity did not square with Inquisition ideology.

That this is right is supported by the parallel story of Pozzuoli. In antiquity, the key Roman port of Puteoli was far richer and more important than either of the Vesuvian cities. Never affected by volcanic eruption in antiquity, it continued to flourish into the Middle Ages, and the Temple of Augustus on the summit of the promontory turned seamlessly into the cathedral and seat of the bishop. Grave damage was done to the town, as we have seen, by the nearby eruption in 1538, and various efforts were made to rebuild the city until the arrival, in the early seventeenth century, of the vigorous Spanish bishop, Martino de Leòn y Càrdenas. His predecessor, Monsignor Lorenzo Mongiojo, had been disgraced for greed and witchcraft; it is a good guess that he had been poking around in the ruins of the ancient city for marble statues, by now collectors' items in Rome. In any case, when Martino de Leòn started his vigorous campaign of building a new city above the ruins of the old, he took no care to extract antiquities. On the contrary, a spectacular collection of statues was found in the 1990s, virtually intact, beneath his building rubble. In this Counter-Reformation world, pagan antiquity was simply too dangerous to rediscover.

Something of the same story can now be told at Herculaneum, on the basis of the reopening of earlier tunnels. It was standard practice among the early explorers of the site to backfill tunnels after extracting the treasures they were hunting, typically slabs of coloured marble, always good for recycling. They backfilled because to bring all the material

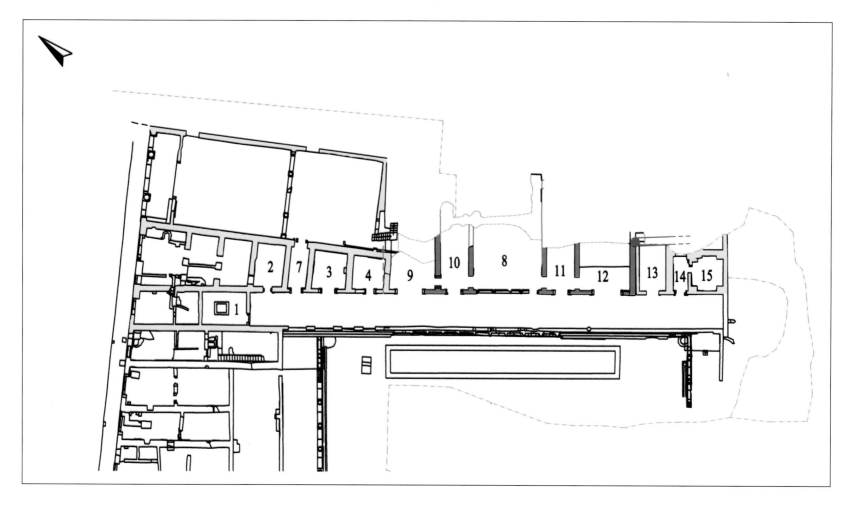

to the surface was hard work, and pointless. In the process, these explorers left traces of themselves. By emptying carefully the backfill, we can get an idea of when the tunnels were explored. The most astonishing finding is that the pottery left by the tunnellers is not just of the eighteenth century, the period of Bourbon tunnelling, but of the seventeenth and sixteenth, and even the Middle Ages. Sometimes these ceramics can be dated with considerable accuracy. A rather handsome plate, broken into several pieces, but nevertheless nearly complete, showing a soldier in brightly coloured trousers, belongs to the 'Harlequin' series of the Montelupo pottery, dated closely to the period 1590–1630. It is not very obvious why Bourbon tunnellers should have taken this plate down over a century later; it surely belongs to an earlier, unrecorded phase of exploration.

In another case, we seem to be looking at an exploration closely datable to the Middle Ages. The down-shaft of a well hit an ancient pavement, then travelled laterally across it. Where the tunnellers went,

*Top: Plan of the upper terrace above the Palaestra. The medieval well and tunnel are located in Room 13 (marked in green).*

*Above: Fragments of pottery dated to the twelfth or thirteenth century found in this test trench.*

they removed the marble plaques of the pavement. The pottery they left behind was all medieval, from the thirteenth century, a period when, thanks to the model of the Cosmati brothers in Rome, patterned pavements in coloured marbles were popular. The inhabitants of the village above Herculaneum, then called Resina, were probably aware of this local resource for centuries, though they will not have been too keen to share their knowledge with the authorities, let alone the world at large.

In fact, the Bourbon tunnellers themselves came across these earlier attempts to explore and rob the site, though they attributed them to the ancient Romans. Thus Father Piaggio, the antiquarian who made his name by his machine to unravel papyri, noted:

> It frequently happens that during excavation they encounter similar tunnels made by the ancients, but so low and so narrow that one cannot understand how a man could walk. Upon finding one of these, they can be certain that some precious statues already have been carried off.

Whether statues had such a high value in antiquity as to be worth risking life and limb may be doubted. The pottery finds that have emerged to date point to the later Middle Ages and early modern periods, though it cannot be ruled out that there were antique explorers too, as is certainly the case at Pompeii.

Clear evidence of the knowledge of the site of Herculaneum in the sixteenth century comes from the manuscript of the Neapolitan antiquarian Fabio Giordano, whose *Historia Napolitana* belongs to the second half of the century. In it he reports the 'recent' discovery of a long inscription 'in the village of Resina, four miles from the city [of Naples], by the ancient town of Herculaneum', where were dug out 'from an ancient building of wonderful elegance' some iron and bronze smithing tools, and a long honorific inscription. It is notable that though

the inscription itself does not specify the name of Herculaneum, only a 'municipium', Giordano had no hesitation in identifying it correctly.

The story of Prince d'Elbeuf, which traditionally represents the first stage in the 'discovery' of the site, belongs within this older tradition of local exploration. Emmanuel-Maurice de Lorraine, later promoted to the title of Prince d'Elbeuf, was a commander of the Austrian army, which for a brief period at the beginning of the eighteenth century controlled Naples (1707–34). In the course of building his vast villa on the port of Granatello, a kilometre or so north of Herculaneum, he became interested in stories of locals finding marble underground, and specifically a local smallholder called Cola Aniello Nocerino, nicknamed (in local style) 'Enzecchetta'. He bought up his land, and conducted excavations under his own authority, finding himself directly above the ancient theatre, rich with coloured marbles (some of which ended up in the church of Saint Etienne in his home town of Elbeuf sur Seine) and with statuary, the most famous examples of which, the 'Herculaneum women', he had to surrender to his commander, Prince Eugene of Savoy, who took them off to his new palace in Vienna. D'Elbeuf, just as generations of explorers before him, did not announce to an expectant world that he had rediscovered an ancient city, but kept it strictly under wraps, hoping to hang on to the finds, only to find his cover blown.

Our story thus changes complexion. No longer can it be a question of how the cities that were lost were triumphantly rediscovered, but rather a question of how what had been local knowledge, suppressed on account of a mixture of greed and fear, became a matter of public concern and excitement. The answer, inescapably, is political. In general, major excavations are far too expensive to make sense except in a context of public opinion and political strategies. Excavation is an ideological activity, impossible when the dominant ideology is hostile (the Inquisition), only desired when a regime sees it as serving its direct purposes, as with the establishment of the Bourbon dynasty, the establishment of the new nationalist regime of the Risorgimento, and the Fascist era. Spanish rule in the south of Italy, over the 'Two Sicilies', went back to the fourteenth century, yet the arrival of Charles Bourbon was a new start in many senses.

In the delicate balance of powers in Europe, the death of Charles II of Spain in 1700 and the succession to the Spanish throne of Philip d'Anjou, grandson of the French Louis XIV, as Philip V, provoked turmoil. The Emperor Leopold of Austria laid counterclaim to the throne, and the British under Queen Anne and her general, the Duke of Marlborough, supported Austria for fear of a unification of the crowns of France and Spain. The battle of Blenheim (1704) was fought to keep the French and Spanish in check. In 1707 the Austrians seized the kingdom of the Two Sicilies. The War of the Spanish Succession ended with an agreement to keep the French and Spanish crowns permanently separate. Philip V therefore had to respect the idea of a balance of powers, and to recover his lost Italian realm without upsetting the balance. The solution was to send out his son, Charles, to make for the first time an independent kingdom, one that would not threaten the Austrians or the other European powers. Charles arrived in Italy in 1732, to take possession of the Duchy of Parma inherited from his mother Elisabetta, last heir to the Farnese dynasty. Within two years he wrested Naples from the Austrians. A new deal was cut with the European powers that allowed the Bourbons to reign in the Two Sicilies provided they remained independent from Spain, an arrangement that was to survive through his heirs for 127 years.

The archaeological ambitions of the young king are the direct outcome of his political ambitions. Charles Bourbon needed to establish the validity of his dynasty, its quasi-independence from Spain, and keep the other European powers happy. One tactic was to make his court one of the most spectacular and attractive in Europe. He built magnificent modern palaces, at Capodimonte, at Portici and, rivalling Versailles, at Caserta. He changed the face of the Grand Tour. In increasing numbers, the aristocracy and educated elites of Europe made their way to Naples, drawn by the glittering court life and the romance of what was one of Europe's most populous cities. But above all, archaeology worked for him. Already he had, from his mother, the finest collection of antique statues in Italy, built up by the Farnese family, which were eventually moved down to Naples. But the knowledge that more statues were emerging to grace the court of Vienna, from a site only 10 kilometres from his palace in Naples, was an irresistible pull. Excavating more made sense for the first time in terms of Realpolitik.

A further twist was that his new bride, Maria Amalia of Saxony, happened to come from the very court at which the statues of the Herculaneum women had ended up through diplomatic exchange in Dresden. It was said that she recalled as a girl seeing them unpacked, 'wrapped up like sardines in a box'. There is no need to attribute the excavations of Herculaneum to Maria Amalia's girlish enthusiasm; rather she is a vivid illustration of how the news of Prince d'Elbeuf's hot finds were travelling around the courts of Europe creating excitement, and offering an obvious incentive to a regime keen to make friends and cut a figure.

Charles Bourbon arrived in Naples in 1734. By 1736 he was at work on his new palace at Portici. So close to the site of Herculaneum is it that the south-eastern edge of the palace gardens overlaps with the north-western corner of the Villa of the Papyri. By 3 November 1738, a major royal project of excavation was under way. Inescapably, the project picked up, in location and in method, where the last episode of tunnelling had left off, in the Theatre. Now the project was under military engineers, with Rocque Joaquim de Alcubierre in charge. Military engineering probably brought a quantum leap in sophistication

Left: View of the new royal palace at Portici by Giovanni Battista Lusieri.

Below: Plan of the area around Resina (Ercolano) in 1796 with the Villa d'Elbeuf bottom left, by Francesco La Vega.

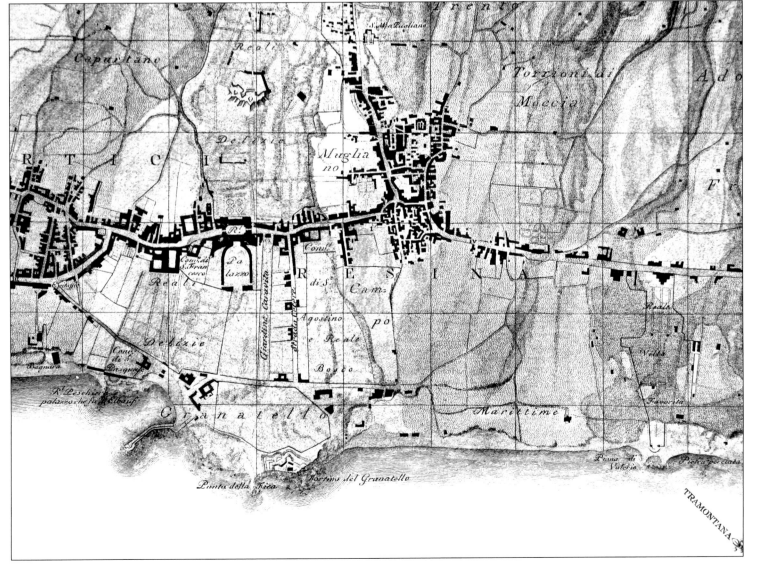

compared with the furtive explorations of previous tunnellers. They could use forced labour (prisoners of war), easily disposable manpower in tunnels that were dark, dusty, liable to collapse and afflicted by the noxious gas they called 'mofeta', probably pockets of carbon dioxide. Today, too, the tunnels are dangerous, but the radon gas that lurks in them is thought not to constitute a risk to life except after prolonged exposure.

The excavations, despite a good deal of acrimonious dispute, characteristic of the Neapolitan court, moved with astonishing speed. The Theatre rapidly gave up its crop of statues, and within a year a new dig had been opened up, in the area just east of the via Mare, the ancient track that led down from the centre of the village of Resina to the sea. The new dig hit the monumental core of the town. The military engineers not only dug more quickly and efficiently, but made accurate plans of what they excavated. The major public building, a portico, which they called the Basilica, is still only known from the plans made by the engineer Pierre Bardet de Villeneuve, refined by the French architect Jérome Bellicard, who happened to be doing his Grand Tour in 1745. Their plans show not only the cluster of three public buildings which stood at the heart of the town, but a dense pattern of private houses to the north of the principal street, which today lie under the modern town. Challenging though it was to explore an ancient city like some great coalmine by subterranean tunnels known as *cunicoli*, they recovered an astonishing amount of information. Despite the difficulties of surveying in tunnels (the instrument, the 'circumferentor', could not even turn round, as it had to do to work, in some), at least fourteen plans were produced between 1739 and 1750.

*Above: Aerial view looking north-west from the site (bottom) to the nearby Royal Palace at Portici (top right).*

*Right: Plan of Resina in the late nineteenth century, showing fields and houses covering the site (in red, the excavations carried out in this period).*

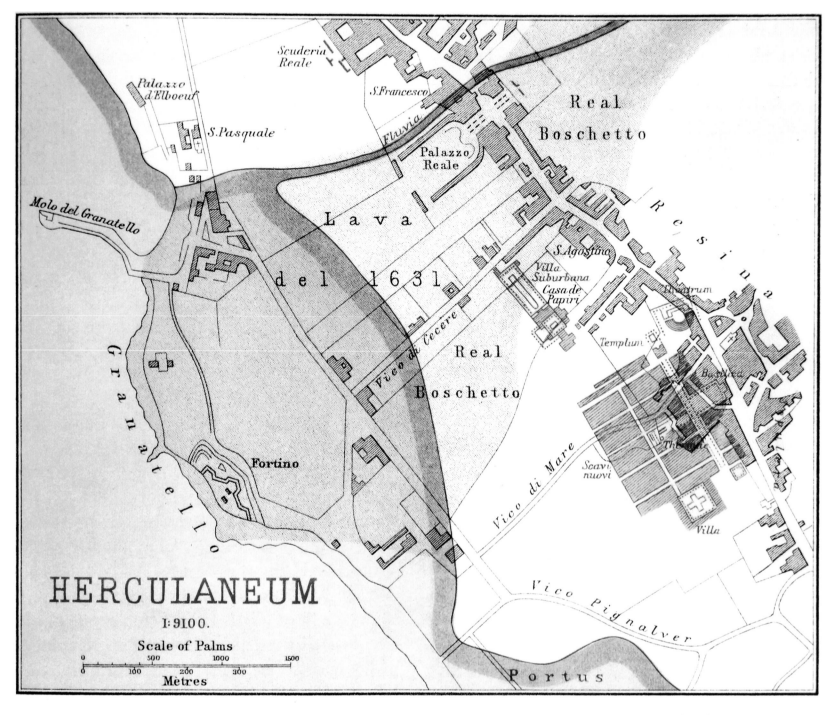

HERCULANEUM

1:9100.

Scale of Palms

Métres

*Plan of Herculaneum in the late nineteenth century, showing in red the location of buildings mapped by the Bourbon excavators.*

The 1740s and 1750s were the glory years of excavation at Herculaneum. Under a succession of engineers (Alcubierre from 1738, Bardet displacing him from 1741–5, Alcubierre back 1745–9, handing over to the Swiss Karl Weber from 1750 to his death in 1764, to be replaced by Francesco La Vega), the city was extensively explored. When Amedeo Maiuri launched the modern excavation of the site in the early twentieth century, he complained of the difficulties of excavating structures already undermined by a diabolical network of Bourbon tunnels. They reached a good deal further than the known plans reveal. To reopen their tunnels is to discover just how astonishingly thorough they were, crisscrossing buildings in a dense maze, with nodal points where as many as six tunnels converged, each opened up progressively, often over a period of many years.

The fruits were an astonishing collection of marble and bronze statues, fresco paintings, inscriptions and a host of household objects and furnishings, particularly in bronze: lamps, candelabra, basins, jugs, pans, ladles, tables, stools, ornamented couches, braziers and water-heaters. Gathered and displayed in the palace at Portici, they attracted the admiring gaze of visitors from all over Europe. Charles Bourbon's policy started to reap its rewards, and the heavy investment paid back (the engineers constantly complained at court of underfunding, but the costs were enormous). It was in these years that Herculaneum revealed its most important buildings: the Theatre, the so-called Basilica and the so-called Galleria Balbi (now the Basilica Noniana), the Palaestra complex and a series of private houses, among which pride of place went to the Villa of the Papyri, explored by Weber from 1750, with its unparalleled crop both of statues and carbonized papyri. A total of as many as 1,800 carbonized scrolls containing literary texts caused a sensation throughout Europe, dangling the prospect of a lost ancient library and the recovery of precious texts.

As the fame of these finds spread round Europe, the Grand Tour definitively shifted its terminus to Naples: 'see Naples and die' meant that until you had been there, your life was not yet complete. So effective was this propaganda that tourism has never flagged, with numbers gradually mounting over the years to

*Above: A point where six tunnels converge, showing the red bricks of a triumphal arch collapsed on its side.*

*Below: The access shaft to the Theatre.*

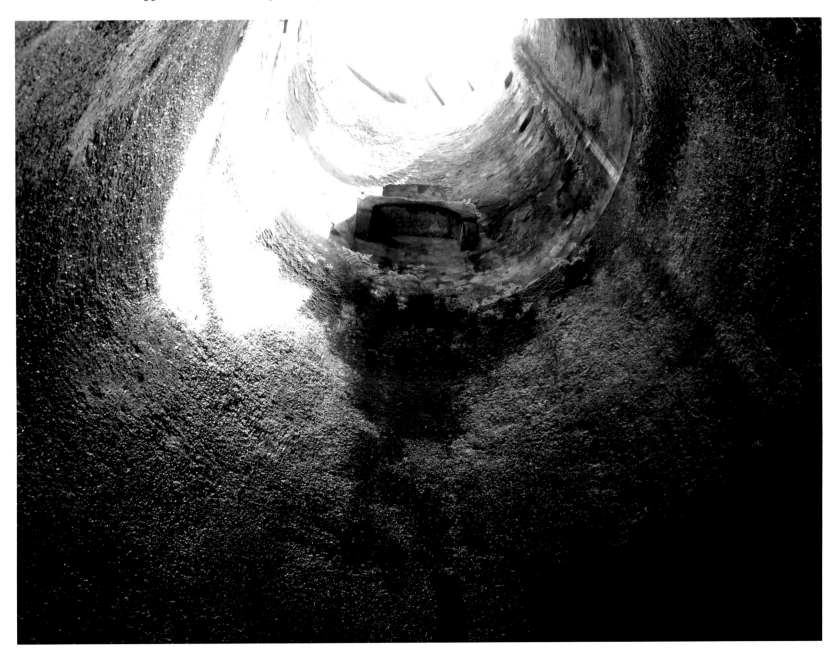

the many millions today. It is a sort of virtuous circle: the more people who visit the Vesuvian cities, the more coverage they receive from the media, so providing free advertising and stimulating yet more visitors and encouraging local authorities to invest in and promote tourism for the benefit of the local economy. All that has its origins in the reign of Charles Bourbon; he might not have envisaged the scale of mass tourism in a global economy, but at least he could try to persuade the wealthy elites of Europe to come.

It is remarkable how soon they came, and how enthusiastically they commented. Already in 1741, two English gentlemen, Horace Walpole, son of the former Prime Minister, and his Etonian friend Thomas Gray, Fellow of Peterhouse, Cambridge, and budding poet, made their visit. Although by then only the Theatre and Basilica had been explored, Gray could say that the king's workmen, in looking for statues, 'came to what one may call a whole city under ground'. He was less than impressed by their methods:

*Left: The Theatre: detail of the proscenium.*

*Opposite left: La calata nelli scavi (Visit to the Excavations of the Theatre), by Giacinto Gigante (1806–76).*

*Opposite right: L'escalier du théâtre d'Herculanum (anon.), engraved by Migliorato (1865).*

The work is unhappily under the direction of Spaniards, people of no taste or erudition, so that the workmen dig, as chance directs them, wherever they find the ground easiest to work without any certain view. They have been fearful of the earths falling in, & with reason, for it is but soft, & crumbling, so that the passage they have made, is but just sufficient for one person to walk upright in.

('Notes on Travel', from Gray and his Friends: Letters and Relics, Cambridge University Press, 1890)

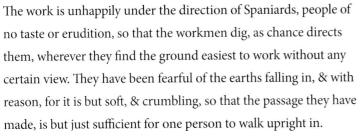

Thomas Gray reckoned they had excavated about a mile of such a winding passage, and saw 'buildings of brick with incrustations of marble, & here & there a solid column of it', saw plaster 'painted in square compartments, either green, or red, & sometimes little figures', and saw 'a mixture of woodwork amongst the brick, all black, as a coal, & tho' so firm as to show one even the Grain distinctly, yet upon being touch'd, moulders away into dust'. Gray's experience can still be reproduced in the tunnels of the Theatre. One senses the mixture of excitement at touching the crumbling remains of the past, combined with dismay at the methods of the excavators.

In this period, Herculaneum, not Pompeii, was the name to conjure with. The exploration of Pompeii started a decade later than that of Herculaneum, in 1748, and despite the considerably greater ease (and lower expense) of excavation, initial results were disappointing. There were two reasons for this. One is that the conditions of its preservation, a blanket of 5–7 metres of light *lapilli*, easily shovelled away, meant that Pompeii had been systematically ransacked from antiquity onwards, and there were fewer statues and objects of value to find. If you were looking for marbles and bronzes, the deeply buried Herculaneum offered a far richer seam. The second is that, even in antiquity, Herculaneum seems to have been a wealthier place, with an extraordinary density of fine houses, and a far more lavish use of coloured marble claddings than in Pompeii. So long as the priority remained the discovery of finds which could be carried to the surface and installed in a new setting in the Portici palace, Herculaneum was more promising.

But priorities changed under the impact of a series of external factors. In September 1759, on the death of his half-brother Ferdinand, Charles Bourbon left to become Charles III of Spain, leaving his eight-year-old younger son, another Ferdinand, to succeed as King of Naples. The regime of a minor, under the regency of Bernardo Tannucci, and closely watched over from Spain, was more sensitive to foreign criticism than that of his father, consolidated over twenty-five years. It was at precisely this time that the excavations, mildly criticized by those like Thomas Gray, came under a blistering attack from an authoritative foreign visitor, Johannes Joachim Winckelmann. Visiting Herculaneum first in 1758, then in early 1762, he experienced enormous frustration. First, he was appalled by the uncollaborative approach of the Bourbon officials; despite a letter of introduction from Frederick Christian, Elector of Saxony, to his sister Maria Amalia, he experienced constant difficulties of access to the material. If the court treated a well-recommended visitor like this so poorly, it is clear that they did not understand the promotion of cultural tourism. Indeed, it is to this period that belongs the extraordinary policy of destroying frescoes that were not brought to the palace at Portici, for fear that they be sold off to foreigners. Winckelmann took remorseless revenge in his *Sendschreiben von den herculanischen Entdeckunden* (Account of the Discoveries at Herculaneum), excoriating the excavators, especially Alcubierre, notoriously characterized as having as much to do with antiquity, in the Italian expression, 'as the moon with crabs', and the antiquarian Camillo Paderni, 'as much an impostor as a nitwit and an ignoramus'. While rubbishing Bourbon archaeological technique, by the entire structure of his letter he underlines the importance of archaeological context. He is not, as art historian, content to describe the artworks in the museum, but precedes it with a careful account of the site. And he pays full tribute to the intelligent Karl Weber for his insistence on making exact plans of the buildings discovered.

Winckelmann's observations were not original: Spanish excavation methods had been under fire from the first, and Weber had been long insisting at court on the importance of the recording of context. What mattered was the shockwave of bad publicity for the Bourbon court of the *Sendschreiben* of 1762, and the more so (since German could be to some extent ignored) of the French translation of 1764. The court of the boy king Ferdinand was highly sensitive to such high-profile criticism. To look like a European prince, it was no longer enough to have a fine collection of statues: you had to take account of the opinions of foreign visitors. Antagonizing Winckelmann by the usual dog-in-the-manger tactics was a PR disaster. It was time for a shift of tactics.

At the same time, Pompeii came to the rescue. After some years of rather frustrating results, excavations started to concentrate on the area of the Theatre, and a new policy was adopted, impossible at Herculaneum, of leaving the excavated structures exposed to visitors. In August 1764, work started, under Francesco La Vega, replacing Karl Weber, on the Theatre of Pompeii. By November, the nearby Temple of Isis was beginning to emerge, and work continued without a break until September 1766. Then, in October 1766, work started on the portico behind the Theatre, excavations which continued into summer 1768, producing sensational finds: the gladiators' barracks, complete with gladiatorial armour, the stocks in which the gladiators were confined, together with a number of skeletons, including that of a lady with much jewellery. The Theatre, the Temple of Isis and the barracks produced a sensation that had little or nothing to do with statues. Here was ancient life, in its most extreme forms, being laid bare: an exotic Egyptian cult and the most brutal of entertainments. The international interest was immense. Numerous artists captured the Temple of Isis, during and after excavation, in a way unparalleled at Herculaneum.

Public attention thus shifted decisively from Herculaneum to Pompeii, and this was never to be reversed in the popular imagination. True, as the finds of the two sites started to be published in 1757, in the magnificent series of folio volumes issues by the Royal Press in Naples, they were still titled, despite reporting material from both sites, *Le Antichità di Ercolano Esposte*, just as their production was supervised by the Royal *Herculaneum* Academy of Archaeology, established by Charles in 1755. That the name of Herculaneum still had significant resonance was increasingly due to the circulation, often in pirated versions, of *The Antiquities of Herculaneum*. The first, unauthorized, English translation, by two Fellows of Sidney Sussex College, Cambridge, Thomas Martyn and John Lettice, came out in 1773, and was promptly brought to a halt at the request of the court of Naples. Something of the impact of the name can be caught in the choice to name the pottery at Toxteth in Liverpool, producing neo-classical pieces as fine as those of Josiah Wedgwood's 'Etruria' pottery, the Herculaneum Pottery.

But in the meantime, from the death of Weber in 1764, exploration at Herculaneum fell off dramatically, and the site was virtually untouched for the next sixty years. Francesco La Vega continued work in the Theatre, principally in order to complete the plan begun by Weber, but there were few new finds. As far as visitors were concerned, although the visit to the subterranean theatre had its charms, for the rest of the site, the experience of going down tunnels by torchlight could not compete with the experience Pompeii now offered, of a dead city 'brought back to life'. Only in 1828, after the accession in 1825 of a new sovereign, Francis I, at the end of the long reign of his father Ferdinand, did attention return briefly to Herculaneum, and the first attempt was made to give the site something of the appeal of Pompeii by 'open-air' excavations, exposing a short stretch of street (Cardo III) and the houses of Argus and Io

*La Decouverte d'Herculanum (H. Robert), engraved by C. Guttenberg.*

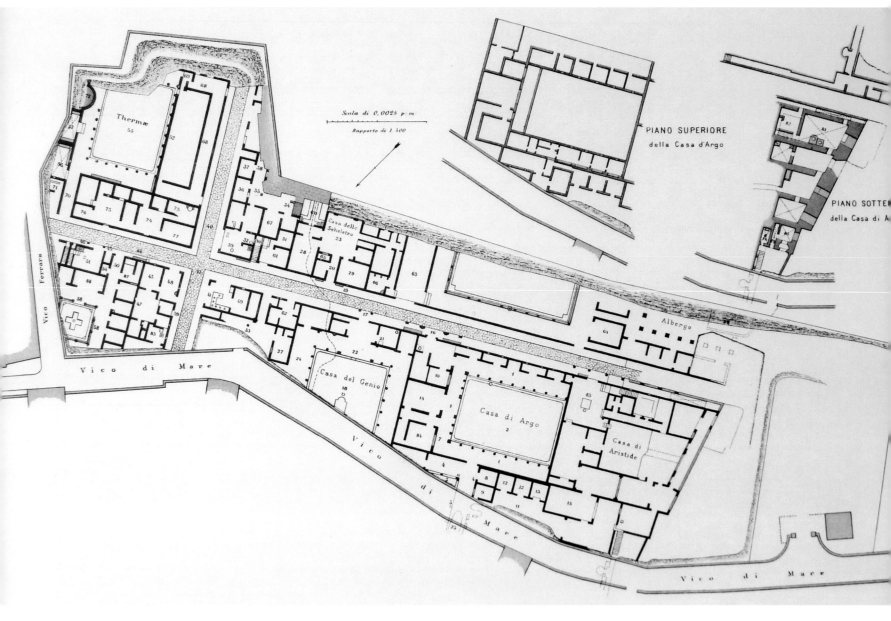

and of the Skeleton. But work was suspended on 18 March 1837 by royal rescript, and the funding for excavation was transferred to the Amphitheatre at Pozzuoli. The moment for Herculaneum had not yet come. Activity was resumed briefly in the 1850s, when the House of Aristides, with its precious upper floors, had to be propped up, an early sign of the problems of conservation that were to dog the site.

The melancholy feel of Herculaneum in the 1830s is vividly evoked by the Countess Blessington's memoirs, *The Idler in Italy*. She visited the site in the company of the indefatigable Sir William Gell, author of the much-read volumes of *Pompeiana*, who in the 1820s and 1830s introduced so many English

visitors, including the novelist Edward Bulwer Lytton, to Pompeii, and helped further to spread the fame of that site. She records:

12th– Went to Herculaneum yesterday, accompanied by Sir William Gell. This excursion may well be called a descent into the grave of a buried city. . . .

The wild and grotesque figures and animated gesticulations of the guides, waving their torches, which cast lugubrious gleams of light around this sepulchre of a dead city; the dense and oppressive air, and the reverberation of the sound of the carriages passing and repassing through the streets

*Plan of excavations of Herculaneum between 1828 and 1875 (E. Tascone).*

above it, have an indescribable influence on the mind. One consequently ascends into light and life again with feelings of melancholy, which not even the beautiful scenery that courts the eye can banish for some time.

The Bourbon 'kingdom of the Two Sicilies' collapsed in 1860 as Giuseppe Garibaldi successfully advanced through the south. The last of the Bourbons, Francis II (Francischiello, 'Little Francis'), was manoeuvred into abandoning his capital without a blow. The deal had been negotiated between Garibaldi at Salerno and the principal figures of the government, led by the liberal Liborio Romano, through the mediation of Alexandre Dumas, author of *The Three Musketeers*, who, having followed Garibaldi's advance, moored his yacht, the *Emma,* beneath the windows of the royal palace in Naples. Dumas asked for, and received, as his reward, responsibility for Pompeii, but his position proved untenable, and he was rapidly replaced. His successor was the ambitious young scholar, Giuseppe Fiorelli, who had for some time served the king's uncle, the Count of Syracuse, as secretary, publishing his collection of coins, and also drafting a famous letter in which the king was urged to adopt more liberal policies.

Fiorelli's period in prison after the uprising of 1848, when he had incited the guardians of Pompeii to arm themselves against the regime, gave him credibility as an anti-Bourbon, and had also given him the leisure to pull together the old records of excavations at Pompeii as *Antiquitates Pompeianae.* A staunch supporter of the new national government, he would receive his reward in promotion to national Director of Antiquities in 1875. He is rightly remembered as one of the principal figures in the archaeology of Pompeii, rather than of Herculaneum. Yet he did not completely neglect the site, and in 1869 he reopened the excavations abandoned in 1837, inviting King Vittorio Emanuele to a grand opening ceremony

*Photograph of the nineteenth-century
excavations, viewed towards the houses on the
via Mare.*

on 8 February 1869: the moment was memorialized in a contemporary photograph and a large oil painting based on the photograph, now in the Naples Museum. It seems to trumpet a grand new beginning. For four years the excavations produced results, including the exceptional silver bust of Emperor Galba (see page 185), found outside the house consequently named the House of Galba, though the bust had been swept down the street by the pyroclastic surge many metres from its place in a public building. But with Fiorelli's departure for Rome in 1875, the excavations ground to a halt again.

Late nineteenth-century guidebooks were singularly unenthusiastic about Herculaneum. Typical is the John Murray handbook of 1892:

> The Scavi Nuovi are entered by an iron gate
> on the l[eft] of the Vico di Mare, 5 min. from
> the entrance to the theatre; for those who have
> already seen Pompeii a sufficiently good idea
> of the whole can be obtained from the entrance
> without.

The iron gate can still be seen, hidden behind a low wall and bushes, on the left (as you go downhill) of the Vico Mare: a reminder of how small and unappealing the site was until transformed by Maiuri's excavations. But though the public had deserted the site, there were scholars who understood its importance and potential.

Charles Waldstein was primarily a Greek archaeologist. Born in New York, he took up a post in classical archaeology at Cambridge in 1880, and became Director of the Fitzwilliam Museum, Director of the American School of Archaeology at Athens, and Slade Professor of Fine Art at Cambridge, a career of some distinction, even if he was not always welcomed by the British establishment. By the end of the nineteenth century, he was an international authority on Greek art, respected for his work on the sanctuary of Hera at Argos and on the Greek sculptor Pheidias. What caught his interest about Herculaneum was its exceptional potential as a source of *Greek* art. He knew that the ninety-eight sculptures found in the Villa of the Papyri were among the best collections of 'Greek' works yet found; he belonged to a period when the most interesting thing about the art of Roman sites was its potential to reconstruct the lost masterpieces of classical Greek art.

> . . . the fact remains that, from the actual finds
> made in earlier excavations, we are justified to
> hope, nay, bound to expect, that discoveries
> of valuable works of Greek art will be made in
> the future, and this to a far higher degree than
> at Pompeii or any other site hitherto known in
> classic lands.
>
> (From *Herculaneum Past Present
> and Future*, 1908, page 12.)

His prophecy has indeed been borne out, at least to some degree, by subsequent excavations, though we are less inclined to define the works of art as 'Greek', rather than contemporary Roman versions of older Greek works.

Waldstein led a vigorous international campaign to raise funds for the excavation of Herculaneum between 1903 and 1907. In a remarkable model of a spirit of internationalism, urging that the vast costs of excavation were beyond the reach of any one nation state, and that our ideal must be to overcome the barriers of chauvinism and national rivalry, he set about finding support at the highest levels: King Edward VII, President Roosevelt and President Loubet of France promised patronage, and the Giolitti government was talked round, not without difficulty. Finance was forthcoming, with the support of figures such as Pierpont Morgan. From the first Waldstein stressed internationalism, leaving Italy in the lead to avoid any hint of the

*Funerary urn of Charles Walston (Waldstein), a Roman vase donated by Amedeo Maiuri (courtesy James Walston).*

familiar colonialist venture of so much nineteenth-century archaeology. Nevertheless, the Italians, including the great Giacomo Boni, excavator of the Roman Forum, had deep misgivings, and in the end his scheme was blocked, the Italian State undertaking to do the excavation itself. The Italian funds, as Waldstein realized when he published his account – full of enthusiasm cut with bitterness – were simply not forthcoming, and the venture had to wait a full twenty years for the arrival of a Fascist government, committed as none since Charles Bourbon to archaeology as a source of national prestige. Waldstein died in 1927, but not before he had taken a final cruise to the Mediterranean, disembarked at Naples, and gone to visit Amedeo Maiuri on site at Herculaneum, just as the new excavations were beginning. Maiuri was deeply moved to be able to realize the dream of a dying man, and when Waldstein died shortly after, Maiuri sent his widow an original Roman glass funerary urn from his excavations, in which the ashes lie still.

The Herculaneum we see today is essentially the result of Amedeo Maiuri's work. A man of astonishing energy, he combined a deep knowledge of classical antiquity and an exceptional capacity to communicate with the ability to organize with military precision a massive project of engineering and complex reconstruction that demanded the close co-operation of numerous trades and skills and the co-ordination of hundreds of workers. Without the willingness of Mussolini's government to invest in recreating 'ancient Rome', he could never have started, and a large proportion of the excavation was indeed carried out between 1927 and the collapse of the regime in 1943. Nevertheless, he kept his project going not only through the war but into the post-war period, and played a crucial role in relaunching the Bay of Naples as a prime destination for the new post-bellum mass tourism. He was not only the excavator and restorer of ancient Herculaneum, but its principal publicist,

writing a series of popular works and guidebooks, reaching a culmination in his monumental publication of 1958, *Ercolano: i nuovi scavi (1927–1958)*, printed with all the elegance and style of which the Poligrafico dello Stato, the Italian State press, was capable. With his retirement in 1961, the period of new exploration came to a halt, and extensions since then have been intermittent, notably the excavation of the seashore in the 1980s, and of the area towards the Villa of the Papyri in the 1990s. There are many grounds on which Maiuri can be criticized, as we shall see: his restorations ran ahead of the evidence, and sometimes his narratives involved distortion or falsification of the evidence. Nevertheless, it is to his drive, vision and skill that Herculaneum owes the reversal of the fall from grace that it has experienced ever since Winckelmann's letter of 1762. Waldstein understood the importance of the site, ranking it higher than Pompeii. Maiuri gave reality to that vision.

# 3
# RUINS RESTORED

We think of the traces of the past buried beneath the earth's surface as having been 'lost', and the role of the archaeologist as being to 'save' them. Lost to sight, certainly. But at least what is below the ground is in a more or less stable condition. The damage has been done, and it has reached some sort of equilibrium with the environment – until, that is, human action comes to disturb it again. The moment we 'expose' antiquities (in the words of the Bourbon publication of *The Antiquities of Herculaneum Exposed*), we subject them to new damage, and to the risk of a second, and this time terminal, destruction.

This reflection, familiar to a modern world in which conservationists have made their voices heard, never troubled the Bourbon tunnellers. They treated the remnants of the past with a strange mixture of reverence and contempt. Statues and frescoes instantly achieved the status of 'lost masters' and were reverentially taken to the royal palace for display. Heaving them up to the surface, often pieces weighing several tons, via the rabbit warren of their *cunicoli* ('burrows', as these tunnels were known), was no joke. Frescoes presented a particular difficulty, because they formed part of the integral decoration of walls. Some were relatively easy, panels only a few centimetres wide and deep, depicting still lives, or landscape vignettes, or cupids at play. These could be hacked out of their original decorative context. This did a permanent damage to that context, as Maiuri was to discover when, for instance, he excavated the House of the Stags to find all the vivid still lives hacked from the walls of the portico. But at least one could re-establish what came from where. Much more challenging were

the mythological scenes that occupied the walls of the great public buildings, the scenes of Theseus and the Minotaur, Hercules and Telephus or Achilles and Chiron, each with dimensions ranging from 1 to over 2 metres. It was an enormously delicate job to remove these from their walls in a single piece, let alone carry them up to the surface without damage. The workmen cut through the thick layers of plaster, and then secured the works in frames of solid wood, reinforced behind with slates to keep the plaster rigid. The weight was enormous, but the frescoes were in the end well preserved in the dry atmosphere of the palace museum. What might seem like vandalism turned out to save them.

Not everything was treated with the same respect. Whatever was not a masterpiece could be destroyed. Frequently the tunnels cut straight through frescoed walls and fallen structures. What did not seem worth preserving was often smashed, and as the suspicions of the court grew that workmen were illicitly selling fragments to tourists, the king, anxious to maintain his monopoly, ordered that frescoes not brought to the surface should be gouged to render them unusable. We can still see in the Villa of Arianna at Stabiae the results of this wilful barbarism, which upset many observers at the time. Not even material brought to the surface was safe. Numerous bronze fragments were found of a group showing an emperor in a four-horsed chariot, probably from the top of the arch by the Basilica. The task of reassembling these proved to be too much of a challenge, and Winckelmann lamented that they were first abandoned in a heap in the courtyard of the palace, and then partially melted down to make a statue of the Bourbon king himself.

*Archival photograph (1930s) of the shop in the front of the House of Neptune and Amphitrite, with reconstructed balcony and wine-rack, and amphorae, grain and a lamp on display.*

The Bourbons had not moved all that far from their predecessors who thought the classical past was best left buried.

But voices of concern over the cause of conservation were raised from an early stage. Winckelmann's protests rang out across Europe, and King Ferdinand needed to repair his reputation as a barbarian. In July 1766, Conte Coppola, the Royal Chamberlain, commissioned an architect, Ferdinando Fuga, and a painter, Francesco di Mura, to report on the condition of the frescoes in the royal collection. Both reported extreme concern at the damage done by the application of modern varnishes to 'preserve' the paintings. Fuga pointed out, correctly, that the paintings were not pure frescoes, but also had layers of colour applied after the plaster was dry, which consequently had a tendency to flake off. The varnishes exacerbated this tendency, and he urged careful research into the different pigments and varnishes. The painter di Mura was even clearer. He said the varnish only did damage to the paint and made it darker, and that the sort of plaster on which they were based would tolerate neither this nor any other sort of varnish or preparation.

> Wherefore in all humble respect to Your Majesty, in my feeble opinion I would say that to conserve as much as possible of the air and spirit of antiquity of these noble paintings, it is not at all appropriate either to tint them or bathe them in varnish or in any other type of liquid, but simply to keep them guarded and protected from the air and the sun's rays.

The authorities did not listen. They continued to apply ever-more modern and scientifically advanced preparations up to the paraloids of the late twentieth century, each doing damage. In the nineteenth century it was standard practice to hurl a bucket of water over a fresco to 'freshen it up' for the visitors, doing incalculable damage, and leaving them ultimately faded to nothing. In the twentieth century, a mixture of wax and paraffin was designed to rub into the frescoes to keep them bright for longer than the water. Two hundred and forty years after Francesco di Mura, the modern conservator would say the same thing: protect them from the damp and the sun, and put no liquids and no chemical preparations on them.

At first it seemed that the priority was to deter the Bourbons from hacking paintings from the walls. Sir William Hamilton, newly arrived as ambassador to the Bourbon court in 1764, was soon offering advice to the Prime Minister, Tanucci. The following year, in a letter dated 12 November 1765, he reports:

> The Marquis Tanucci . . . has lately shown his good taste by ordering that for the future the workmen employed in the search for Pompeii should not remove any inscriptions or paintings from the walls, nor fill up after they have searched, so that travellers will have the opportunity of walking the streets and

*Above: Frescoes damaged by Bourbon excavators. A panel cut out of the Basilica (above) and a figure deliberately scored through, from the Villa of Ariadne at Stabiae (below).*

*Inside: Panoramic view of the Atrium of the Suburban Baths.*

seeing the houses of the ancient city (which is infinitely more considerable than Herculaneum) as commodiously as Naples itself.

Such advice turned Pompeii into the visitor attraction it is. But it also created new levels of risk for the remains. None saw that as clearly as the other English knight whose name became so closely associated with the site, Sir William Gell. In 1832, after more than a decade of repeated visits to the site, he expressed his deep concern:

> It has often been noticed, during the winter months, that the stuccoes which
> had been observed perfect, during a first visit to a newly-discovered edifice,
> had entirely disappeared on a second examination; so that, no traces being left,
> many of the prettiest fancies of antiquity are irrecoverably lost; while the order
> continues to prevent strangers from drawing till three or four years have expired,
> and the objects become defaced.

Gell was of course expressing a personal frustration that he himself, a consummate draftsman, was being prevented from recording new finds, thanks to a monopoly granted to an Italian architect, who did not even bother to exercise his right to make images. Even today, the state authorities jealously guard their copyright over the images in their sites, and restrict access to 'unpublished' buildings (which remain such for many decades). A more enlightened viewpoint might suggest that images are better conserved by allowing access than by restricting it.

Once the policy had been adopted at Pompeii of preserving material in the position found on site, a deep, new problem of conservation was created. If you leave frescoes on their broken walls, open to the weather (let alone 'refresh' them with buckets of water), you guarantee their destruction, and any visitor to Pompeii today can see the acres of devastation left by this policy, which lasted at least a century. The only way to save such frescoes (save removing them from site, which is maybe not such a stupid policy, after all) is to put a roof over their heads. But in that case, you have to decide what sort of a roof. Most of the houses of Pompeii had upper floors, yet only the ground floor was preserved under the blanket of *lapilli*.

Those who leapt to publish the excavations, with François Mazois, the architect supported by Caroline Murat, the French Queen of Naples, dominant during the period of French occupation (1801–15), and William Gell in the vanguard after the Bourbon restoration, took particular pleasure in re-imagining the houses as they were before the eruption, and juxtaposing 'before' and 'after' views. The views of the post-excavation state reveal the absence of roofs; the reconstructions put back the original antique roofs (along with the missing decoration, the furniture, etc.). Consciously or unconsciously, such publications influenced the excavators, and when it became clear, under Fiorelli, that it was necessary to

*Left: Drawings of the House of the Tragic Poet by Sir William Gell. The actual state (above) and the proposed reconstruction (below).*

*Right: Photograph of Amedeo Maiuri, excavator of Herculaneum (1927–61).*

re-roof a house in order to conserve it, the conclusion seemed obvious that a 'reconstruction' of the original condition was the way to go. By the end of the century, when the House of the Vettii in Pompeii was excavated in a remarkable state of preservation by Fiorelli's successor Giulio De Petra, it was equipped with a series of rooflines that certainly evoked the impression of a Roman building, even if the use of cement and iron was modern. It was thus not until the 1890s that the model of 'reconstruction' that was to become typical was born.

Hence, by the time that Amedeo Maiuri set about excavating Herculaneum in 1927, the experimentation of a previous century of restoration determined the broad approach he would use. Material should be left, so far as possible, on site in its original position, not sent back to the museum in Naples, and the structures, where the conservation of valuable decoration demanded, should be restored so far as possible to their original condition in the original style. There was already a cautionary tale on site that underlined the importance of immediate reconstruction. When

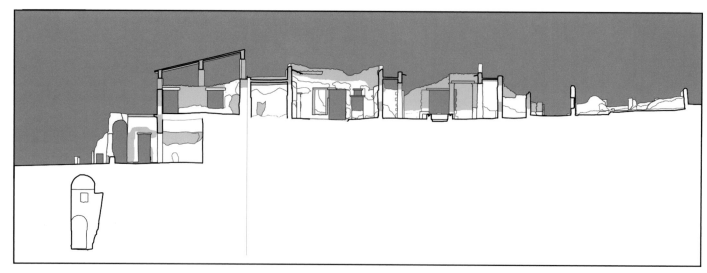

Reconstruction by Maiuri    Original structures

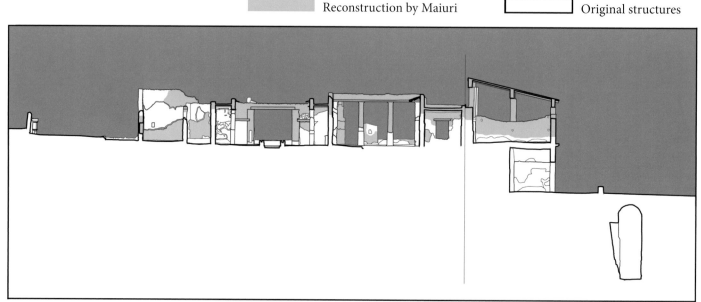

the House of Argus was excavated in the first half of the nineteenth century, it was found to have a partial upper floor (something exceptional in Pompeii, but normal in Herculaneum), including a considerable quantity of carbonized foodstuffs stored there. The upper floor was left unprotected, and, already weakened by earlier tunnelling, it started to collapse. With great regret, the architect Carlo Bonnucci, who was in charge of excavations from 1828 to 1855, was forced to demolish what remained, something that later to Maiuri seemed a scandalous loss. He did not intend to make the same mistake himself.

The consequence, one which every visitor to the site needs to keep in mind, is that what we see is not an ancient town as preserved by an eruption, but fragments painstakingly pieced together, stabilized, reinforced and 'restored' by Maiuri. In one house

where careful volumetric measurements have been undertaken, the House of the Telephus Relief, the architects calculate that no more than 50 per cent of what is standing is antique: the rest is Maiuri's reconstruction. We have to remind ourselves continuously that what we see is not the raw evidence, but a re-presentation, one done with consummate skill by an outstanding archaeologist, but incorporating his own interpretations.

Because these excavations were documented photographically, and occasionally even filmed, as well as painstakingly recorded in the daybooks of the excavations, we can follow the process in detail. In doing so, our admiration for Maiuri only grows. He was fearless in using modern technology. A splendid Ingersoll-Rand compressor powers his pneumatic drills, and is proudly recorded for posterity. Tracks

*Above: North–south cross-sections of the House of the Gem and the Telephus Relief, looking west (above) and east (below). Parts shaded in blue are modern reconstruction (drawing by Gionata Rizzi).*

*Right: Archival photographs of Maiuri's excavations, showing the compressor for pneumatic drills (above left), trucks for spoils (above right) and horses for towing (below).*

are laid for a railway for removing the spoils, with iron skips pulled by horses. (The tracks were also recycled as joists for reconstructing concrete lintels.) The army of workmen, whose names are daily recorded in the diary, are carefully co-ordinated. They move with seamless speed from excavation to reconstruction.

Three shots from the same spot taken over three successive years show the progress of the reconstruction of the atrium of the House of the Telephus Relief. In 1934, the tops of three columns peep shyly from the volcanic shroud. A year later, the columns are not merely exposed, but have had an architrave and roof restored above them. In the foreground two other columns can be seen, these without architrave. In the final shot, belonging to 1936, the reconstructed architrave is complete, turning the corner closest to the camera. Between the columns the original marble plaques have been suspended, called *oscilla* because of their oscillation in the wind, to reveal fine low-relief carvings on both sides. In the background, the excavation appears to have been pushed back to embrace the peristyle garden. The scene is decked out festively for the arrival of Mussolini. The speed of reconstruction is admirable, and the impact on visitors, with the original marble decorations in place, impressive (the viewer cannot see behind their right shoulder the larger marble plaque depicting the healing of the wounded Telephus by Achilles, a magnificent neo-Attic relief – moved for the convenience of visitors from its original position elsewhere). The whole is a careful composition, with the visitor in mind. It is also in part false, because the central basin, or *impluvium*, with its high edging, shows that the atrium roof originally covered the central space. Maiuri has used the columns which supported an upper floor to turn it into a peristyle-type atrium.

Another eye-catching example of visitor presentation is the House of Neptune and Amphitrite, or rather the shop with flat

*Right: Archival photographs of the excavation of the atrium of the House of the Telephus Relief in 1934 (top), 1935 (middle) and 1936 (bottom).*

*Opposite: Archival photograph of the site c.1937, looking over the House of the Gem and the House of the Telephus Relief from the south-east. Note the relief after which the house is named is still in its original position.*

*Overleaf: Marble neo-Attic relief showing Achilles consulting the Delphic Sybil (left), and healing the seated Telephus with the rust from his spear (right).*

above in its frontage. The fact that the street where it is located, Cardo IV, is rather narrow and rises steeply, combined with the fact that the pavement opposite is unusually high, means that the visitor can see this house as a sort of cross-section or cut-away, operating on two levels. Below, the shop is revealed in more intimate detail than any other surviving Roman shop. The counter is visible with its earthenware containers (*dolia*), rendered easier to see by the partial collapse of a part of the counter. The *dolium* at the end of the counter has been filled with the carbonized grain it 'originally' contained. On the counter is displayed in a glass case a range of the pottery used in the shop. Behind, to one side, the 'original' carbonized wooden rack supports the 'original' amphorae from which various wines were served. At the back, even more amazingly, is the 'original' wooden partition with screen, creating a small backroom for the shop, with a storage area above, and amphorae duly stored there. From the beam hangs – delightful detail – an 'original' bronze lamp; below it is the cooking hearth. But then, step back and look into the upper portion of the cut-away. Because no upper wall has been restored, we see directly into the bedroom, with a small marble table, and a leg of the 'original' bronze couch attached to the wall. Here is an independent flat, with its own stove and latrine. Ancient life reaches out to touch us with extraordinary immediacy.

Yet it is all stagecraft. The wood is not original – it is largely modern reconstruction, with some fragments of carbonized wood prominently incorporated. We know from the excavation diaries that, where necessary, Maiuri had no scruples about displaying artefacts actually found elsewhere. There is no reason to be confident that this grain was found here, not (as so often) in an upper storey. The amphorae may be reassembled from this and other houses. What we are looking at is a skilful composite, true to the spirit of the original, but not actually archaeological evidence of what was found.

TABERNA DELLA CASA DI NETTUNO E ANFITRITE · INTERNO

*Left above: Archival view of the façade of the House of Neptune and Amphitrite, showing 'cut-away' effect of restoration of upper floor.*

*Interior of the shop in the House of Neptune and Amphitrite, in an archival photograph (above) showing the display of artefacts on the counter, as well as amphorae and a suspended lamp, and in a watercolour reconstruction by Maiuri (opposite).*

*Above: View of the upper floor of the House of Neptune and Amphitrite.*

*Opposite: Detail of bed.*

In another case, the shop of the 'weaving girl', Maiuri's passion for a good story evidently carried him away. As displayed to the public, the backroom of the shop contained the skeleton of a teenage girl lying on a couch. By her couch is the little loom, on which she was weaving before the eruption, a small stool with marquetry decoration in front of it for her to work from. A small marble table rests against the left-hand wall, and a bronze candelabrum provides illumination on the right. The excavation diaries tell a very different story. They report the bed and the skeleton of a 'young boy', and otherwise 'no finds'. Maiuri has carefully put together this composition, and the entire story of the weaving girl. Deeply touching, but not actually true.

It is not clear that Maiuri was actually in the business of misleading the public. It was a new, and inspired, idea to display a good selection of the objects excavated actually on site, so restoring a sense of 'real life', aided by the survival of carbonized wood and grain, going well beyond what was possible at Pompeii, as in the House of the Vettii. In moving things around, like the fine Telephus relief, he did not want to deceive (he left the hole from which it was removed clearly legible) but to save the visitor effort, to give them a more immediate experience. In his guidebook, published with great promptness, he explains precisely where the Telephus relief was found, and the fact that the atrium had a Tuscan roof above a second floor, so that the roof above the columns of the peristyle was not the original one. But gradually, the reconstructions came to assume the value of original evidence, and by 1958, in his principal publication of the site, he had completely fallen for his own story of the little weaving girl.

From the point of view of presentation of evidence, Maiuri does not pass today's much higher standards of purism. His reconstructions have come to be seen as a sort of falsification. Might it have been better to leave the ancient structures stabilized but not reconstructed, and instead create some great shelter over them, like the structure that now covers a block of houses at Ephesus in Turkey? This is a conservation debate that will long rumble on, reflecting the changing ideological priorities of each age. What Maiuri, however, achieved very effectively was the reliable conservation of the remains. Seen from the modern approach to the south, the site gives the impression of a little hilltop town, with charming tiled roofs sloping down, and palms, pines and pomegranates growing in the gardens. For a moment, you can believe this is how the town

looked. Closer inspection reveals that 70 per cent of the roofed spaces have modern flat roofs in poured concrete. It is a clever solution, because they are virtually invisible from above, and save the archaeologist from having to reconstruct what he knew to have been there: an upper storey. And they work well to protect the frescoed walls and marble-inlaid floors below, so long, that is, as they are properly maintained, gutters and downpipes unblocked, plants kept at bay from the roofs and wall-crests. The modern crisis of Herculaneum started when the maintenance programme established by Maiuri stopped.

Just how well he did, and how far short more recent times have fallen, is clear when one considers the excavations of the 1990s that made a first step towards the planned excavation of the Villa of the Papyri. The project was proposed and financed as a project of pure excavation without provision for conservation of the site. The excavation revealed (as excavations always do) many surprises. Instead of finding an empty seashore separating the villa from the town, it revealed an impressive series of buildings, the lower, seaward parts of the most westerly blocks of the town, then a bathing establishment, and finally the lower terrace and swimming pool associated with the villa. Unlike Maiuri's excavation, restoration did not go hand-in-

*Above: The 'room of the little weaving girl' as reconstructed by Maiuri, showing the skeleton on the bed, the loom, and furniture. Everything except the bed and skeleton has been moved from other locations.*

*Left: Detail of the same loom.*

*Right: Aerial view of the site c.1955, before the expropriation and demolition of the houses in the north-western corner.*

hand with excavation, and archaeological supervision was minimal. Workmen with heavy earth-moving equipment tore through ancient structures, leaving the marks of metal teeth in wooden beams, plaster-work, even gouged deeply into brick masonry. There was no money, and no time, to put shelters over what had been found, and large plastered surfaces were left exposed to the pitiless elements. Only the atrium of the villa itself was given a temporary cover, and one so crude and flimsy as to offer as much damage as protection. Concrete footings were laid on mosaic floors, and the plastic sheet roofing, bombarded by rubbish hurled from the modern town above, soon

allowed the water to penetrate, destroying the mosaics below. To make matters worse, the pumps necessary to keep a site such as this dry, lying partly below the water table, were underspecified, and rapidly broke down, causing a major inundation.

The entire site was at risk, and voices from abroad, the modern successors of Charles Waldstein, pleaded desperately for the excavations to continue. What they did not understand is that excavation, in itself, does not save a site: it subjects it to the risk of destruction. Until, after over two and a half centuries of excavation at this site, we learn to save what we expose, we must continue to ask: 'Why do we dig up the past?'

*View of the site from the south, looking over the House of the Stags towards Vesuvius.*

*Left: Excavation trench running to the Villa of the Papyri, seen in 2006 before conservation work.*

*Below left: Details of structures scored by the teeth of a mechanical digger.*

*Below right: Flooding of the seashore in 2000 caused by the breakdown of the pumps.*

# 4
# THE TOWN
# AND ITS SETTING

*Cardo IV viewed from the north. Note the columns to support the upper balconies, and the lead pipes running close to the surface of the pavement.*

Why this town here? Location, location, location. The Augustan geographer Strabo, in his sweep around the Bay of Naples, speaks with particular enthusiasm of the position of Herculaneum, 'set on a promontory that juts into the sea, and wonderfully exposed to the breezes of the south-westerly Libyan wind, making it a healthy place to stay'. The eruption so dramatically transformed the landscape that it is now hard indeed to imagine this promontory kissed by the sea breezes. The shoreline moved outwards by 400 metres in a matter of 24 hours, and Ercolano now forms one unbroken strip with neighbouring Portici and Torre del Greco. Gone too are the rivers about which a Roman historian wrote (his history survives only in fragments – if only the Villa of the Papyri would restore us texts like this!). Cornelius Sisenna, before his death in 67 BC, wrote about the Social War of 91–89 BC, the brutal civil war in which many of Rome's Italian allies, especially those who spoke not Latin but Oscan, made a bid for independence. Herculaneum, like its neighbour Pompeii, took sides with their fellow Oscan-speakers against Rome. In a citation that survives by chance, he describes a Roman commander approaching Herculaneum as 'a town on a steep rise by the sea, with little walls, between two rivers beneath Vesuvius' (he made the Latin for 'river' feminine not masculine, and so caught the eye of a grammarian). The soft volcanic tufo is easily gouged by torrents descending the steep slopes of the mountain, and since Herculaneum is at the point of the coast closest to the crater (most of which still lies within the jurisdiction of the

Municipality of Ercolano), such ravines would be particularly deep. Herculaneum lay on soft rock, formed by an eruption perhaps no more than 8,000 years before the present, and then modified by water into a promontory with steep sides.

Its south-westerly exposure and its flanking rivers also made Herculaneum a good anchorage. Another Greek writer, Dionysius of Halicarnassus, in his *Roman Antiquities* written in the late first century BC, attributes the name of the town to Hercules (in Greek Herakleion, named after Heracles) and to the fact the hero anchored his fleet in the safe haven here, adding that 'it has safe moorings in all seasons'. Strabo's gentle Libyan winds meet Dionysius' safe haven, and conjure up an image of a spot that was truly blessed, between the fertile green slopes of Vesuvius and the glittering crescent of the bay. It is harder to imagine today, amid the discordant chaos of one of the most densely inhabited areas in Europe; yet in the evening, when the setting sun bathes the site in golden light, you can catch for a moment the advantages of the south-westerly exposure, and understand why the rich were so keen to build houses on the lip of the promontory that caught the healthy breeze and enjoyed the incomparable view.

How long before the eruption had this promontory been inhabited, and by whom? To recognize Hercules as the founder was inevitable: the busy hero in his travels around the Mediterranean founded many cities in his name, including Iraklion (Herakleion) in Crete, the harbour of the Minoan palace of Knossos. He thus links two famous archaeological sites. Hercules had been busy in Italy, and

*Panoramic view of the site from the south.*

more specifically at Rome, getting rid of the monster Cacus, and the historian Dionysius suggests that after founding Herculaneum, the Italians gave him divine honours in thanks for everything he had done for them. Certainly, by the time it was a Roman city, Hercules was worshipped in Herculaneum, and the inhabitants were doubtless well aware of the Roman links. The town, as we will see, was very conscious of its divine patron.

Nevertheless, the archaeologist is hard pressed to give substance to this story. Of course, you cannot excavate the founding of a city by a mythological hero, but at the very least, the story should imply continuous inhabitation since the

distant past, from before historical times. On the Bay of Naples, historical times begin with the arrival of the Greek colonists in the eighth century BC. First was the settlement on Ischia, which they called Pithecoussa, 'Monkey Island'; then in the late eighth century BC came the foundation of the important colony of Cumae, named after the Euboean city of Kyme, which had particularly strong presence here, and left its variant of the alphabet for locals to imitate. Finally came Neapolis, the 'new city' of the fifth century that replaced the older settlement (in retrospect, Palaeopolis, but named mythologically Parthenope) of the seventh century. A foundation by Hercules implies something earlier than these.

*Left: View of the site from the south at sunset.*

*Below: View from the north-western corner looking south.*

Strabo, more prosaically, says that Herculaneum had the same story as Pompeii, being held first by the Oscans, then by the Etruscans, next by the Samnites, and finally by the Romans. This rather schematic account would also push the foundation before the arrival of the Greeks, since the arrival of the Etruscans in Campania in the seventh and sixth centuries was a response to the Greek presence, and Strabo is suggesting there was a local Oscan settlement before ever the Etruscans arrived. Strabo may not be the only source who located Etruscans in Herculaneum. The Greek philosopher and botanist Theophrastus, writing his *History of Plants* in the early third century BC, talks of a noxious herb called 'ephemerum' against which there is no remedy, favoured by slaves trying to poison their masters, about which, he throws in casually, 'the Etruscans in Heraclea' have made sufficient researches. Our 'Heraclea' is the only one within Etruscan territory.

On one point all these ancient sources are agreed, at least by silence. Nobody wants to say, despite its name, that Herculaneum/Herakleion was a Greek town founded by Greek colonists. We had better assume they knew what they were talking about, as Greek colonial foundation myths were proudly treasured by their inhabitants.

To return to location: Herculaneum is very close indeed to Naples. It is 5 kilometres to the outskirts of Naples, 10 to the centre. Nor, apart from the rivers that once flanked the promontory, are there any significant geographical obstacles. The route is flat, and indeed attracted the first railway line built in Italy, by the Bourbon Ferdinand II in 1839. This proximity means that whoever lived in Herculaneum had to take account of Naples. Even if Oscan was their first language, they are liable to have been Greek speakers too, so long as the Greek language was dominant on the northern bay (as it still was

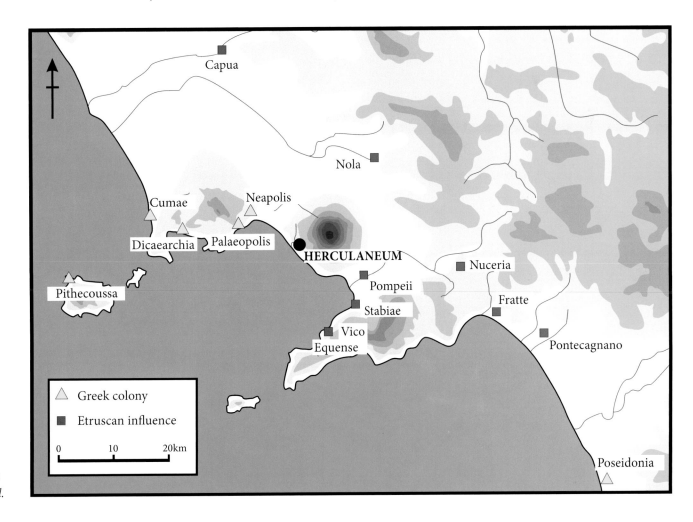

*Plan of the Bay of Naples, indicating the location of Greek colonies founded in the eighth to sixth centuries BC, and the local Oscan foundations under Etruscan influence in the same period.*

in the first century AD). One of the striking features of Greek colonization of southern Italy is how, having occupied an unbroken stretch of coast from the heel of Italy to the colony they called Poseidonia, and the Romans Paestum, there is a break, without Greek settlements, from Salerno to Vesuvius. The north of the Bay of Naples then forms an island of Greekness, after which, north of Cumae, no further settlements occurred. Evidently the people from the sea had tough negotiations with the locals, and lines were drawn. And much though they doubtless would have liked to continue the settlement strip southwards from their first foothold in Ischia, the locals were strong enough to keep them out. These locals, speaking the central Italic language called Oscan, had links through to the peoples of the interior, including those whom the Romans called Samnites. They were also reinforced in their separateness, at least from the seventh to the fifth centuries, by the Etruscans, who left traces of their own language from Pompeii to Salerno. Hence Herculaneum represents the northernmost bulwark of a non-Greek block.

It would be fascinating to recover traces of what Herculaneum was like in this period, as has been done for Pompeii. But the archaeology of the site is obstinate in disgorging no sign of life earlier than the fourth century BC, a period in which Greek influence, after a series of defeats, was very much on the wane, and the Samnites of the interior were, as Strabo states, dominant. Perhaps the oldest visible feature of the site is its street plan. It forms a grid of rectangular blocks, or *insulae*, sloping down to the seawall, with which it aligns. The pattern is one familiar from many Italian cities. In Roman towns, a distinction was drawn between the broad streets that cut horizontally across the town, preferably west–east (*decumani*), and the narrower vertical streets that dropped from north to south (*cardines*). (The Latin word *cardo* also means the hinge of a door, that is, the vertical axis on which it turns.) Herculaneum fits this pattern; if we take Vesuvius as north, as is traditional for sheer convenience, the three visible *cardines* are north–south, though of course the south-westerly orientation that so impressed Strabo means

*Left: Cardo IV viewed from the south.*

*Right: Detail of Cardo IV, with the tenements of the House of Wattlework (a Graticcio).*

*Overleaf: Panoramic view of the central portion of the site, with Cardo IV, from the north.*

*Panoramic view of the western edge of the site, with Cardo III, seen from the north.*

that, more precisely, they run from north-east to south-west.

The excavated portion we can see consists of two *decumani*: the more northerly is significantly broader, and is evidently the main street of the town, hence called, following Latin practice, Decumanus Maximus. Three 'vertical' *cardines* are visible, traditionally numbered, from west to east, Cardo III, IV and V. Two further *cardines* were marked on the plans made by the Bourbons, hence numbered from the west I and II, and the steps at the bottom of Cardo II have been found in the new excavations towards the Villa of the Papyri. The same excavations verify the Bourbon maps in suggesting that the westernmost block of the town was thinner than the others, with an offset profile, narrowed by the steep drop in the land presumably caused by the passage of the westernmost

of Sisenna's two rivers. There is evidently more of the town to the north of the Decumanus Maximus, since houses disappear into the escarpment. If the Decumanus Maximus bisected the town through the middle, as is often supposed, then there may be two rows of *insulae* or blocks of houses missing; but the lack of evidence emerging from under the modern town, north of its main street, the Corso Resina, might give pause to wonder. We cannot rule out the possibility that only one row of *insulae* is missing.

The layout, as we have seen, can be described in the standard terms of a Roman town. But it can equally be described in the terms of a Greek town. Naples, according to our valued guide Strabo, was divided into broad *plateiai* and narrow *stenôpoi*. The word *plateia* itself indicates 'broad' and is the origin of

*Panoramic view of the eastern edge of the site, seen from the north.*

the modern *piazza* or *plaza*, while *stenôpos* indicates 'narrow'. The street pattern of fifth-century BC Neapolis is still clearly legible in the heart of modern Naples, and its four *plateiai* have become the central via Tribunali ('Spaccanapoli') and its parallels. Naples is a grid of four *plateiai* by twenty or more *stenôpoi*, an order of magnitude greater than little Herculaneum. If Strabo was right that Herculaneum went back to antiquity like Pompeii, we cannot see it. The visible remains belong to a city laid out in the fourth century BC at the earliest, and maybe later, with a street grid broadly imitating that of its neighbour Neapolis.

We can add another significant element to the argument. Recent excavation

down at the ancient seafront has revealed extensive traces of quarrying. The spur of tufo, which made up this promontory, will originally have sloped gently out to sea. The impression of a cliff face, along which the town walls run, is not natural but manmade. By quarrying out the stone below, they both made the town more defensible against attacks from the sea, and provided a ready source of building material for construction of the town walls themselves (though it must be admitted that the earliest walls we can see are made of river-washed boulders). Cutting the cliff face also provided the alignment on which the road system is based, so it should all have happened at the same time. Who the enemies they feared were, we

*Left: Views of the junction of the Decumanus Maximus and Cardo IV, from the west (above) and the north (below).*

*Right: View down Cardo IV from the north, with the Superintendent, Piero Guzzo.*

can no longer tell, Greeks, Samnites, Carthaginians coming in from the sea, Romans, or just pirates, ever a scourge of the Italian coast. Strabo calls the town a *phrourion*, meaning a 'garrison' or 'hill fort'. Maybe it was the last outpost of the local Oscans against the Greeks, but respectfully modelled on their ideas.

Important new light on the shape of the town has been cast by recent geological studies. The eastern (strictly south-eastern) side of the town disappears rather abruptly into the escarpment, on the top of which runs the access road established by Maiuri. This escarpment cuts off the town before its edge: the Palaestra visibly disappears into the rock face, while to the south, the garden of the House of the Telephus Relief and the associated range of rooms similarly disappear. Ironically, as a series of geological core samples have demonstrated, the excavation stops only just too soon. The natural tufo spur drops off steeply to the east of Cardo V. Both the Palaestra and the House of the Telephus Relief are constructed on artificial terraces, ramping out the natural slope to the east, and so enabling construction on several levels. Instead of respecting the alignment of the street grid, they are built at an angle, responding to the contours of the land as it drops. The edge of these terraces is only a matter of metres further east, stepping down towards the sea.

If one of Sisenna's rivers sliced down to the east of the Palaestra, it is surely here we should be looking for the harbour of the town, so sheltered as to attract a Hercules. At the foot of the tower-like building constructed above the shore at the most southerly point of the House of the Telephus Relief, there are numerous signs of damage by the sea, coming in from a south-easterly direction. Had there been further buildings in this direction, this could not be so. The mouth of the harbour will lie just beyond, approximately under the new ticket office for the site.

On the other flank, we can be reasonably confident of the location of Sisenna's second river. As

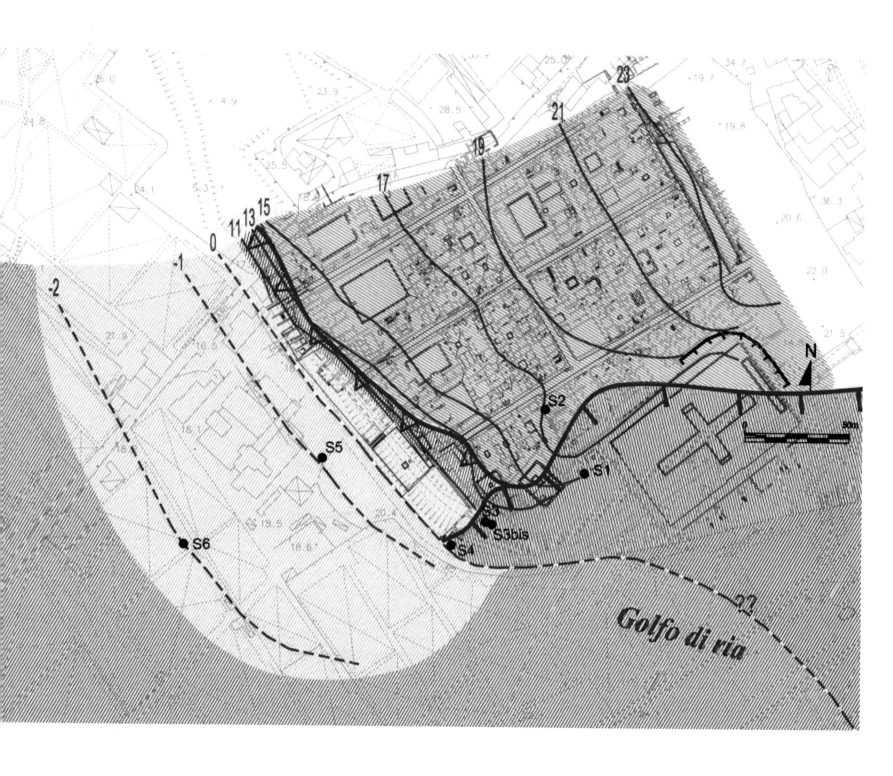

*Above: Plan of site, showing
isomorphs which reveal
the underlying shape of the
natural terrain (heights above
modern sea level marked in
metres).*

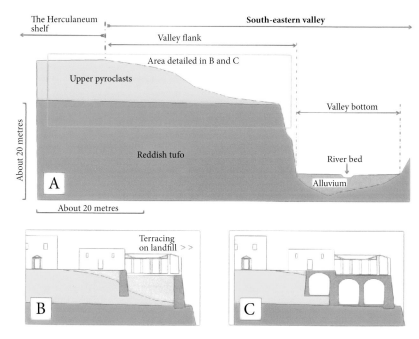

South-eastern valley

Valley flank

Area detailed in B and C

Upper pyroclasts

Valley bottom

About 20 metres

Reddish tufo

River bed

Alluvium

**A**

About 20 metres

Terracing on landfill > >

**B**

**C**

*Left: Sections showing the House of the Telephus Relief terraced out over the natural drop in levels.*

*Below: Test trench in the Vicolo Meridionale to the south of the Palaestra, showing steep drop in natural terrain to the east.*

we have seen, the *insulae* to the west are narrowed, curtailed by the edge of the ravine. The westernmost building of the town is the Theatre. This is slightly off alignment with the main street grid. Presumably, like the Palaestra to the east, it had to take into account the steep contours of the land. Then, between the western *insulae* and the Villa of the Papyri itself, there is a sort of blank without ancient constructions, which has been taken to mark the mouth of the river. The villa itself, distinctly built like a country residence as opposed to a town one, must be outside the town walls, and is on a different alignment from the town, responding instead to the angle of the coast.

We have, then, not a bad idea of the outlines of the town, to south, west and east. The only real uncertainty is how far it stretched north. The present excavations, at their widest dimensions roughly 200 × 230 metres, cover approximately 4.5 hectares. The full town must have been at least 15 hectares, perhaps 20 at the most. Compared to Pompeii's 66 hectares, Herculaneum is truly a pocket city, not even a third, maybe a quarter the size of its neighbour. Pompeii in turn is much smaller than the 90 hectares or so of ancient Neapolis. Scale makes a big difference. By modern standards, Herculaneum is no more than a village of at best a few thousand inhabitants.

The basic outline of the town, then, probably goes back to a local Oscan-speaking settlement of the fourth century BC, if not before. Its origins lie in the period when the main players in the area were the Greek colonists of the south and the Samnite peoples

of the interior. But of this settlement, scarcely a trace remains except in its street pattern. The context of the Bay of Naples was transformed by the arrival of Rome, first as an ally of Naples in 327 BC, and tightening its grasp of the area in the early third century BC. Just how hard it is to see pre-Roman Herculaneum is reflected in the fact that one solitary public inscription has been found in the Oscan language, in contrast to the dozens known from Pompeii. A marble altar top bore the dedication to Venus by a local magistrate: 'Lucius Stlabius, son of Lucius, Aucilus the *meddiss tvtiks* had it made for Herenteis Erucina'. He has the authentic title of a Samnite chief magistrate, *meddix tuticus* as the Romans transliterated it, and Venus, recipient of a famous cult at Eryx in Sicily, has her Oscan name of

Herenteis. The dedication is enough to remind us of a pre-Roman past largely deleted by the buildings of the first centuries BC and AD.

What spelled the end of this phase when Herculaneum spoke a language other than Latin, and called its magistrates and gods by non-Latin names, though nevertheless fighting alongside Rome as an ally, was the Social War of 91–89 BC. Herculaneum, as we have seen, featured with its two rivers in the narrative of the Social War by Sisenna. It was probably the scene of the siege and capture of Herculaneum by Sulla's legate, Titus Didius, supported by the loyal Hirpinian commander, Minatius Magius of Aeclanum, from whom the Roman historian Velleius Paterculus was proud to trace his descent (Velleius, *Histories* 2.16). Being on

*Above: Excavation trench leading to the Villa of the Papyri, after conservation work and new protective shelters (2009). There is no sign of a river between the town and the Villa of the Papyri.*

*Inside: Panoramic view of Cardo IV from outside the House of the Wooden Screen.*

*Above: View of the Sanctuary of Venus on a terrace outside the town walls.*

*Overleaf: Aerial view of the site towards the north-east.*

the wrong side of Sulla was no comfortable experience, and Herculaneum doubtless suffered severe punishment, including confiscation of lands. This might explain in part why it is hard to see the Oscan town – but only in part, since Pompeii, which fell to a Sullan siege, preserves many traces of this past.

By the first century BC, the degree and character of the Roman presence in the area was much changed. The turning point is marked by the foundation, by Scipio Africanus, the Roman general who defeated Hannibal, of the Roman colony of Puteoli in 194 BC. Deliberately competing with the old Greek centres of Cumae and Neapolis, it created a naval and commercial base for Rome that rapidly established itself as the most important harbour in the western Mediterranean, and a key to Rome's

imported food supply. Where business (*negotium*) led, leisure (*otium*) followed. Near modern Pozzuoli, its Roman phase now dramatically visible beneath the earthquake-damaged centre, the sulphur springs of Solfatara still attract intermittent tourist interest. The sulphur springs were more active in antiquity, especially at Baiae, across the bay immediately west of Puteoli, and the hot steam attracted the interest of Greek doctors like Asclepiades of Bithynia, who recommended hot steam baths as a cure-all. Just as centres like Bath and Brighton flourished in Georgian England under medical advice, and generated an entire social life in its own right, so Baiae flourished in the first century BC, and attracted crowds from Rome. The cocktail of good health, Greek culture and fashionable company offered

by the area turned the entire Bay of Naples into a centre for *villeggiatura*, the Roman rich on holiday. Few members of the Roman elite of this period are not attested as owning villas, which stretched, in Strabo's words, like a continuous development around the entire crescent of the bay. It is this massive presence of Roman wealth, both through the trade of Puteoli and the spending of the leisured rich, that is the context for the transformation of visible Herculaneum.

By no coincidence, Herculaneum is as well known for a single villa outside its walls as for the town itself. The relationship of the Villa of the Papyri to the town is emblematic of the relationship of Roman to local. When the elder Pliny took a squadron of ships into the path of the erupting volcano, it was not to rescue the local population, but to respond to the urgent message of a villa owner: Rectina the wife of Tascius, or Cascus or Caesius (Pliny the Younger, *Letters* 6.16.8). By a bold leap of etymology, the Bourbon antiquarians saw in her name the origin of the name of the village that was then still named Resina, until its renaming as Ercolano in 1969. The idea still occasionally reappears, in the context of the relaunch of a tourist jetty called Portus Resinae. The connection will not work, because, even if Rectina could become Resina (as opposed to Rettina), Roman naming conventions would ensure that the villa, if called after her rather than after her husband, would be in adjectival form, ending '-iana', and based on her (unknown) gentile name. Nor, it is clear, was the Villa of the Papyri her villa. But the point is that the admiral of the Roman fleet could unthinkingly give priority to a villa over a city, something that the sheer wealth of the Villa of the Papyri makes a little less incomprehensible.

Since its exploration by tunnelling, at the hands of the excellent engineer, Karl Weber, between 1750 and 1760, this villa has held an exceptional place in the popular imagination. This is due only in part to its size; its seafrontage, from the Belvedere in the

west to the unexplored limit to the east, exceeds 220 metres, and is comparable to the excavated seafront of the town. Contemporaries complained of villas built like cities, and this sort of scale shows why. But it was the finds that gave the villa its fame and name: first the exceptional collection of statues, some sixty-three in bronze and some twenty-four in marble, and then the 1,800 or so carbonized rolls of papyrus. Much has been written of this villa and its collections, and the papyri themselves are of such outstanding importance as to merit a learned journal in their own right. There is no need to add to this discussion here, except in so far as the understanding of the villa adds to that of the town.

Herculaneum, like any Roman town, had a surrounding territory under its jurisdiction. The territory of the present Comune di Ercolano stretches as far as the crater of Vesuvius, though it is bounded to the west by that of Portici, and to the east by Torre del Greco. Such settlements did not exist in antiquity, and the boundaries of the ancient town must have been with Neapolis to the northwest and Pompeii to the south-east: where exactly we cannot tell. It was a territory rich with farmland, and we will meet (page 143–5) documents in which

*Above: An example of partly unrolled papyrus scroll from the Villa of the Papyri.*

*Overleaf: Panoramc view of the newly excavated room on the lower terrace of the Villa of the Papyri.*

landowners like Cominius Primus bought and sold properties, argued over boundaries, and cared for their valued vineyards and woodlands. At the heart of each of these estates, *fundi*, was in all probability a farmhouse or villa. It is only in modern times that 'villa' has come to indicate a lavish building. The basic distinction in Latin is between a town house, *domus*, and a country house, *villa*. The architect Vitruvius, writing towards the end of the first century BC, had considerable qualms about suggesting any particular recipe for the construction of a villa other than the provision of suitable farm buildings, cow-byres, stables, haylofts, threshing floors and the like. Rather grudgingly, he concedes that those wishing to build more 'delicately' can apply exactly the same rules as for building a town house, though he is sarcastic about this taste for 'suburban' comfort.

As Vitruvius was well aware, his ideology was out of step with contemporary practice. Luxury villas were a major expression of wealth and status, and had developed an idiom of their own, characterized by spaciousness, *laxitas*, built round successions of colonnaded porticoes or 'peristyles'. Vitruvius ironically expresses the villa as an inversion of the town house: whereas in the town, the atrium precedes the peristyle, the suburban villa proceeds from peristyle to atrium. That succession, which is far from being a universal rule, can be seen in the Villa of the Mysteries at Pompeii, the Villa of the Papyri at Herculaneum – and also the Villa of Arianna at Stabiae and the villa at Settefinestre, near Cosa in Etruria. But the cases are very different. The peristyle of the Villa of the Mysteries at Pompeii is part of a working farm: the rooms that open off it include the kitchens and the wine-pressing room, and none of the elegant reception rooms of the house open on this space, but instead concentrate around the atrium. There is a distinct contrast of rustic and urban, utilitarian and luxurious. The Villa of the Papyri also has fine reception rooms around its atrium, which cannot be the entrance area to the complex since it stands over an edge dropping down to the sea, allowing magnificent views for those rooms. But on the other hand, there is nothing remotely rustic about either of its peristyles, both of which were crammed with valuable works of art. The Villa of the Papyri therefore represents a large step further away from the rural origins of the villa ideal. It does not form part of the integral relationship of town and country, the symbol of the rural productivity that supports the town, but represents a rupture.

With good reason, the original owner of the villa has been identified as Lucius Calpurnius Piso, consul in 58 BC, father-in-law of Julius Caesar, and target of one of Cicero's most spectacular invectives, the speech *Against Piso*. The evidence is circumstantial, not documentary. Of the papyrus scrolls that have been painstakingly unfurled and deciphered, a very large proportion contain works of Epicurean philosophy, in which the work of Philodemus of Gadara is dominant. Piso was a prominent patron of Epicurean philosophy, and Cicero represents him in his invective as living on particularly close terms with a particular Epicurean philosopher, a man of great learning and humanity (unlike Piso himself). The philosopher is not named, but is surely, as the ancient commentators claimed, Philodemus, who explicitly dedicated to him his essay 'On the Good King in Homer'. It is a little difficult to imagine who would have kept such a comprehensive collection of the works of Philodemus in his library, if not Piso.

Whether or not Piso was the owner, the villa is anything but the country house attached to a country estate of one of the population of Herculaneum. It only makes sense as the luxury villa of a member of the high Roman aristocracy. It is not difficult to imagine that the villa was built on land confiscated by Sulla from Herculaneum after the Social War, and awarded to one of his friends. Nor is its collection of statues the usual garden furniture that Vesuvian town houses, or even a grand villa like that at Oplontis, could display. Cicero, who used his friend Atticus as agent in his pursuit of suitable sculptures for his own philosophical villa, the 'Academy' at Tusculum, could never rise to the level of this collection. It is at a level to which only the high elite of the late Roman republic could aspire, ransacking the east for statuary and libraries in their desire to look like eastern kings. The model is neither the country *villa* nor the town *domus*, but the palaces of the Hellenistic kingdoms. This is a *mouseion*, a place dedicated to the Muses, to collections of art and philosophical texts. By no coincidence did J. Paul Getty use it as the basis for his own museum at Malibu; the architecture, which makes no sense either for a Roman farmhouse or for a Californian ranch, is perfect for a collection of antiquities. The modern world constantly reproduces effects designed in antiquity. The modern tourist industry, in turning the Bay of Naples into a world of hotels, seemingly living in a parallel universe to the local social and economic realities, reproduces the effect established by the Romans with their luxury villas.

Our understanding of the Villa of the Papyri and its relationship to the town of Herculaneum will be limited until the modern campaign of excavations is carried to a more satisfactory conclusion. The campaign of excavation undertaken between 1996 and 1999 uncovered no more than a corner of the villa, limited to its atrium area. Yet it gave results of fundamental importance for the understanding of the villa's context. By opening a vast trench to connect the villa to the main site, and by taking the excavation down to the level of the ancient shore, it demonstrated that both the villa and the houses on the western edge of the town had lower levels reaching down to the shore. The hasty and crude work of the initial excavation was put right in part by a campaign conducted by the Soprintendenza in 2008. It confirmed the magnificence of the lower terrace of the villa, with its pool close to the seashore, and its exquisitely carved furniture in wood and ivory. Simultaneously, it demonstrated the splendour of the house at the western edge of the town, decorated with handsome neo-Attic reliefs. What is missing is the gap in the middle, a stretch of about 50 metres between the edge of the villa terrace and the baths, which represent the westernmost building of the town. In that gap is supposed to be the outlet of Sisenna's second river, and possibly a secondary port or haven. Further excavation should answer these questions.

Opposite: Ivory relief depicting a scene of vintage, discovered in conservation work near the Villa of the Papyri.

This page: Marble relief depicting a religious scene, Zeus and a dancing Maenad, at the moment of discovery in a house in the south-western edge of the town (left), and after restoration (above).

Overleaf: View of the eastern end of the Decumanus Maximus.

# 5
# INHABITANTS

I n the vaults down by the seashore, the bodies of the last inhabitants were found in their hundreds, crowded by the dozen into each space. There they took refuge from a catastrophe that they hoped they might survive, one in the form of a tremendous earthquake, only to find themselves overwhelmed by the catastrophe they had never imagined, a pyroclastic surge that reduced their bodies to skeletons in a matter of seconds, if not fractions of a second. When someone dies of thermal shock, their tendons involuntarily contract into the 'pugilist' position of a boxer in self-defence. The sight is familiar in the victims of catastrophic fires and bomb explosions. But so swift was their death that the process of involuntary contraction was not even complete before they died. What is left, after careful excavation, is a shocking sight. One can only look with dismay at the remains of fellow humans so instantaneously snuffed out. The effect of the intense heat is to deprive the skeletons of their humanity, of all the elements that enable us to recognize someone, to 'put a face to them'. Yet the paradox is that this state of frightening anonymity is, after all, legible. Advances in forensic science and palaeo-osteology, the science of study

*Left: Bronze portrait from the House of the Bronze Herm.*

*Right: Skeletons from the seashore, as discovered in 1984.*

*Skeleton of a 'wealthy matron'*
*found with a bag of jewellery*
(National Geographic).

of the bones of the past, mean that each skeleton can be carefully individuated, by gender, age, medical history and (to some extent) social condition.

Much, as we will see, can be said about these victims. Yet nothing will restore their names. We do indeed have names of the inhabitants in great abundance. Inscriptions and dedications allow us to reconstruct much about the town's ruling elite over at least a century. The largest and most important inscription preserved in Herculaneum gives us more than this: the names of up to 500 inhabitants, all male and of free status. Even more precious, we have dossiers of wooden tablets, archives from no less than eight of the houses, totalling some 160 separate documents. These not only illustrate vividly the life histories of a select group of inhabitants, but, thanks to the Roman insistence of having every legal document witnessed by at least seven people, provide hundreds of names from the last two decades of the town's life, as many as 650 separate individuals. It is rare, anywhere in the Roman world, to have the evidence of hundreds of contemporary skeletons, or to know hundreds of contemporary names, let alone to have both such sources of information. But that is not, of course, all. We have a good proportion of their houses too, the residences, shops and flats in which they lived. And in one extraordinary case, which we will look at in detail, we have, thanks to the great sewer or cesspit that ran under the block of shops and flats by the Palaestra, the organic remains that enable us to analyse in detail the diet of several dozen inhabitants over the course of a couple of decades. And indeed, if more was needed, we actually can put faces to a few dozen of the more wealthy inhabitants, thanks to their fondness for portraits in marble and bronze. It is hard to imagine any other ancient population that can be known in such close-grained detail.

This chapter will try to pull together some of these clues, to build up a picture of the sort of human society which the last inhabitants of Herculaneum represent. To piece together a picture of antiquity is to work with a giant jigsaw puzzle in which many or most of the pieces are missing, and those that survive can only too easily be confused for something else. How rewarding it would be to take a skeleton from the arches, give him or her a name, assign them a house, find their dossier of legal documents, identify their portrait, and then recount the details of their diet. It is never going to work like that. We have to operate at a more generic level, characterizing the sort of population they were, what their names, documents, houses, portraits and diet may tell us about them. Like ghosts, their faces will slip in and out of focus, at one moment vividly present, at the next frustratingly out of reach and unknowable.

The skeletons are a good place to start. We have the advantage of knowing that they are all precisely contemporary, though on which day exactly they died we can no longer say, since the scientific evidence piles up against the traditional date of 24 August AD 79 being right. To judge from the ripe pomegranates and other botanical evidence, it was a day in late October or November. The date of 24 August given in the younger Pliny's vivid description is, after all, only one of a number of variants given by the manuscripts, and another source speaks clearly of the 'late autumn'. In any case, the same point of death has the rare advantage, archaeologically speaking, of freezing a cross-section of the population, of different ages and social standing. The excavations that discovered the skeletons, amid considerable international excitement, had been instigated by the then director of excavations at Herculaneum, Giuseppe Maggi. Funding for new work had effectively dried up with Maiuri's retirement in 1961, and gradually the skilled team of workmen and restorers he had built up was reduced to a rump. Maggi, as director from 1971, watched helplessly as the site began to disintegrate for lack of funding. Then in 1980, despairing of support from the Ministry of Culture, he turned to Paolo Martuscelli, responsible for special funding for Naples. Funds were provided for a project to

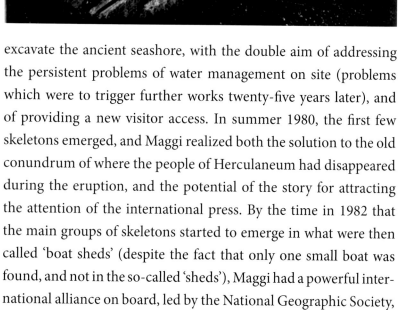

excavate the ancient seashore, with the double aim of addressing the persistent problems of water management on site (problems which were to trigger further works twenty-five years later), and of providing a new visitor access. In summer 1980, the first few skeletons emerged, and Maggi realized both the solution to the old conundrum of where the people of Herculaneum had disappeared during the eruption, and the potential of the story for attracting the attention of the international press. By the time in 1982 that the main groups of skeletons started to emerge in what were then called 'boat sheds' (despite the fact that only one small boat was found, and not in the so-called 'sheds'), Maggi had a powerful international alliance on board, led by the National Geographic Society, enabling the involvement of American scientific specialists, Sarah

*Above: Archival photographs of excavations of the seashore in the 1980s.*

*Right: Archival photographs of the boat as discovered on the ancient shore.*

Bisel for the anthropological study of the bones, Haraldur Sigurdsson for the volcanology of the eruption and Richard Steffy for the marine archaeology of the boat. But just as Charles Waldstein's proposed international project had run aground in 1907, so in 1984 the voices of local chauvinism, against which Waldstein had railed, made their corrosive impact. In an account published in 1985, Maggi asked whether the voices that 'we should do it all ourselves' ('potremmo fare tutto da noi') would bring about a repetition of history. They did: Maggi's directorship was terminated and the international collaboration came to an abrupt end, with disastrous results for the study of the skeletons. Some 139 had been excavated for study by Sarah Bisel. These were then handed to another group of Italian experts, with less established claims to international recognition,

and the remaining skeletons were left as a tourist spectacle, gradually to disintegrate and disappear under a growth of weeds. Not till 2009 was excavation resumed.

Modern scientific study of skeletons has advanced by leaps and bounds over recent decades, and even if the study of the 300 or so bodies had been completed in the 1980s, it would be desirable to repeat the study, with new techniques, like the potential of strontium isotope analysis to reveal the composition, and thus the origin, of the water consumed by the individual in various growth stages, so distinguishing those locally born from immigrants from elsewhere. In a population with an abundant supply of slaves, this can be particularly revealing. The studies to date, then, are partial and to some extent contradictory. Even so, they evoke a vivid picture.

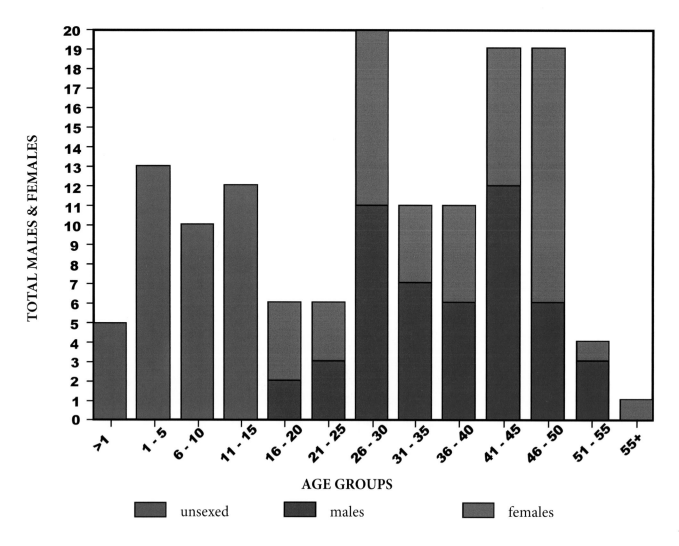

*Age and sex distribution of skeletons studied by Sarah Bisel. Note the shortage of young people.*

Of the 139 skeletons studies by Bisel, 51 were males, 49 female, and 39 children (thus harder to sex reliably). This sounds like a normal population, and the spread of ages from unborn foetuses to people over fifty-five sounds normal enough. But a surprise is the lack of young people in their teens and early twenties. Numbers peak at those in their late twenties, of whom there are four times as many as those in their late teens or early twenties. Luigi Capasso's study of a marginally larger group (143 individuals) gave a different distribution, with a more equal distribution of people in the early and late twenties, but a similar dip for those aged fifteen to nineteen. He also came up with a large proportion of males (81) to females (61). There are too many judgement calls involved for anyone to be certain of the age of a skeleton, but both authors were confident of a big dip in numbers of teenagers. They offered different explanations. Sarah Bisel pointed to reduced fertility and inability of the population to replace itself, Capasso to the impact of the earthquake of AD 62/63, which might have led to a reduced birthrate for a number of years.

But there is another factor to take into consideration. In a society with a high proportion of slaves, where humans are acquired from the slave market and not from reproduction, there might be a peak of numbers in the year groups when slaves were at their most active and useful, that is, in their twenties. Perhaps, if this sample is remotely representative, we are looking at a population distorted by the operation of the slave market.

Nevertheless, even though many of these individuals must have been slaves or ex-slaves, they are notably healthy. Their average heights seem to be above those for Naples in the mid-twentieth century (around 160 cm for men, 150 cm for women), though new research suggests that the formula used for extrapolating heights may have led to exaggeration. Their teeth are remarkably low in caries, though this will have been helped by the exceptionally high levels of fluoride – the local bottling plant in Ercolano was closed down only recently because it exceeded the maximum levels permitted by European legislation. Levels of lead are not particularly high, despite the

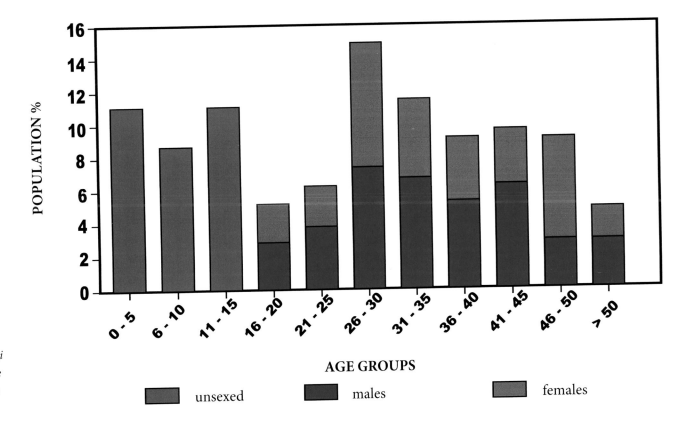

*Age and sex distribution of the skeletons studied by Luigi Capasso: he suggests that the big dip in numbers coincides with the earthquake.*

well-known use of lead piping in the Roman world, and the use of lead in sweetening wine and other foods. Anaemia was quite common, which suggests a paucity of meat in the diet, but in a seaside town fish may have provided a commoner source of protein: Neapolitans remain dedicated fish-eaters. However, though reasonably well nourished and growing to good heights, a high proportion of the skeletons showed signs of stressful hard work: excessive development of limited muscle groups and injuries, both breakages and conditions like arthrosis and hernias. Many of the young too were overworked.

The impression is indeed of a population with a number of rich people, but a significant proportion of slaves, or of those who still carried the scars of servitude on their bodies. Case studies illustrate the potential of the study of skeletons to tell individual life histories. Sarah Bisel, whose premature death deprived us of a full study, offered some vivid illustrations. Skeleton Erc65 was one who caught the eye of the National Geographic photographers, thanks to the rich haul of jewellery and money with which she was found, including two handsome gold snake-headed bracelets. A woman in her middle years (around forty-six), she had excellently formed teeth, but was suffering from periodontal disease. Above average in height (157.2 cm), with strong bones, she may have had two or three children. It is not hard to see her as a well-off Roman matron, a *materfamilias*. Erc10, by contrast, is taken to be a slave girl, found together with a baby, taken to be her master's. Only fourteen years old, her bone development suggested 'a lot of running up and down stairs or hills'. Grooves of hypoplasia in the enamel of her teeth are attributed to severe malnutrition while still a baby herself. Erc 26 is a soldier of around thirty-seven, at 174.5 cm well above the local average height. That he was a soldier is inferred from the sword he carried, but the signs of his calling can also be seen in the remains of a stab-wound on his left femur, and three missing front teeth. Erc27 is a middle-aged (forty-six years)

man suffering from conspicuous signs of overwork, thin bones suggesting poor nutrition, overdeveloped upper body muscles, and a spine with seven thoracic vertebrae fused by disease.

Potentially, each and every skeleton can offer a vivid life history, though we need to resist the temptation generated by the constant media interest in this site to let imagination run away in the telling of heart-breaking life stories. So Capasso offers a characterization for each of the skeletons: the consumptive, the cart driver, the spinning woman, the flautist, the boxer, the old horse rider, the young shepherd, the limping Maltese, the woodcutter, the young fisher, the soldier, the old sailor, the porter, the javelin thrower, the little rower, the hunchback, the old tailor, the swimmer, the shepherd with sandals, and so on and so on. It evokes a colourful picture of a varied society, and one in close contact with the sea, but the cautious may ask whether the osteological evidence can bear this weight of interpretation. Only when the remaining 150 or so skeletons have been fully analysed can we be on firmer ground.

For real life histories, we are better off with documents, and in these Herculaneum abounds. It is the population of the final century, and above all of the last few decades before the eruption, that reveals itself most clearly: the people of pre-Roman Herculaneum, and even of the last decades of republican rule at Rome, are largely invisible, and everything changes with the rise to power of Augustus as emperor, and the new social order he established. Inscriptions in public places were designed to commemorate, to ensure that future generations would not forget the names and faces of the leading citizens. Among these, none is so conspicuous as Marcus Nonius Balbus, the great (but by no means the only) benefactor of the town, one who rose to the rank of praetor in Rome, and to the governorship (with rank of proconsul) of Crete and Cyrene. We meet him in the building that bears his name, the Basilica Noniana, where his portrait, in the toga of a citizen, is accompanied by

*Funerary altar dedicated to Nonius Balbus, with his statue behind.*

*The funerary altar of Nonius Balbus today (above) and at the moment of its discovery in 1941 (below).*

that of his father, with the same name, his mother Viciria, probably his wife Volasennia, and possibly his daughters. We meet him in the Theatre, where his statue in heroic nudity left the impression of his face in the tufo. We meet him and his father again, each on horseback, in a public square outside the Theatre, where the inscription recalls his benefactions to the town, the building of the Basilica and the rebuilding of walls and gates. Finally we meet him on his terrace below the walls, in the armour of a Roman commander, by the funerary altar that bears the full text of the honorific decree passed by the local council after his death, providing that an equestrian statue should be erected to him in the most crowded place in the town (if only we knew just where it was found, we would have found our forum), that a marble altar be put up to him at public expense (the one we are looking at), that on the day of the Commemoration of the Dead, the Parentalia, the procession should start here, that a day of the annual athletic festival be dedicated to him, and finally that an empty place should be left in his honour in the Theatre. There was no getting away from Nonius Balbus, wherever you turned.

Who was he, and how did he rise to this prominence? By chance, his name survives in a passing mention in a historical account, that of the historian Cassius Dio. The year 32 BC was a critical one for Octavian, the future Augustus. The pact between him and Antony called the 'triumvirate' was disintegrating, as they squared off for their final showdown. Each accused the other of being the obstacle to peace and the return to normal life. The consuls at the beginning of the year were both supporters of Antony, and took the opportunity of the opening of the year's proceedings to launch an attack on Octavian. The consul Sosius, whom we now remember for the elegant Temple of Apollo by the Theatre of Marcellus in Rome, was on the point of introducing measures against Octavian when Nonius Balbus, one of the ten tribunes of the people,

used his power of veto to block him. If Balbus were not, thanks to Herculaneum, someone known to us, we would pass over his name, which never comes up again in the history books. But evidently, his intervention at a critical moment won the future emperor's gratitude, and the reward of promotion to the praetorship and a province, Crete and Cyrene, which offered exceptionally rich pickings. Indeed, to judge by a long inscription that survives in Cyrene, governors like Balbus pushed their luck too far, and elaborate measures were set up, not long after Balbus' tenure, to limit the rapacity of the provincial government.

Where does this place our Balbus on a Roman scale? By no means one of the Roman nobility, he did not make it to the peak of a senatorial career in a consulship (who knows, maybe protests from the fleeced provincials may have stopped him in his tracks). He is what the Romans called a 'new man', one whose family had not made it to office before: the inscription to his father Nonius Balbus Pater lists no claims to distinction. He came from an insignificant provincial town, not Herculaneum but Nuceria, at the other end of the Sarno valley from Pompeii. We know this much because his fellow townsmen, 'Nucherini municipes sui', put up a statue to him in Herculaneum. There were plenty of people living in the area who outclassed him by far: people like Lucius Calpurnius Piso, if it is right that the Villa of the Papyri belonged to him, consul and father-in-law of Caesar, member of an old and distinguished Roman family; or Appius Claudius Pulcher, consul in 38 BC, member of one of the most famous Roman families of all, who shared the stage of the Herculaneum Theatre as an honorand with Balbus.

The fascinating thing about Nonius Balbus is that he was not, beyond the confines of Herculaneum and his native Nuceria, all that important. He played a bit part in history, and got his reward. But he behaved like a good Augustan. Just as the emperor enriched the capital with buildings, turning it famously 'from brick to marble', so Nonius Balbus enriched his little seaside town, making a disproportionate impact such as he could never have made at Rome. One of the clearest traces he leaves of his importance is in the survival of his name in the next generations. Whether he had a son, we do not know, but every time an owner formally freed a slave, so making him a Roman citizen, the slave took his first two names, the *praenomen* (Marcus) and the *nomen* (Nonius). We meet endless men named Marcus Nonius in the next generations in Herculaneum: men with names of Greek origin typical of slaves, like M. Nonius Anthus, M. Nonius Eperastus, M. Nonius Hermeros, M. Nonius Stephanio or M. Nonius Terpnus, and men with ambiguous names that could be slave or free, like M. Nonius Carus, M. Nonius Celer, M. Nonius Ianuarius, and M. Nonius Severus. Twenty-five can be counted on one inscription alone, the great album of 500 names, and adding in witnesses from documents raises the score to fifty. No single name occurs so frequently in the town as M. Nonius.

But there were others too in the league of big spenders. Another frequently recurrent family name is that of Lucius Mammius. A group of inscriptions celebrated an important local figure together with his father and a cousin, both of whom made the rank of equestrian military tribune under Augustus (equestrians ranked second only to senators). We are told that Augustus made a point of encouraging towns to recommend local men for promotion to military rank at equestrian level, and these might be examples. Evidently the family were local benefactors. The man who financed the orchestra of the Theatre, Lucius Annius Mammianus Rufus, must have been born into the Mammii, and given in adoption (as the tell-tale ending 'ianus' shows) to another family, that of the Annii. One of the biggest benefactors of the town during the reign of Claudius was Lucius Mammius Maximus, who built or rebuilt the Macellum, the market, and dedicated a batch of statues to members of the family of the Emperor

Claudius, including Antonia mother of Claudius, Agrippina his wife, and Germanicus, his father-in-law. The historian Tacitus records that it was one Mammius Pollio who as consul designate in AD 49 proposed that the young Nero should be engaged to Claudius' daughter Octavia, a recommendation that was followed (*Annals* 12.9). It is clear that this Mammius enjoyed high favour at the imperial court. L. Mammius Maximus on the other hand was a freedman and Augustalis, but the family links seem

*Above: Marble portrait of a young man, found in the Suburban Baths.*

*Right: Portrait of 'Terentius', from the Bourbon excavations near the Theatre, now in Naples Museum.*

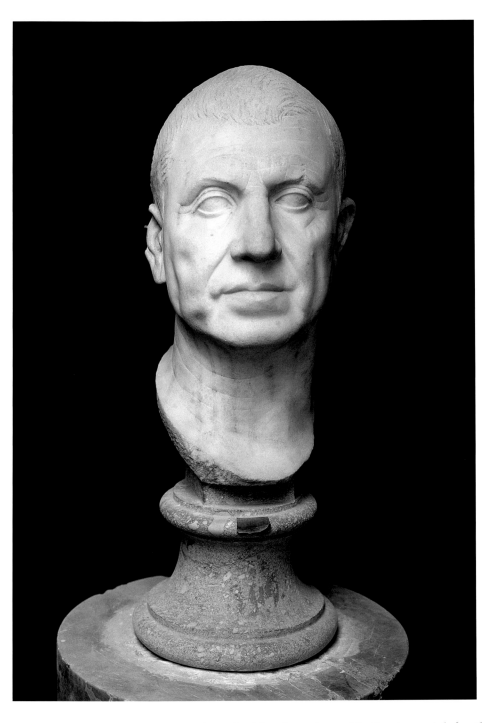

relatively small group of families, whose prestige was marked by the reciprocal deal of benefaction in exchange for honour, or, in the Greek expression, 'euergetism'. The rich paid for the public buildings of the town, and celebrated them by offering public dinners to the townsfolk, especially the two 'orders of dignity', the *decuriones* or members of the local council, all of whom (at least in theory) had to be freeborn, and the *Augustales*, members of the quasi-religious order dedicated to the cult of the emperor, who were typically slave-born freedmen. The return for acts of generosity was 'honour'. Election to a magistracy itself was regarded as an honour by the people, as was election to a priesthood, and to be a member of the priestly college of the imperial cult was equally an honour. But serious generosity merited further honours, escalating from a mere statue to the sort of extraordinary posthumous honours Nonius Balbus enjoyed. The richness of the public buildings of Herculaneum, despite its small size, shows that the system was working well for them. There was real wealth on the Bay of Naples, and it ended up benefiting the community as well as private individuals.

But in a sense, the fact that Herculaneum had a rich elite and fine public buildings makes it like so many other cities around the Roman world. We do not need the eruption of Vesuvius to tell us this. What is special about Herculaneum is that it allows us to look at a far broader social spectrum. You could call them 'ordinary' people, if it wasn't for the fact that the set-up of a slave-owning society makes it so extraordinary to our own eyes. Who were the 'ordinary' people? The less-well-off freeborn, who mostly, however poorly off, will have had slaves of their own, the slaves who did so much of the work, or the freed slaves who, by that arrangement so distinctive to the Romans, acquired full citizen status on gaining their freedom, and who consequently were so keen to set a visible distance between themselves and those who were still slaves? The norms of ordinariness read

to show in his obsession with the imperial family. Another of the family, Lucius Mammius Flaccus, was one of the two senior magistrates of the town in AD 61. Other big local families, whose names are recurrent in the lists, are the Quinti Junii, probably linked to the senator Q. Junius Blaesus, and the Marci Calatorii, a name rarely met outside Herculaneum. M. Calatorius Rufus, like L. Mammius Maximus, enjoyed the honour of a statue in the Theatre.

The town, as was normal, was dominated by a

*Bronze statues of Marcus Calatorius Quartio (left) and Lucius Mammius Maximus, Augustalis (right), both found during the Bourbon excavations near the Theatre, now in Naples Museum.*

rather differently for this Roman imperial world than for our own.

The first document that takes us into the world of the 'ordinary', or rather the rank and file of free people, is the great album of names. Numerous fragments, with names carefully cut into handsome white marble slabs, emerged from the earliest Bourbon excavations, on 26 May and 1 July 1739. Because at the time there were two excavations, at the Theatre and at the 'new excavations' ('nuevas grutas' in Spanish) near via Mare, there was continuous confusion over what came from where, and it was long believed they came from the Theatre. Only when, at the end of his career, Amedeo Maiuri was exploring the area of the Basilica did three new fragments emerge, one of which matches perfectly an old fragment. Not even the excavation reports of the time are precise about the find-spot, but it appears to have been between the outer wall of the Basilica and the raised platform that blocks the road that defines the western edge of the excavations, Cardo III. Their importance was not recognized for over a decade.

The great Roman historian Theodore Mommsen, who published the initial fragments in 1883, did not attempt to specify what the list was, beyond saying 'fragments of some album' (an 'album' being simply a list) and recognizing that it included names of tribes, the basic Roman subdivision of the citizen body. By Maiuri's time, the conviction spread, driven by the high proportion of freedmen's names, that it was a list of the *Augustales*. Maiuri, who was extremely attentive to the phenomenon of the rich freedman, was convinced that the neighbouring building was the 'College of the Augustales'. Hence, when the new fragments were published by Guadagno, the assumption persisted that they were all *Augustales*, and many (including the author) repeated the assumption. Simple maths should have told us we were wrong. Something like 500 names survive. But the inscription is fragmentary. There must have been at least six panels, each measuring about 3 × 5 Roman feet;

there was space for three columns of names on each panel, each about sixty-six names long. Six panels with 200 names each suggests 1,200 names, and of course there is no guarantee that there were no other panels. One cannot imagine more than a few dozen *Augustales* for a small town like this. In any case, if the standard guess of 4,000 to 5,000 inhabitants is right, given that half should be women and a good half of the men children or slaves, we cannot imagine that the entire adult, male, free population much exceeded 1,200. If the *Augustales* were a privileged group (as was certainly the case), they should not have numbered more than a hundred at most.

So what did the list represent? It is still too early to be sure, but it looks like everyone entitled to a vote locally. Roman citizens born in a *municipium* such as Herculaneum were automatically voters; those born elsewhere, like Nonius Balbus from Nuceria, who took up residence in the town counted as *incolae*, inhabitants, and they too were entitled to the vote. Those passing though were not. Nor were those who did not enjoy full Roman citizenship. There was an important category of these, known as 'Latins'. Originally applied to the citizens of Latin towns around Rome which did not enjoy Roman citizenship, since by the first century BC these all automatically were Romans, the term was reapplied by an Augustan law, the 'lex Junia', to a special category: those ex-slaves who had been given freedom by their owners informally, without respecting the strict terms of the legislation. They could thus be referred to as 'Junian Latins'. Romans in the period of Augustus fretted about the excessive number of ex-slaves making their way into citizenship, in a way not completely unlike contemporary European anxieties about illegal immigration. Augustus imposed strict terms on how many slaves you could free, and at what age. The minimum age was thirty, and given the short life-expectancy of antiquity, especially among those exposed to heavy labour, many slaves could not expect to live much longer (the skeletons

*Fragments of the great marble list of names, as discovered in the eighteenth century, with names of freeborn citizens (top left), the new fragments found in 1961 (top right), and the join between old and new fragments (below). The first two columns of names are those who have neither fathers nor masters named; the third column names freedmen with masters.*

examined by Sarah Bisel actually included plenty in their thirties and forties, and the steep drop off comes in the fifties).

Thus a slave freed under the age of thirty counted as a 'Junian' Latin, lacked the right to vote, and lacked the ability to inherit or leave property, since all reverted to the owner. Yet perversely, those freed under thirty were the lucky ones, their owner's favourites. A mechanism was needed to convert their disadvantage into an advantage, and this was found in the legislation which allowed a Latin who had a child that survived to the age of one by a legitimately married wife to declare the birth to the magistrates and claim promotion to full citizenship. As we will see, Herculaneum preserves the one known case study of this law in action. Does the list, then, include Latins or former Latins?

One of the mostly puzzling features of the list is that names are given in not two but three forms. The two standard name forms for citizens were those for the freeborn (*ingenui*) and those for the freed (*liberti*). The freeborn were flagged by the use of the patronymic, the father's name: Marcus Nonius *son of Marcus* Balbus (Marcus Nonius Marci filius Balbus, abbreviated to M. Nonius M.f. Balbus). The freed were flagged by the name of the former slave-owner: Marcus Nonius *freedman of Marcus* Anthus (*Marci libertus*, abbreviated

to M.l.). On this document, just to underline the difference between the two classes, the freeborn also are given the name of their voting tribe, though freedmen too were assigned to voting tribes: thus M. Nonius. M.f. Men(enia) Fuscus, Marcus Nonius son of Marcus *of the Menenian tribe* Fuscus. The two categories are kept rigidly separate: on no fragment are freeborn and freedmen listed mixed up together.

But there is also a third category which is neither the one nor the other, neither freeborn nor freed, neither fish nor fowl. With equal consistency, there is a group that has just three names, and neither patronymic nor name of patron. They cannot be freeborn Roman citizens, otherwise they would have their fathers' names. Even bastards had to have a father's name, Spurii filius, 'son of Spurius', abbreviated Sp.f. There is just one of these, M. Livius Sp.f. Sabinus, and he is indeed listed among our third category. But if they were all bastards, they should all be called 'Sp.f.' In theory, they might not be Roman citizens at all. They might be *peregrini*, foreigners who were not Roman citizens, but not slaves either. On the other hand, it was a serious offence for a non-Roman to pretend to be a Roman by having 'three names' – the *praenomen*, *nomen* and *cognomen*. Claudius had banned *peregrini* from using Roman look-a-like names and had men executed at

*Peristyle of the House of the Black Saloon, possibly owned by Venidius Ennychus, whose documents were found in an upper room on the far side of the peristyle.*

the Esquiline Gate for pretending to citizenship. There was a lot in a name. They might be Junian Latins and others who could legally use the three-name formula but were not full citizens. But this can be ruled out because on one of the panels, there are two columns of these people preceding a third column of freedmen. Romans were insistent on hierarchical precedence when they listed people: thus witnesses always occur in their social rank order, freeborn before freed. No list could give precedence to non-citizens over citizens, so citizens they must be.

How people could achieve this halfway house remains to be fully explained, and there may be several routes. But at least one was the route that L. Venidius Ennychus took, because he is one of the names on the list. And at this point we are helped out by his surviving dossier, and to this we may turn before going back to the album of citizens. Ennychus lived in one of the swankier houses in town, that of the 'Black Saloon', or at least it was here that he left on an upper floor a basket full of at least thirty-nine of his documents. Important legal records were kept on bundles of wooden tablets, either in two or (from AD 63) three pieces, with the text given twice, once scratched with a stylus (*graphium*, whence graphics) on a thin wax film, and once in black ink. Often there was also an index or summary of contents written in ink on the edge of the tablets, so that some elements of the document were given three times, a great help in revealing carbonized fragments, where black ink is against blackened wood and the wax of the interior has disappeared, leaving only scratches in the wood left by the point of the stylus.

The bundle was of crucial importance to Ennychus, because they guaranteed his status. The earliest seems to date to AD 40–1, recording a loan of money to one L. Mammius Rufus. Another loan dates to AD 52, to one Volusius Crescens. Money lending was a classic way of making a fortune in this booming economy, and by the year AD 60, he was ready for some social acknowledgement. The first in a series of documents records that on 24 July AD 60 he officially declared the birth of a daughter by his wife Livia Acte. The name Acte shows that his wife, like Ennychus, started life as a slave, but the family name 'Livia' shows that she had been freed. Their daughter will have been called Venidia. The declaration must have been made on the day of her birth. The next is a document of exactly a year later, dated 25 July AD 61, and records that in the Basilica Noniana in Herculaneum, the magistrates M. Antonius Rufus and

L. Mammius Flaccus with the *decuriones* made a decision. What that was emerges from the third document, dated 22 March AD 62. Here the Roman praetor, L. Servenius Gallus, states that he has been approached at his tribunal at Rome in the Forum of Augustus in the Julian portico (even the number of the column is specified, but lost in a gap) by a delegation from Herculaneum, led by the magistrates Marcus Ofellius Magnus and Tiberius Crassius Firmus, to report that they have examined the case of Lucius Venidius Ennychus and Livia Acte, who have had a daughter by a legitimate marriage who has survived to the age of a year, and declares his finding that under the terms of the lex Aelia Sentia, they are now Roman citizens. Before finding these documents, we knew from the Roman lawyers that a Junian Latin could be promoted to citizen on the survival of a child to the age of a year, but we had no idea of the elaborate procedure it might involve, requiring not only a meeting of the local council, but a delegation to the praetor in Rome. Ennychus had reason to be proud of these documents, as of the later ones, in which he applied to the council for promotion to the order of the Augustalis, and named ten good men and true who could be warranty for his standing and character.

Ennychus' dossier gives us an important insight into the great list of names. Since he belongs to the third category, those who had neither a father (freeborn citizen) nor a patron (legally freed former slaves), it follows that the third group comprised those citizens who were neither freeborn nor regularly set free or 'manumitted', but who had nevertheless, like Ennychus, been promoted to full citizenship. It might be imagined the group were not citizens, including people like Junian Latins who had not been promoted. But the fact that this group comes *before* the lists of freedmen on one panel is a clear indication, in a society where questions of rank order were observed scrupulously, that they ranked higher, and must therefore be citizens. This does not mean that all followed the same route as Ennychus, of declaring the birth and survival of a year-old child. This was just one of the incentives to reproduce which Augustus introduced. But promotion to citizenship was offered as an incentive to others: by the Emperor Claudius to those who built a ship of a certain capacity and brought grain to Rome for at least six years; by Nero to those who built a house of a certain value in the city of Rome; by Trajan to those who ran a bakery in Rome for at least three years. Full citizenship was an important inducement to do what the State considered advantageous.

*Wooden tablet from the archive of Venidius Ennychus.*

What this list of people, born or officially resident in Herculaneum, who were full Roman citizens, reminds us is how little we understand about this society with its rigid distinctions of slave and free, but numerous and complex ways of passing from one status to the other. Slavery is a theme we meet again and again in these legal records. We meet records of sales of slaves, like the girl Olympias, bought from Ennychus by M. Nonius Hermeros (another of the M. Nonius clan) on 30 November AD 47. There is C. Iulius Phoebus, who sells a slave girl to one Calatoria and guarantees her to be free of hidden fault: buying a slave could be a risky business if they proved to be a runaway or improperly acquired. Or we find Lucius Cominius Primus making a loan of 600 sesterces from his strongbox to M. Nonius Fuscus, and receiving the slave

*Fragment of marble inscription from the Basilica, possibly naming Viciria, mother of Nonius Balbus.*

It may seem to us astonishing that so essential a piece of information as Justa's birth status was not properly documented and agreed by all. It was agreed that her mother, Petronia Vitalis, was the freedwoman of Gaius Petronius Stephanus, the husband of Calatoria Themis. The point at dispute is whether Justa was born while Vitalis was still a slave (in which case, so was she) or after her manumission, in which case she was born a Roman citizen, even if to an unmarried mother. This in itself may surprise us: the child of an unmarried ex-slave mother would even so have full citizen status. But the Roman rule was that you took your status from your mother, not your father, who was a figure harder to be sure of in days before DNA testing.

To settle the argument, a number of witnesses were called to give evidence. Their depositions are curiously circumstantial and inconclusive. Among those who were sure that Justa was freeborn was Gaius Petronius Telesphorus, surprisingly enough the legal tutor of Calatoria Themis. Swearing the customary oath by the gods and by the genius of the Emperor Vespasian and his children, he stated that he knew that Justa was born free to his fellow-freedwoman, Vitalis, and had made an agreement with Petronius Stephanus and Calatoria Themis that she should have her daughter returned to her, in exchange for payment of the costs of upbringing. From this emerges the surprising fact that, even if she was freeborn, the baby Justa was left behind in the household of Vitalis' former owners and brought up by them.

This much was confirmed by another witness, Quintus Talmudius Optatus. Swearing the same oath by gods and emperors, he recalled Petronius Stephanus saying to the mother, Petronia Vitalis, something to the effect of, 'Why do you grudge us your daughter, when we treat her like a daughter?' That, to Optatus, showed she was freeborn, though in truth it might have shown the opposite, for a slave born in the home could be a favourite, treated like a child, but even so legally a slave, and waiting to the age of thirty before receiving legal freedom. The freeborn Publius Arrius, son of Publius (his last name does not survive) bore witness to the same effect.

Another witness, the freeborn Marcus Vinicius, son of Marcus, Proculus swore that he had heard Petronius Stephanus, at the time he freed the mother Vitalis, state that she was his only slave. It followed that the daughter Justa could not be a slave. But others were convinced of the opposite. Sextus Vibidius Ampliatus, who claims

girl Nais as security. Strange indeed to think of humans used much as we use documents in mortgage deeds. But we also find slaves as trusted agents of their owners, engaging in business, like Venustus, the slave of Ulpia Plotina, to whom Cominius Primus repaid a loan on 19 July AD 69. There is a good chance that Ulpia Plotina was the aunt of the future Emperor Trajan and a major local landowner. Her slave agent could be an important figure.

The most moving example of an argument over the difference between slave and free has always been the bundle of wooden tablets found in 1938, just two hundred years after the first excavations, in the House of the Bicentenary the case of the so-called Petronia Justa. The story has been told many times; but we still await the new edition by Giuseppe Camodeca, which, to judge by his patient and skilful re-readings of so many other documents, may put an entirely new complexion on the story. As it stands, the story is as follows. A court case is in progress to determine whether the woman who calls herself 'Petronia Sp.f. Iusta' is, as she asserts, a freeborn citizen, albeit born without a legal father, 'daughter of Spurius', or is rather, as one Calatoria Themis asserts, slave-born and her freedwoman. The parties give bail to appear before the urban praetor in Rome: very precisely on 7 December AD 74, in the Forum of Augustus before the praetor's tribunal at the second hour.

*Marble statue of Viciria Archais, mother of Nonius Balbus, found in the Basilica Noniana.*

to have been a close friend of the family, was present when some (now illegible) transaction took place that for him proved that the girl was the freedwoman of Calatoria Themis. If so, calling herself Petronia Justa was quite wrong. Presumably on this scenario she was inherited by Calatoria from her husband Stephanus on his death. If she was Calatoria's freedwoman, her name would be Calatoria Ɔ.l. Iusta: Calatoria Justa freedwomen of a woman (women did not have first names, *praenomina*, so a reversed C was used to indicate a woman or Caia). Another witness, Marcus Calatorius Marullus, an illiterate, and possibly a freedman of Calatoria, was equally confident that Calatoria Themis had manumitted the girl.

On the one hand, it is curious that there were no birth certificates or manumission certificates to prove the matter one way or other. On the other hand, the survival of these wooden tablets shows the importance people attached to hanging on to legal documents that could demonstrate their own status (think of Venidius Ennychus) or their claim over others (like the slaves they bought, sold, or left as warranty for loans). The documents show above all how important, and at the same time slippery, issues of status were. Maybe Justa was indeed born a slave and left behind in her owner's household; maybe Vitalis came into money, and saw the chance of buying her daughter back, repaying costs of upbringing, as happened in cases of the assertion of free-birth, and entering into a quiet conspiracy that she had been freeborn all along. And maybe Calatoria, after the death of the husband who treated the slave girl like his daughter and fudged the issue of her birth, decided to grab back a slave whom she regarded as part of her inheritance.

It is a society in which your legal status has an overwhelming importance. But at the same time, it is a society characterized by movement between status groups to a degree that may astonish us. It is too soon to tell just how many of the citizens of Herculaneum were born free; but on the six marble panels that carried their names, just over three panels carried the names of freedmen, just under two carried the names of those who were neither freedmen nor freeborn, and only one carried the freeborn. There may be other panels yet to emerge, but on today's count only a sixth of the Roman male citizens in Herculaneum could name their freeborn fathers. Even if we double the proportion to a third, it leaves them massively outnumbered.

# 6
# THE PUBLIC FACE
# OF THE TOWN

Once we come to terms with the scale of the town, the most remarkable thing about it must be its evident wealth, at least in its final phase, and the magnificence of its public buildings. Herculaneum is most familiar to us as a place to look at Roman *private* buildings, in their intimacy, and ranging from the swanky residences of the rich to simple upstairs lodgings of humbler folk with flimsy wooden partitions. If the modern visitors want public buildings, they head for Pompeii. It is sometimes hard to remember Herculaneum has public buildings at all, because the most important ones are at least partially buried: the Theatre, the Basilica and its larger neighbour, the 'so-called Basilica', and even the Palaestra, disappear under the rock face. Then there are the public buildings down by the seafront: the Suburban Baths (these indeed are impressive), and the two temples on the terrace of the Area Sacra, so easy to overlook because they have never been reconstructed. It requires an effort to see the public life of the town at all.

Even so, if we peel back the volcanic cover in our imaginations and see the town as a whole, we get a different picture. This tiny settlement is dominated by its main drag, the Decumanus Maximus, its equivalent of Spaccanapoli, the main street of old Naples. A handsome broad road, it defines the public face of the community. To the west is the (still buried) Theatre: not the biggest in the Roman world, but with its 1,350 seats not bad for such a town. To the east is the Palaestra, with its great cruciform pool, built out on terraces stepping down, if our reconstruction is right, to the harbour. The road between is lined with

shops and houses, mostly handsome town houses of a decent size. In the middle, where Cardo III marks the central point, there is a cluster of public buildings. The road itself becomes heavily monumentalized, with lavish use of marble linings. A double arch made of brick-faced concrete, originally clad in plaster, marks the beginning of this monumentalized part to the east; a symmetrical brick double arch also marked its western edge, though this suffered heavy damage in the eruption, and partially collapsed into the façade of the Basilica. To the south of the Decumanus Maximus, flanking Cardo III, are two significant buildings, the Basilica Noniana, and what is currently known as the College of the Augustales (see pages 177–8). To the north of the main road is the largest known public building in town, and the one which, after the Theatre, produced the greatest density of statues and inscriptions, often referred to as the 'so-called Basilica'.

The frustration, and indeed the mystery, of the site has always been the location of its forum. The forum was the heart of a Roman town. Around it clustered the principal public buildings, the Curia where the local senate met, the Basilica where legal cases were heard, the temples where the most important gods were worshipped. Without its forum, Herculaneum is little more than a pleasant suburb. Maiuri was frustrated to find his excavations stopped, by shortage of time and finance, but above all by the buildings of modern Resina above, at a point where he believed the most exciting discoveries were yet to be made. He had not excavated the public heart of the town: the Basilica and the 'so-called Basilica' lay maddeningly

*Left: Aerial view of the site seen from the south-west.*

*Inside: Panoramic view of the Area Sacra outside the walls, with the Temple of Venus.*

*Views of the portico of the large house to the north of the Decumanus Maximus, seen from the street (left) and the pavement (right).*

*View of the triumphal arch over the Decumanus Maximus.*

Left: Detail of the triumphal arch over the Decumanus Maximus.

Below: Plan of the three public buildings excavated in the 1740s, according to Jerome Bellicard.

on the edges of the site, and somewhere beyond, he was sure, must lie the Forum and a crop of monuments, statues and inscriptions that would beggar those of the so-called Basilica. There is, however, a problem, a big problem. The Forum should lie, if anywhere, at the centre of the town, on the intersection of the Decumanus Maximus and the central *cardo*. We may imagine it was immediately to the west of the trio of public buildings so thoroughly ransacked by the Bourbons. But if so, how was it that they never found this space, potentially full of statues and inscriptions? If there was empty space west of the Basilica, why should it be that when Bellicard drew up his plan in 1745, he marked the Decumanus west of the Basilica as flanked by shops and houses? When Francesco La Vega came to make his own plan of the town as a whole in 1796, he too showed blocks of buildings west of the centre.

Far from placing the Forum by the Basilica, La Vega marked as the Forum an open area immediately south of the Theatre, that is to say, on the extreme western edge of the town. He also placed here a temple, the basement of which can still be seen from the tunnels extending from the Theatre. We cannot exclude that Herculaneum was so eccentric as to place its Forum on its very edge, but it would be hard to find a parallel. The Forum belongs in the heart of the town, more or less the centre: if Pompeii's Forum is well west of centre, it is clear that it is because the city spread eastwards after the location of the Forum was fixed. But if the Herculaneum Forum isn't to the west, where is it? It may be time to cut the Gordian knot. Perhaps the monumental heart of the town was precisely the group of three buildings we know about. What you see is what you get, sometimes at least. Rather than assuming that the town had a number

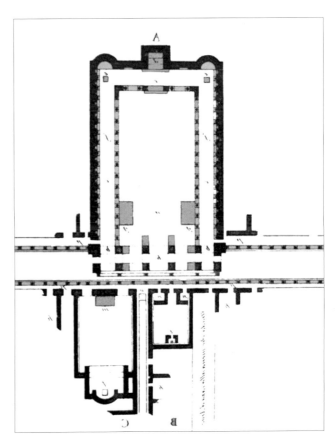

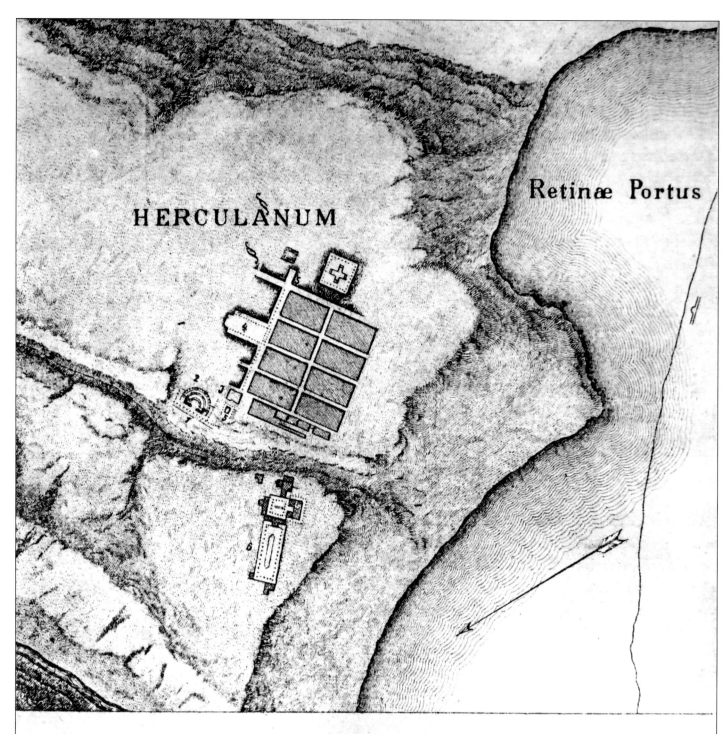

Retinæ Portus

HERCULANUM

1. Puteus ex quo prima consepultae urbis rudera et signa emerserunt. 2. Theatrum. 3. Forum. 4. Basilica. 5. Templa. 6. Domus pseudourbana, ubi volumina sunt reperta. ⊸ Hac linea designatur quousque in praesenti litus procurrit. ϟ Sepulcretum

Metà di un miglio da 60 a grado o metri 925.925.

100   200   300   400   500

Nola
Gate

Sarnus
Gate

Vesuvian
Gate

Herculaneum
Gate

Nucerian
Gate

Stabian
Gate

Marine
Gate

0    100 metres

Left: Plan of the site by Francesco La Vega, 1796.

1 Well from which first evidence of the site emerged
2 Theatre
3 Forum
4 Basilica
5 Temples
6 Domus Psedourbana (Villa of the Mysteries)
The tildas mark the Sepulchretum, or burial ground

Above: Plan of Pompeii, marking location of public buildings. Note clusters around Forum, Theatre and Amphitheatre.

1 Forum
2 Temple of Apollo
3 Building of Eumachia
4 Curia
5 Basilica
6 Temple of Fortune
7 Triangular Forum
8 Large Theatre
9 Small Theatre
10 Temple of Minerva and Hercules
11 Temple of Isis
12 Temple of Aesculapius
13 Samnite Palaestra
14 Temple of Venus
15 Amphitheatre
16 Large Palaestra
17 Forum Baths
18 Stabian Baths
19 Central Baths
20 Suburban Baths

of major missing monuments, it is worth looking more carefully at the ones we do know about, and starting from the opposite assumption, that these are in fact the principal public spaces of Herculaneum.

Public buildings in Roman towns have a distinctive distribution. They are not spread at random through the urban fabric, but cluster. So in Pompeii, the Forum represents the heart of public life, and round it cluster many of the principal buildings: two temples (of Apollo and Jupiter), a number of buildings associated with imperial cult, the great porticoed space constructed by the local benefactress, Eumachia, of disputed function (some have seen the wool exchange, others a slave market), a cluster of what seem to be administrative buildings including the Curia, in which the local senators, *decuriones*, met, and the magnificent Basilica, traditionally the seat of legal cases. The two northern exits to the Forum are marked by triumphal arches, designed to support statue groups of emperors in four-horse chariots. The Forum then has what we may think of as a northern extension, marked by a broad stretch of road culminating in a further triumphal arch. To the right of this stretch of road is another temple, that of Fortune, and to the left a set of public baths.

A second cluster in Pompeii is the theatre quarter, next to the so-called 'Triangular Forum', with two theatres, one large and open, the other small and enclosed, and three temples, of Minerva/Hercules, of Isis, and the minor shrine attributed (erroneously) to Zeus Meilichios, more probably that of Aesculapius, the god of healing. There is also a gymnasium, or palaestra, called the Samnite Palaestra, to the east of the Triangular Forum, though the enormous four-sided portico behind the Large Theatre may have replaced its function, before it ended up as the barracks for the gladiators in the final phase.

Thus public buildings of various types, religious, administrative and for leisure and entertainment, cluster around two 'central spaces', one major, one minor. There are further public buildings that defy this pattern of clustering, and instead seem to patrol the extremities of the city. The Temple of Venus stands at the south-western point of the town, looking out to sea from its elevation, while the Amphitheatre occupies the south-eastern corner, fitting neatly into the angle of the walls, while next to it in close association opens the Large Palaestra. The Temple of Venus and the Amphitheatre are the sentinels of the city, patrolling its furthest reaches, while the Forum and Triangular Forum are the double core. These apart, the only type of public building that is truly scattered through the urban fabric is the baths: in addition to the Forum Baths at the edge of the Forum complex, the Stabian Baths lie a little apart from the theatre complex, on one of the principal intersections of the road system; the Central Baths are in the middle of a dense area of housing, and the Suburban Baths are found outside the 'sea-gate'.

Herculaneum too concentrates its public buildings in distinct clusters. Baths, as in Pompeii, are relatively scattered. The Central Baths occupy the bottom half of an *insula* (VI), but do not adjoin the Decumanus Maximus and the monumental complex. With their careful separation of (larger) men's and (smaller) women's baths, each with their

*Above: Detail of the mosaic floor of the Central Baths of Herculaneum.*

*Overleaf: Panoramic view of the apodyterium (changing room) of the Central Baths.*

sequence of changing room (*apodyterium*), warm room (*tepidarium*) and hot room (*caldarium*), they offered a facility to all free inhabitants, male and female, at the topographic middle of the town. Two other, more recently constructed, sets of baths marked the western and eastern extremities of the town, standing outside the town walls, like the Suburban Baths at Pompeii, in order to benefit from the proximity of the sea. The Suburban Baths to the south-east are among the most impressive bathing spaces found in the Roman world, thanks in part to the quality of their preservation. Built out, as we have seen, over the ancient shore, on top of the tufo platform created by quarrying, the traces of sand trapped under the foundations show that they date from the period when the sea had retreated as a result of the slow expansion of the earth's crust. It must have seemed to the inhabitants of the early first century AD like a gift from the gods to be able to spread out beneath the sea walls, and benefit from the gentle sea breezes. They were built in two episodes: first, the standard cluster of entrance (the tall, atrium-like lightwell at the centre with its red columns and arches makes this space particularly evocative) followed by cold, warm and hot rooms. This *caldarium* is small and intimate, but its luxury is seen in the delicate stucco work and in the glazed bay window, fragments of glass from which remain embedded in the tufo mass, which retains the impression of the circular basin (*labrum*). The second phase added a new *caldarium*, but on a wholly different scale. With its own furnace, operating by direct heating immediately under the bronze 'samovar' in the middle of the pool, it offered an area of warm water big enough for up to twenty to swim in. This second hot room is an enlargement belonging to the final years of the town, after the earthquake of 63. Even so, there was time for it to suffer severe damage as the land sank and the sea returned a second time, with greater violence, damaging the new building severely.

*Left: Atrium of the Suburban Baths.*

*Right above: Decorative stucco in the tepidarium (warm room) of the Suburban Baths.*

*Right below: The calidarium (hot room) of the Suburban Baths. To the left is visible the impression left in volcanic ash by the marble basin (labrum) to the right.*

It is remarkable how many bathing establishments a small Roman town could offer, though we should remember that they served more than the locals, attracting visitors from the surrounding area, the bay being famous as a bathing resort. The association of Hercules with hot baths was old, and his city was a natural place to join the god's leisure. One of the major surprises of the excavations of the late 1990s, intended to launch the rediscovery of the Villa of the Papyri, was a large apsidal building, its roof still perfectly preserved. Initially, it was taken for a temple. What emerged was a vast bath building, equipped, like the extension of the Suburban Baths, with a direct, 'samovar' heating system, and again offering capacity for a large number of bathers. It was only part of a thermal complex, of which a colonnaded portico is visible, but the rest remains buried. A flight of marble steps led down from these baths towards the sea, through an area with pools, fountains and gardens. This too belongs to the period we may regard as the calm before the storm, between earthquake and eruption, when the sea seemed an attraction not a threat.

Baths are impossible without a water supply. Up to the end of the first century BC, the inhabitants relied on the rainwater collected from their roofs (especially via the catchment basin called the *impluvium*) and stored in cisterns. Many of these survived from earlier phases and continued to function. What made the big difference, and enabled public baths, was the arrival of piped water from an aqueduct. It has been assumed that Herculaneum was served by the great

aqueduct constructed under Augustus, the Aqua Augusta, bringing fresh water from the springs at Serino in the Hirpinian mountains to Pompeii, Naples, and ultimately to the imperial fleet at Misenum (the aqueduct that plays so memorable a role in Robert Harris's *Pompeii*). But the Serino supply was heavy with limescale, and left thick deposits on the pipes. Pipes in Herculaneum are free of these deposits, and it seems likely they had their own supply locally. The local water is rich in fluoride, and that shows up in analysis of the teeth of the inhabitants. But though it was separate from the Aqua Augusta, it was surely built around the same time.

Apart from supplying the baths, the aqueduct supplied a series of public fountains and many of the grander houses. We can see at the top of Cardo IV, where it meets the Decumanus Maximus, a brick tower to support a water tank, to ensure sufficient

*Far left: The large calidarium (hot room) added to the Suburban Baths, with underfloor 'samovar' heating.*

*Left: The South-western Baths, with an abandoned flight of marble steps.*

pressure. On it, two local officials have painted an announcement to deter the pollution of the water supply by dumping rubbish nearby. Another pressure tower is found further down the same street. We can also see, close to the surface of the pavement, the lead piping that runs downhill from the tower. Public fountains formed part of a public water supply, and three are visible, each distinguished by a divinity: one close to the water tower itself with the figure of Venus at its head; one at the east end of the Decumanus Maximus with the face of Hercules; one on the junction of Cardo V and the Decumanus Inferior with the figure of Neptune. It is possible that the choice of gods was determined by the street names. The one south Italian city of which we know the ancient street names, Thurii, called them after gods, so Herculaneum may have had a via Herculia, a via Veneria and a via Neptunia. As important as the water supply is the drainage system, and Herculaneum, unlike Pompeii, was well supplied with drains under the streets, of which the one under Cardo III is the most easily visible.

Baths, then, plotted the city, marking its corners and centre – what happened further uphill, we cannot tell. Other public buildings are limited to two areas. Of these, the less important is the strip outside the town walls. One of the benefactions of the great Nonius Balbus to his town was to repair the walls. We can see how he monumentalized the southern wall towards the sea, encasing it in the 'network' technique of *opus reticulatum* that was standard in the period of Augustus (see page 22). He may also have helped to improve the terraces beneath the walls. In any case, his statue and funerary altar were given pride of place on one of them, by the entrance to the Suburban Baths. To the west, there had already, probably since the second century BC, been a small temple, of which the podium has been glimpsed in an excavation. This may be the temple of the goddess Herentas Erycina, the Oscan cult name of Venus, which is mentioned in the one surviving

inscription in Oscan. It was replaced, perhaps as part of Balbus' programme, by two small temples, probably both dedicated to Venus. Four handsome reliefs in the style of early Greek sculpture, showing the gods Minerva, Mercury, Neptune and Vulcan, do not necessarily indicate who was worshipped. More worship of Neptune, god of earthquakes, and Vulcan, god of fire, might seem to have been called for. The recently reconstructed dedicatory inscription from the pediment reveals that it was indeed the Temple of Venus, repaired and partly rebuilt (not necessarily

*Below and right: The fountain and water tower at the top of Cardo IV.*

*Details of the fountains decorated with different deities: Venus (above left), Neptune (above right) and Hercules (left).*

after earthquake damage) by the largesse of two local benefactors, Vibidia Sabina and her son A. Furius Saturninus. Both were born slaves, Vibidia being the freedwoman of a famous Vestal Virgin ('Virginis liberta'). They paid lavishly, not only reconstructing this building, but contributing to the repair of the Capitolium, the Temple of Jupiter echoing that on the Capitoline in Rome, and making a distribution of cash to members of the local council, the *augustales*, and the priestly college of Venus, as well as a gift to the town of 54,000 sesterces in recognition of their promotion to honorary membership of the local senate. Rich freedmen had no qualms about spelling out the deal by which they traded money for status and recognition.

The effect of the terrace beneath the town walls is to create a strip of public land, comprising sacred area with temples, funerary altar of Balbus, and baths. It may be thought of as a sort of quid pro quo for the reduction of public land above. A town wall, if it is to serve a defensive function, needs to rise to a good height above ground level, and to have a strip of open land behind it for the defending troops to pass along. But Balbus' wall provided instead a pleasant low parapet, over which the rich houses that were built up to and over the walls could enjoy their treasured sea view.

We may now return to the main public area of the town, the Decumanus Maximus. While Pompeii clusters its central buildings

*Above: The interior of a drain running down Cardo III.*

*Below: Terraces beneath the southern walls of the town.*

around a core, Herculaneum stretches them out along a string. The public buildings at the west and east end mark the edge of the city, rather like the Temple of Venus and the Amphitheatre in Pompeii. The Theatre forms part of the Augustan transformation of the town. Built in concrete, faced with *opus reticulatum*, and its steps carved from tufo blocks, it was, according to an inscription, paid for by the magistrate Lucius Annius Mammianus Rufus, and designed by the architect P. Numisius. Though Nonius Balbus did not build this one, he certainly made his presence felt. On either side of the front stage were dedications by the citizens of Herculaneum, one to Nonius Balbus, the other to a great Roman noble, Appius Claudius Pulcher, consul in 38 BC (and nephew of the rabble-rousing tribune, Clodius Pulcher). A ghostly image of Nonius remains today in the ceiling of one of the tunnels by which the Theatre was explored. The ash set round the marble face of Nonius Balbus, standing in the full-frontal nudity appropriate to an athlete. The statue is in the Naples Museum; his face still looks down from the ceiling (see page 172).

*View of the Temple of Venus.*

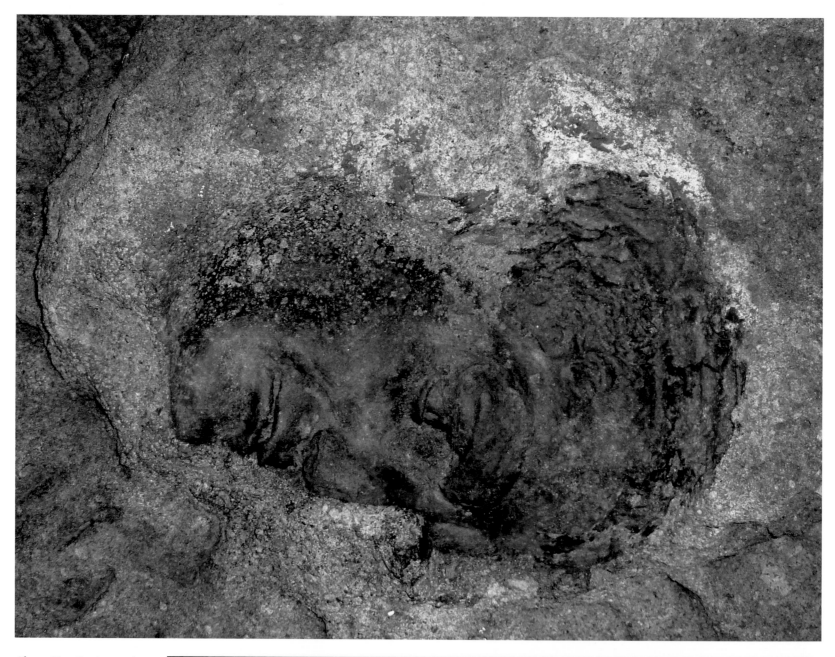

*Above: Negative impression in the volcanic ash of the face of the statue of Nonius Balbus in the Theatre.*

*Right: Dedicatory inscription of the same statue.*

*Marble statue of Nonius
Balbus in heroic posture,
found in the Theatre.*

Eighteenth-century tunnellers, led by the Prince d'Elbeuf, and followed by the engineers of Charles Bourbon, made a thorough job of stripping the Theatre of its marble cladding and decorative statues, but the case of Balbus shows how important it was as a place for honouring the big names of the town, as was the practice in the Greek east. It was from the Theatre that two of the most famous marble pieces came – the 'large' and 'small' Herculaneum women – which made their way to the court of Dresden. Both are standardized types, used in cities across the Mediterranean to celebrate the virtues of the leading women, especially those who had made generous donations. The types have their origins in the Greek world, and have been found in hundreds of copies in cities from one end of the Mediterranean to the other (the current count on the more popular 'large' woman stands at 207, that on the 'small' woman at 169). They are the visual equivalent of the repetitive inscriptions found in Greek cities, with the citation 'for piety and sobriety' – the modest virtue of *sophrosynē* was often cited: the restraint of a faithful and obedient wife, corresponding visually to the dress wrapped so comprehensively around the body as to suggest minimal hint of female form. Other honorific statues (if the reported location is correct) included bronze portraits of leading citizens in togas, like Lucius Mammius Maximus and Marcus Calatorius Quartio. This was a portrait gallery in which, if you wanted be anyone in Herculaneum, you needed to be seen.

At the other edge of the town, to the east, the Palaestra represented a type of structure which, like the Theatre, was considered essential to any self-respecting town in the Greek world: the *gymnasium*. The Romans were coy about admitting that they built *gymnasia* – the architect Vitruvius goes out of his way to deny it, suggesting that the Italic *palaestra* was something very different. Architecturally, they were variants on a theme; socially, they may indeed have been different, since the *gymnasium* was the principal place for the physical training and intellectual education of the young citizen, something which to the Roman viewpoint, disapproving of what it interpreted as an incitement to paedophilia, was inappropriate. We cannot tell whether Herculaneum's Palaestra had such an educational function, only that it offered space, in its long colonnades and exterior walkways, for exercise, walking and running, and in its cruciform pool for swimming.

Left: Portico around the Palaestra.

Above: Detail of capital from the portico.

It seems to have been constructed in two separate phases. The first involved only the strip of land to the north, which was built up under Augustus. Half a century later, perhaps under Claudius, a programme of extension was carried out, involving major engineering works to the terracing on the edge of the eastern ravine. It was in this episode that the three-storey block of shops and apartments was constructed, which formed the profitable rental side to an expensive public monument. To this we will return, but it is worth underlining the subtle but significant modification that is made to Cardo V in the course of this operation. The new building is set at a slight angle to the road, enabling the road itself to be gradually widened as it slopes downhill toward the sea (the widening can be seen in the paving of the road, which changes colour). The result is that by the time the road reaches the next crossroads, where the main entrance to the Palaestra was located, it has formed a 'largo', a broad area outside the monumental entrance with its two columns. When this entrance was constructed, the access to the Palaestra had shifted away from the Decumanus Maximus. Even so, that left a large and grand public space opening off the Decumanus, now referred to as the Upper

*Far left: Western portico of the Palaestra.*

*Above left: Archival photograph of the bronze statue of the Hydra (the many-headed monster killed by Hercules) found in the Palaestra.*

*Above right: Fresco representing an actor as king, found in the Palaestra.*

Aula, that led to a series of grand rooms above the Palaestra. The precise function is not clear, but it was suitable for grandiose public ceremonies. The paintings that survive from this episode, preserved in Naples Museum, include some of the most famous 'masterpieces' there on display.

We thus have two of the key areas of public leisure and entertainment at either end of the Decumanus Maximus. We may now return to its centre. Three buildings stand, like the Three Bears, large, medium and small, in a cluster at the mid-point of the main road of the town. The monumentalization of the roads between them makes clear this is a special area. No wagons and carts carrying supplies to shops and private houses could pass here: they were blocked off by the triumphal arches. Even Cardo III, running between the two smaller buildings, is end-stopped. A rectangular structure, a little over a metre high, stands in the way of traffic. Its function is not obvious. It has been identified as a tribunal or *suggestum*, from which a magistrate could address the people, or a public crier could make an announcement or hold a public auction. If this is right, the paved space in front of it seems rather cramped. An alternative would be to see it as the base of a small shrine.

Of the three public buildings mapped in the eighteenth century, only one, the smallest, is fully visible today, known to visitors as the College or Shrine of the Augustales. Its shape is unusual, with the four central columns supporting an upper floor giving the impression of the atrium of a private house, and the central *cella* or shrine beyond it raised on a platform and decorated in a rich colour scheme, in the 'Fourth Style' typical of the final years of the city, and mythological scenes twice depicting Hercules. In one, he is bargaining with Achelous, the river god whom he fought successfully for the hand of Deianira, seen in the background. In the second he is seen seated in heaven before the goddesses Juno (with her rainbow) and Minerva (with her helmet). As is the way with mythology, the scenes may suggest a variety of readings. Those who recalled that the river god Achelous was the father of the Siren Parthenope, and hence closely associated with Neapolis, may have seen a local reference. The scene of Hercules' apotheosis, in the context of early imperial Italy, inescapably recalled the apotheosis of emperors. The ultimate mark of posthumous respect was for the senate to declare them gods, Divi, a privilege restricted by the time of the eruption to Julius Caesar, Augustus, Claudius and Vespasian. There were statues of all these 'Divi' in the Porticus building opposite, and, more significantly, statues to Caesar and Augustus in this building itself. The deification of Hercules was both a mythological charter for what happened to emperors and, in the context of the town of Herculaneum, a suggestion of a particular affinity. But if you wanted, you could find subversive readings here too. His wife Deianira was Hercules' undoing, for, tricked by the dying centaur Nessus, she tried to stop his adultery by giving him the poisoned cloak that killed him. Some of the wives of the divinized emperors were uncomfortably reminiscent of Deianira: passing over rumours about Livia, Agrippina was thought to have poisoned Claudius, leading to his apotheosis, and Seneca made fun of his admission to heaven not as 'deification' but 'pumpkinification'.

In identifying the building as the College of the Augustales, weight has been given to two inscriptions, found here or near by. One is the great list of names that was long taken to be the list, or *album*, of the *augustales* (discussed in the previous chapter). It is now agreed that there were far too many names for it to be the members of this exclusive club, and must be the entire citizen body, so one argument falls. The other inscription is a dedication to Augustus by two brothers, Aulus Lucius Proculus and Julianus, of something unspecified, but surely not a building but a statue of the divine Augustus. On the occasion of the dedication, the brothers gave a dinner to the *decuriones* and the *augustales* of the town. Just as Vibidia Sabina and her son Furius Saturninus gave the *decuriones* and *augustales* a distribution of money to celebrate their promotion, these two brothers were buying favour with the influential men of the town. It proves no specific connection of the building with the *augustales*. It might just as well be a meeting place for the town

*The so-called College of the Augustales, possibly the Curia, or Senate House.*

council as for the *augustales*, and indeed it was identified as the Curia in the eighteenth century. In fact, no less than three graffiti on the first column on the right as you enter mention the *curia* or *curia Augustiana* or *curia Augustana*, to which body various candidates are recommended for election. The argument that because this was the College of the Augustales, the word 'curia' must refer to their college should be stood on its head: because it was the Curia, it cannot have been the College of the Augustales. Herculaneum certainly had a Curia, and this could reasonably be it, loyally dedicated to the Divine Augustus, whose life could be seen as a parallel for Hercules, the great benefactor of mankind.

*Above: Dedicatory plaque from the so-called College of the Augustales. It reads: 'Sacred to Augustus. Aulus and Aulus Lucius, sons of Aulus, of the tribe Menenia, called Proculus and Julianus, at their own expense, to mark the dedication gave a dinner to the decuriones and the augustales.'*

*Left: Archival photograph of the discovery of the inscription in 1961.*

*Above: Frescoes from the central shrine of the building, depicting Hercules with Achelous and Deianeira (left), and his welcome to heaven by Minerva (with helmet) and Juno (with rainbow).*

The largest, and certainly most important, of the three public buildings was the one which made the most impact on the Bourbon excavators, but which now is hardest for us to recapture. Exploration started in 1739, and almost at once produced a sensational crop of statues and paintings, which still have pride of place in the collections of the National Museum of Naples. Despite the careful plans and elevations produced by the Bourbon explorers, there has never been agreement as to its function. Alcubierre initially took it for a Temple of Theseus; Weber preferred to see it as a Temple of Jupiter or Hercules. Roofless, it cannot be a temple. Bellicard, following an essay by M. d'Arthenay published in 1748, identified it as the Forum. But the identification as a Basilica took root, and is seen in La Vega's plans. Later, in the nineteenth century, Michele Ruggiero claimed it as the Palaestra. Maiuri, who excavated the real Palaestra, then identified it as the senate house or Curia – another odd suggestion for a building without a roof. Jean-Charles Balty rejected this idea and suggested a market place, or Macellum.

Perhaps we are safest in sticking to architectural form. It had the plan of a Roman *porticus*, that is a great rectangular open space flanked on all sides by porticoes. The closest comparison is the Eumachia building in Pompeii, but since the function of that is still hotly disputed, it may not help us. In broad terms, it was like the type of building that sprang up in Rome under Augustus, for instance in the Porticus of Livia. Essentially an open square, it is surrounded by colonnades. The old voting place of Rome, the Saepta Julia, looked much like this once Augustus had reshaped it, and it has been noted that some at least of the decoration was similar. The end walls, as we have seen, were occupied by grandiose mythological scenes, of Theseus and the Minotaur, Hercules and Telephus, the musical training of young Achilles by the centaur Chiron, and the musical training of Olympus by Marsyas. The elder Pliny tells us that there were paintings of Olympus with Pan and Achilles with Chiron in the Saepta Julia, the painters of which were unknown, even though they were so valuable that the guardians had to answer for their safety with their lives.

The parallel has suggested that the Herculaneum Porticus might have a similar function to the Saepta Julia, where the Romans citizens voted. But in provincial towns, they voted generally in the Forum itself. The Saepta Julia, like most Roman public spaces, was used for many things: voting, gladiatorial shows, athletic competitions, meetings of the senate. We need to get beyond the idea that buildings were restricted to specific functions. The important thing was that Herculaneum now had a big public space just like those in Rome, surrounded by colonnades, full of fine works of art. These included, of course, statues, in profusion, and mostly of members of the imperial family. In the central niche were the Emperor Titus, flanked by the seated Augustus and Claudius; in the side niches, before the scenes of the heroes of old, Theseus and Hercules, were the new heroes, Augustus and Claudius (again), this time standing in bronze. The

*Right above: Fresco depicting Hercules and his son Telephus suckled by a hind in Arcadia, from the so-called Basilica.*

*Right below: Fresco of the young Achilles learning the lyre from the centaur Chiron, from the so-called Basilica.*

*Opposite: Fresco of Theseus and the dead Minotaur, from the so-called Basilica.*

*Above: Bronze statues of Augustus as Jupiter with thunderbolt (left), and Claudius (right), found in the so-called Basilica.*

*Opposite: Silver portrait bust of the Emperor Galba, found in the street outside the House of Galba, perhaps from the so-called Basilica.*

body of the portico had plenty of other imperial characters: Tiberius and his mother Livia, Claudius and his mother Antonia, his uncle Germanicus, his wife Agrippina and his son Britannicus, and some others. Most of these were dedicated by the rich freedman Mammius Maximus, who was duly rewarded with his own statue in the Theatre, and doubtless other privileges. There is a significant absence of dedications to Nero as emperor, which were doubtless torn down on his death with the damning of his memory, but with the arrival of the Flavians, new dedications appeared, to Vespasian, Titus, Julia daughter of Titus, Domitia wife of Domitian, and Flavia Domitilla wife of Vespasian and mother of Titus and Domitian.

The sheer frequency of statues to the imperial family, or rather, a succession of families of 'good'

emperors, has led recent scholars to the identification of the area as one dedicated to the cult of the emperors: an 'Augusteum'. This is supported by dedicatory inscriptions by the *augustales*, recorded in the eighteenth century. But this may be too specific a reading of this space. It was surely a principal, if not *the* principal, space in which citizens could meet. It may be that d'Arthenay and Bellicard were not far out in identifying it as our missing Forum. If it ever started as a forum, the central circulation space of the town in which people met to do business, to pray, to argue over justice and to elect their magistrates, it had been transformed typologically into a Roman *porticus*. We will have to wait for the emergence of the right inscription to know for sure what label they would have given it.

*Above: Exterior of the so-called College of the Augustales, with the possible location of the weights and measures office ('Pondera') in front.*

*Right above: Watercolour reconstruction of the so-called Basilica by F. Morghen (1835).*

*Right below: Reconstructed elevation of interior wall of the so-called Basilica showing dedication by Augustales.*

*Inside: Panoramic view of the so-called College of the Augustales.*

AVGVSTALES·SP

DISEGNO DI DAVIDE PELUSO — 1995

0  1  2  3  4  5  6  7  8  9  10 Mt.

The Porticus is connected to the small building on the other side of the main street (whether College of the Augustales or Curia) by an arcade structure. Its importance is underlined by the use of marble cladding, at least on the Porticus side, and the numerous bases for honorific statues. The similarity in plan to the Eumachia building in Pompeii encourages the identification of this structure as a 'Chalcidicum' (a building type that should have originated in Chalcis in Euboea, though Latin inscriptions frequently invert the spelling to Calchidicum). One further inscription is relevant here.

*Equestian statue of Nonius Balbus, often supposed to be from the so-called Basilica, in fact from outside the theatre.*

A long text, reported in the sixteenth century by the antiquarian Fabio Giordano, records the meeting of the *decuriones* in the Curia, with all present, at which Marcus Memmius Rufus, father and son, duumvirs for the second time ('duumvirs' were the local equivalent to consuls), were thanked profusely for their generosity in putting on games and for building at their own expense 'Pondera, a Schola and a Calchidicum'. The *pondera* or 'weights' will have been an officially checked set of weights and measures, such as are also found in the Forum of Pompeii, against which the weights used by traders could be checked by the local magistrates. The *decuriones* give the Memmii responsibility for future supervision of the weights, and for the provision of a slave to keep permanent watch over them. A *schola* is a space for gatherings, sometimes no more than an *exedra*, or recess within a portico. A Chalcidicum seems to be a type of arcade attached to a public building: Augustus built one, identified as that against the senate house, the Curia Julia, in Rome, and Eumachia built one as part of the building named after her in Pompeii. The Chalcidicum of Pompeii is generally understood to be the arcade that opens on the Forum. If this arcade in Herculaneum is the Chalcidicum the Memmii built, the Weights and the Schola should be the two spaces on either side of the entrance to the so-called College of the Augustales (or Curia). Analysis of the architecture shows that these two spaces form an integral unit of construction with the Chalcidicum that fronts the Porticus. A complex which pulls together Curia, Schola and Pondera, and Chalcidicum makes the area look even more like the public heart of the town. Why look further?

Everything would be clearer if we knew where exactly the two equestrian statues of the Nonii Balbi, which grace the front hall of the Museum at Naples, were actually found. The inscription on Nonius Balbus' altar, as we have seen, provided that an equestrian statue should be erected to him 'at the busiest place in town', *in loco celeberrimo*. That must surely be the Forum. The equestrian statues of Balbus and his father emerged, according to Alcubierre's reports, in June 1746, at a time when explorations stretched from the Theatre to the Palaestra, and there has always been much confusion about their find-spot. They were stated by Cochin and Bellicard, who were there only three years later in 1749, to have come precisely from this arcade, which they regarded as a portico attached to the Forum. They were also so depicted in the imaginative watercolour of Filippo Morghen in 1835. Bardet was already excavating in this area in 1743, three years earlier, and though he does indeed report finding two bases of equestrian statues, he also found fragments of bronze feet attached to them, which means the Nonii (who are in marble) were not here. But this area is rich with bases of the right dimensions for equestrian statues, four visible around the brick arch, and four more in the area of the arcade, and the Nonii need not have come from the ones Bardet mentions. It evidently was an area, just like the Forum of Pompeii, in which the especial honour of an equestrian statue was suitable. Unfortunately, the great honorific inscription on the

tomb of Nonius Balbus states that the statue should be inscribed 'To Marcus Nonius son of Marcus Balbus, praetor, proconsul, patron, the universal people of Herculaneum, in recognition of his merits'. In fact, the surviving inscription is more simple: 'To Marcus Nonius son of Marcus Balbus, praetor, proconsul, the people of Herculaneum'. No mention of him as patron, or of the 'universal' people, or of his merits. So we have not quite got a smoking gun.

Of the three public buildings, only one now seems certain in its identification, and it is here that the best chances of future discoveries lie. This is the partially visible building to the west of Cardo III. We can be reasonably confident in identifying it as the Basilica which Nonius Balbus built, because the records confirm that statues of the members of his family came from there, including himself, his

*Commemorative inscription to Nonius Balbus recording the gratitude of his fellow townsmen, and the posthumous honours voted to him.*

father, and his mother Viciria Archais. Along the now visible east wall of the building are a series of statue bases, and it is almost certainly from these that the gallery of Balbus' family came (and for this reason it was referred to in the eighteenth century as the Galleria Balbi). If confirmation were needed, a fragment of a new inscription found in the same area, put up by the Nucerians (Balbus' fellow townsmen) to a female (the name is lost) points to a missing member of the family portrait gallery.

The dossier of legal documents, which we met in the previous chapter belonging to one Venidius Ennychus, records that at a meeting of the local council on 25 July AD 61 in the Basilica Noniana, Venidius was recommended to the authorities in Rome for promotion to full citizenship. The close association of the Basilica with citizenship, its formal award and documentation, is confirmed by other recent finds. That the Basilica Noniana was where lists of citizens were kept and displayed is suggested by Maiuri's discovery of three fragments of the inscription when he was excavating here in 1961, apparently found in the road outside the building. More recently, there emerged from within the building two broken slabs of white marble, which at first sight appeared blank. On closer examination, traces emerged of faded letters in ink or paint of a list of names. In fact, Maiuri had already discovered a similar fragment during his excavations. If they kept lists of names painted on blank slabs, as well as properly inscribed lists, it suggests the more strongly that the Basilica is where records of citizens were officially stored.

The plan of the Basilica is now known with reasonable certainty. The campaign of cleaning the escarpment, undertaken by the Herculaneum Conservation Project, coupled with reopening of old Bourbon tunnels, allows us to confirm details from the plans by Bardet and Bellicard. And though we may be dismayed by the extensiveness of the warren of tunnels made in the eighteenth century, it is also evident that Maiuri's instinct was right, and much

remains to be discovered from this focal point of the town. Even in the early days of the cleaning campaign, there emerged from the edge of the old excavations the marble head of an Amazon of the highest quality. The Amazon is one of a type, closely parallel to a similar head found in the recent excavations of the lower terrace of the Villa of the Papyri. What makes this

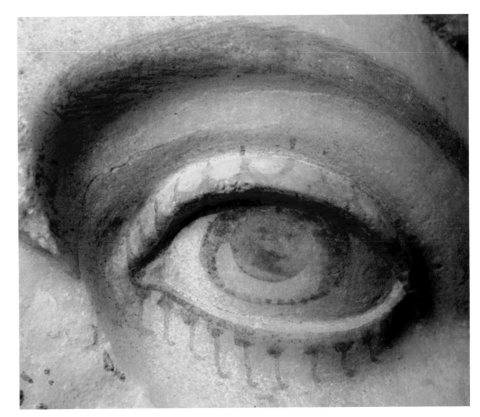

*Left: Mimmo Camardo holds a fragment of a mable plaque dimly inscribed in ink with a list of names.*

*This page: Marble head of a statue of an Amazon at moment of discovery (below), and detail of the painting around the eye (right).*

example particularly valuable is the survival of extensive traces of paint, not only in the hair, but around the eyes, including eyebrows, eyelashes, and pupils. The fact that it was excavated and cleaned by professional conservators does much to explain the survival of these traces of pigment. Too often, marble finds have been scrubbed clean by unobservant excavators.

Our best chance of understanding more about the monumental centre of Herculaneum lies in the full excavation of the Basilica. Already the ground surface above has been cleared of ruinous modern buildings. Reopening the Bourbon tunnels has demonstrated how much they left behind – exquisite details of decoration that were spared their pickaxes. More significantly for the topography of the area, exploration of tunnels to the west of the Basilica has shown that it has other, smaller structures built up against it. This means that it did not immediately flank the missing Forum, though it may still be the case that it is only a narrow row of shops, and the Forum remains to be discovered to the west.

Our evidence is certainly incomplete, and surprises surely await any future campaign of excavation. In the meantime, it is clear that our complex of three buildings at the intersection of Cardo III and the Decumanus Maximus was of central importance in the town; if not *the* busiest place, at least one of them. What else is missing? Certainly a few temples. There was a Capitolium – a temple to Jupiter that imitated the temple to Jupiter Optimus Maximus on the Capitoline. We know that because Vibidia Sabina and her son helped to repair it. And there must have been a temple to Hercules, the patron god of the town. One or other, even both, might be the temple at the west end of the Decumanus Maximus, marked on his map by Francesco La Vega, and today dimly visible in the tunnels by the Theatre. Then there is the mysterious Temple of Mother of the Gods, Magna Mater, restored by the Emperor Vespasian in AD 76: the inscription plaque was found in the entrance to the Palaestra, with which it seems to have no connection. There is a missing Macellum, or market, built at his own expense by the duumvir Marcus Spurius, son of Marcus, Rufus. The unexcavated town undoubtedly has other surprises in store. But from what we can make out, this small community, no more than a modern village, boasted an impressive and well-organized set of public monuments, deliberately imitating the style of imperial Rome with lavish works of art. Pre-Roman Herculaneum is difficult to make out, but imperial Herculaneum, though small, was disproportionately well endowed.

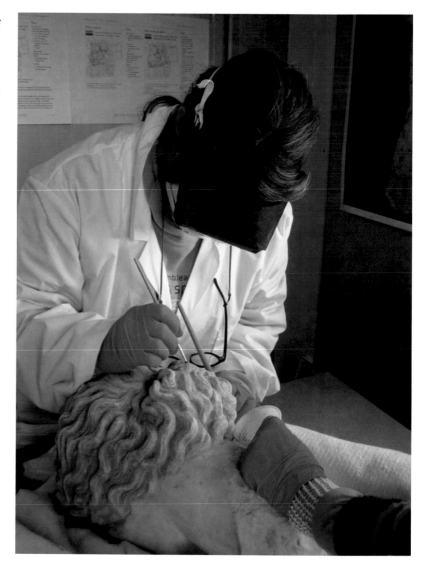

*Above: Cleaning of the Amazon head by conservator-restorer Monica Castaldi Martelli.*

*Right: Marble head of an Amazon (Riccardo Giordano).*

# 7
# STANDARDS OF LIVING

Just like the skeletons, or the inscriptions and wooden tablets with their hundreds of names, the houses of Herculaneum offer us a cross-section and a vivid insight into how people lived, high and mighty, low and servile. When Amedeo Maiuri published his excavations in two magnificent volumes, he divided up his houses not by area but by status, into eight classes. He started with patrician houses of traditional type, followed by middle class houses of traditional type, which he followed by grand houses ('case signorili') and residential houses of a non-traditional type. Here he was evidently torn between two principles of classification, one in terms of the wealth of the owners, the other in terms of the typology of the houses. Why not start with the grandest houses in town? Alas for Maiuri, they were not very traditional, in terms of the dominance of the traditional entrance hall or atrium, so he separates these out. Then he slides down his social scale: middle class houses with attached shops, multiple-residence houses, tradesmen's houses and shops with dwellings, and finally shops and workshops in a multi-storey block.

This complicated classification, applied to no more than sixty units of residence or use, already suggests how diverse the housing of Herculaneum is, in size, wealth, function and architectural style. Maiuri's desire to distinguish houses by social class (flagged by terms like 'patrician', 'signorile', 'middle class' or 'mercantile') reflects an assumption based on modern western cities that people will generally live clustered by class: the working classes in city centre slums or housing estates separate from

*Atrium of the Samnite House with central rainwater basin (impluvium) and upper colonnade.*

professional middle classes in suburbia and upper classes in secluded leafy lanes. These distinctions break down completely in the Roman world. In a world in which status not class is what distinguishes, freeborn or slave-born, foreigner or citizen, ordinary citizen or member of the honoured 'orders' of *decuriones* and Augustales, housing patterns worked differently. For one thing, the richer the household, the more numerous were the slaves, so that the rich lived not in splendid isolation, but surrounded by their dependants. You could not be a Marcus Nonius Balbus, and leave the town teaming with your freedmen and the freedmen of your freedmen, without living in a big house full of slaves and other dependants. We met Venidius Ennychus in the last chapter, the successful businessman whose bundle of legal documents was found in the House of the Black Saloon. Maiuri had some difficulty in believing that this relative 'upstart' could live in such a large, fine house, with its traditional atrium entrance, and indeed we cannot exclude the possibility that he was a lodger or a tenant. But Ennychus was a member of an order of dignity in the town, an Augustalis, and we should expect to find him owning a house that looked dignified.

If we can't start from modern expectations, where can we start? There are few better introductions than the extraordinary evocation of life on the Bay of Naples in the first century AD in Petronius' *Satyrica*, one of the two novels written in Latin that gives us the best insight into Roman imperial society. (Amedeo Maiuri, who himself produced an edition of the text, would not have disagreed.) In the most familiar episode, one among many in a long and rambling narrative, the heroes, a group of literary friends, are invited to the home of Trimalchio, rich freedman and Augustalis. As Trimalchio describes it himself, it is a splendid mansion:

Thanks to the protection of Mercury, I built this house. As you know, it used to be a hovel, now it's a temple. It has four dining-rooms, twenty bedrooms, two marble colonnades, a row of rooms above, a bedroom where I sleep myself, a nest for this viper here [his wife], and a really good lodge for the porter. The guest wing takes a hundred guests.

Scale is vital: there have to be many of everything and space for vast numbers. Trimalchio's household pullulates with slaves. Apart from the hordes of cooks and carvers and pretty-boy waiters and entertainers who circulate throughout the meal, there are unseen crowds in the background, organized by divisions, so numerous that not one in ten knows his master. The vital but arbitrary boundary between slave and free is constantly visible. Trimalchio, whose slaves seem ever in danger of a flogging for trivial errors, nevertheless gives freedom to his favourites with studiedly casual humour: a boy acrobat falls on his master, slightly grazing him, and is granted his freedom 'so that nobody can say Trimalchio was hurt by a slave', and he assures the company he will give freedom to all his slaves in his will (something prohibited by law, which restricted it to fixed proportions), leaving one, Philargyrus, a farm, and another, Cario, an apartment block.

The world of slaves flows constantly into the world of ex-slaves, in the company Trimalchio keeps and the stories he tells about himself and his friends. 'My dear people, slaves are human beings too. They drink the same milk as everyone else, even if their luck has been against them.' This awareness that luck is what makes the difference is pervasive. Trimalchio

was born a slave: as he proudly recounts, he came from Asia no bigger than a candlestick, served the fancy of his master for fourteen years, and ended up his master's heir with a senator's fortune – one he promptly lost in a trading venture, to be rescued by his wife Fortunata, who sold her jewellery to raise the money for a new venture which paid off. Fortunata, he is equally happy to boast, was born a slave, became a dancing girl. Now she counts her money by the sackful. His friends are freedmen too, with their own exotic stories: Gaius Pompeius Diogenes, who started out with nothing, humping wood on his back, but made a mysterious fortune ('stole a hobgoblin's hat'), and has now put up a To Let notice by his shop, declaring he is moving into a house of his own and will let the flat above the shop. Then there's Gaius Julius Proculus, who started free and rich, flourished as an undertaker, but was swindled by his own freedmen and had to auction off his property.

Trimalchio's freedmen friends are hypersensitive about their standing. They feel they are being sneered at by the well-educated narrators. Hermeros flies off the handle:

*Marble table by the impluvium in the House of the Wooden Screen.*

'You a Roman knight, are you? Well, my father was a king!

'Why are you only a freedman?' did you say? Because I went into service voluntarily! I wanted to be a Roman citizen, not a subject with taxes to pay. And today, I hope no one can laugh at the way I live. I'm a man among men, and I walk with my head up.

People so sensitive about status attach importance to the symbols of standing, their houses, their retinues of slaves, and their public recognition. Trimalchio and no less than two of his guests are members of the order of Augustales. When one, Habinnas, arrives late, it is with a fanfare, proceeded by a lictor, and the narrator thinks it must be a chief magistrate arriving, rather than Habinnas, 'Augustalis and monumental mason'. So easily is the successful freedman confused with the local elite. Habinnas' wife Scintilla is dripping with gold jewellery, gold bracelets, anklets and a gold hair net, which her husband claims to weigh six and a half pounds, and calls for weighing scales to prove it. When we find skeletons heavy with jewellery at Herculaneum, we

need to remember they may be Scintillas, not high-born Romans.

Petronius lays on his satire thick, but the point remains: a Trimalchio is as proud of his lavish house, his silver plate, his Corinthian bronzes, his artworks and mythological paintings (however clumsily misinterpreted), his overflowing strongbox, his slave household and quasi-military divisions, as any freeborn Roman citizen. We are going to find a major problem telling freeborn and slave-born apart in Herculaneum, and just because they have a house with a 'traditional atrium' does not mean that they are well-born patricians, any more than that wealth can be read as a sign of free birth. To speak of a 'middle class' in this context is especially misleading. Freedmen traders are as likely to be found in modestly prosperous houses as in workshops and flats above shops, and the good taste of their decoration tells us more about the remarkable skill levels of the workshops of craftsmen that flourished on the Bay of Naples than about the social origins of the householders.

Which houses did the rich live in? Where do we draw the line? It is tempting, and lazy, to imagine the Roman world as having a sharp distinction between rich and poor, the 'elite' of the ruling families, with lavish houses and spreading estates, and the 'ordinary' people with their humble dwellings. As we have seen, it is no easy matter to say who should count as 'ordinary' in a society so full of slaves and ex-slaves. In an open and competitive society, wealth distributes itself in many grades. You can draw no sharp distinction between rich and poor, because too many are clustered around the dividing line, wherever you put it. So it is with the houses of Herculaneum: they come in all shapes and sizes, and signs of surprising luxury can turn up in houses of modest size too.

If there was a standard house at Herculaneum, it was that determined by the plot size of the original layout. Just as the town is divided by its horizontal *decumani* and vertical *cardines*, or in the Greek of

*Detail of marble tragic mask from the House of Neptune and Amphitrite.*

the area, *plateiai* and *stenôpoi*, into blocks or *insulae* of broadly the same size, *c*.3,000 square metres, so each *insula* is divided into a number of standard plots, around 200 square metres each. But over the course of time, boundaries changed continuously, and you have only to look at the plan to see the effects. Property outlines come to form a jigsaw of interlocking shapes, as one neighbour sells another a room here, a garden there. Then some manage to take over a string of properties to make a larger plot, while others subdivide their properties into smaller units, to let out as shops and flats. All this means that, while the norm may cluster around a plot of 200 square metres, there is a spread in virtually every gradation of size, from single-room workshops to spreading properties occupying entire blocks.

The more standard units tend to cluster up and down the side streets, the *cardines*, in the middle portion of the excavated plot. Further north, the Decumanus Maximus, the town's most prestigious street, attracted a string of larger and smarter properties that open directly onto it. Further south, the seawall, which once, as we have seen, represented the

*Plan of the Samnite House.*

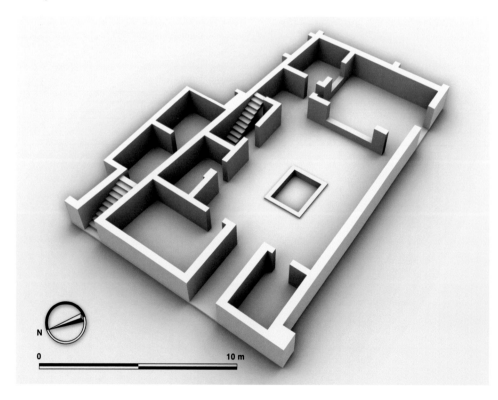

town's military defence against attack from the sea, more latterly, in the peaceful prosperity of the early empire, offered instead an opportunity for grand houses to enjoy the spectacular sea view. The strip of land along which troops must have moved to defend the walls has disappeared to make room for their lush gardens. Let us, then, look at examples of houses from these three areas, the standard plots in the middle, and turn in the next chapter to the grander houses, those to the north, and the most spacious houses to the south overlooking the sea, focusing for now on those which show the signs of wealth that might make us imagine that the rich lived there.

By starting from the 'standard' plots, we can start where Maiuri did, with the Samnite House. Located on the north-eastern corner of what is now the central crossroads of the site, it occupies what looks to be a plot eaten away over the course of time. Its garden peristyle area has been occupied by another little house, distinguished by the 'Grand Portal' that gives its name: in its walls can be seen remains of grey tufo columns which arguably once formed the peristyle of the Samnite House. But even to the north, its boundary has been eroded by the insertion, on a slight diagonal, of a staircase leading to an upper apartment, which was doubtless a valuable source of revenue. Reduced it may be, but the Samnite House has an atrium space so fine that Maiuri could treat it as a model of an older style of living, which he regarded as 'patrician'. There is no denying its elegance. As you enter the narrow *fauces*, or 'throat', which gives access to an atrium, you notice plaster decoration imitating slabs of coloured marbles. It was an older style, one which was common across the Mediterranean in the second century BC, in the days before the new imperial peace encouraged the Mediterranean-wide marble trade and enabled the rich to use real marble slabs. Art historians call this the 'first Pompeian style'. Its antiquity is guaranteed by a painted message in Oscan letters, running right to left, unlike Latin: SPUNES LOPI. Otherwise incomprehensible, it is taken to be a name, possibly of the owner. Hence the 'Samnite' House, because of its clear signs of pre-Roman dating.

The atrium itself is at first glance a textbook example of an atrium. Its floor, in *opus signinum* (crushed pottery decorated with white marble chips), slopes into the central pool of the *impluvium*, where rainwater collected from the roof above, similarly sloping inwards to the central rectangular opening of the *compluvium*. Its edges are decorated with terracotta plaques with lion's head spouts, to direct the flow of water to the basin below. The walls of the atrium are also eye-catching. It is divided as if into two floors. The lower part has decorated plaster, but the other seems to open up into a colonnade. The upper part of the wall at the far end from the door is indeed open to the sky, with a row of elegantly fluted Ionic columns in tufo. The other three walls are all

*Above: Detail of 'First Style' decoration of the entrance passage (fauces) of the Samnite House.*

*Left: Atrium of the Samnite House.*

closed, but the colonnade continues as a decorative feature, half-columns semi-engaged in the masonry, with elegant trellis-work between their lower parts.

Our idea of what constituted a 'traditional' Roman house is dominated by the survival of Vitruvius' ten books *On Architecture*, written early in the reign of Augustus. It is a handy coincidence that his account falls in the middle of the period of architecture best represented at both Herculaneum and Pompeii, the first centuries BC and AD. He devotes the entire sixth book to domestic architecture, and it is natural to look in the remains of the Vesuvian cities for illustrations of the Vitruvian principles of architecture. Maiuri studied his Vitruvius closely, and was always alert to the parallels in what he excavated. But Herculaneum has pride of place in Maiuri's drive to illustrate and recreate Vitruvian typologies. In the site as reconstructed, we can find an illustration of virtually every domestic form that Vitruvius specifies.

But there is a danger here. When Vitruvius talks about the atrium, one of the principal distinctions he draws is in different ways of roofing the space. The 'Tuscan' atrium has an inward-sloping roof, with *compluvium* opening and *impluvium* basin below, and no supporting columns: the Samnite House is a perfect example. The 'tetrastyle' atrium, by contrast, has four supporting columns: the House of the Two Atria gives us an example. The 'Corinthian' atrium had a larger opening, surrounded by a run of columns: the House of the Corinthian Atrium gives us our example. The 'testudinate' ('tortoise-shell') atrium, unlike the others, had outward-sloping roof lines, like those of a modern house, and no *impluvium*: the House of the Stags gives us our illustration. But ironically, the roofing is the element that least often survives in these houses: Maiuri had to put them together again. It is not so much that his reconstructions are at fault, but rather that his strong urge to recreate sloping roofs over the atria of houses, unlike other areas where he frequently inserted flat roofs, was driven by his desire to present the site as

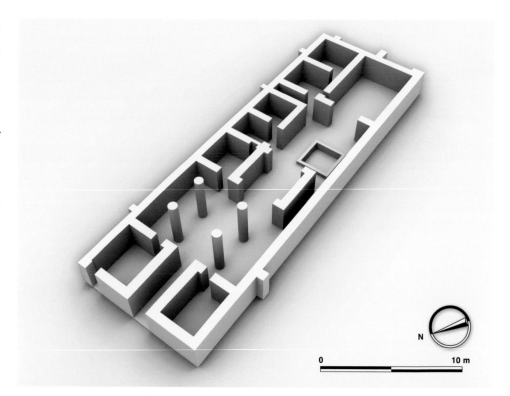

*The House of the Two Atria. Plan (above) and view of the 'tetrastyle' atrium (below).*

an illustration of Vitruvius.

Maiuri was rightly proud of his restoration work in the Samnite House: 'thanks however to the restoration which it has been possible to carry out in this house with the elements and materials recovered in the excavation, we have at Herculaneum the most architecturally complete example of this most unusual type of atrium with loggia.' Climb up on the scaffolding erected for more recent conservation, and you discover that a great deal of his reconstruction is a skilful bluff: most of the elegant tufo semi-columns surrounding the atrium are of modern concrete, as are the 'original terracotta' water-spouts with lions' heads around the roof opening. Again, we cannot say that Maiuri's reconstruction is actually wrong, just that it gives an impression of authenticity that is largely spurious. His projection of a 'Samnite patriciate' which constructed the house is even more a reconstruction based on little evidence.

In fact, this house is far from a classic example of a Vitruvian Tuscan atrium. These are defined not only by roof-lines, but by the layout of rooms, and Vitruvius attaches much importance to the cruciform layout, with two *alae* or 'wings' at the sides, and the ritual reception space of the *tablinum* opening on the central axis of the atrium. As Maiuri was aware, the next house in his line-up, the House of the Wooden Screen, illustrates this pattern far better. The Samnite House has rather a strange layout of rooms. It is such a narrow plot that there is little room for manoeuvre. There are no rooms on the right-hand side as you enter, just the tall wall that borders the street. On the left-hand side, there are three openings, of which the furthest is a vestigial *ala*, which reads visually like a sort of cubby-hole. The *tablinum*, which aligns with the front door and *impluvium*, has a handsome pavement with geometric decoration, but opens not fully on the atrium but with a window. This effect was probably achieved by inserting a low wall to give the *tablinum* better separation, though this was not the original spirit of the *tablinum*, conceived as an open space where the patron could receive his clients of a morning. In a word, this house is much too pokey to count as a classic example of a 'patrician atrium'. Its loggia, especially as reconstructed by Maiuri, is indeed of great elegance, and breathes the spirit of the 'Hellenistic' east so typical of the second century BC. But to leap from this to inferences about the social profile of the owners is hazardous indeed.

The paradox of Herculaneum is that the place which at first seems to illustrate the 'classic' styles of Vitruvian architecture is a great deal more complicated and messy when viewed up close. In particular, far from showing the continued importance of the atrium in AD 79, Herculaneum seems to illustrate how Roman domestic architecture was progressively moving away from traditional forms. Let us move on to the House of the Wooden Screen, which, as we have seen, is a better example of a Tuscan atrium, and was Maiuri's next case study. We find a similar pattern of

*The House of the Wooden Screen, plan (below) and view from tablinum to door (right).*

*Overleaf: Reverse view of atrium towards wooden screen and tablinum.*

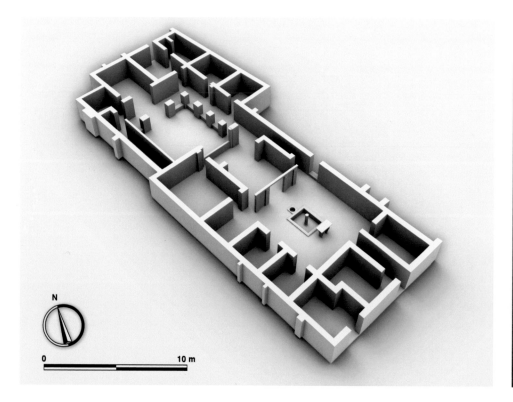

narrow *fauces* passage opening on an atrium, with inwards-sloping floor with geometrical decoration in marble chips, a marble-lined *impluvium*, marked out by marble *cartibulum* or display table, and an elegant fountain at its head; then to the left the open space of the *ala*, and in front the high and wide opening of a classic *tablinum*. Like the Samnite House, this has only rooms opening out on its left-hand side as you enter. There is, however, unlike the Samnite House, plenty of room to the right, only the owners have decided this space is better used for commercial premises opening directly on the street.

And then, just as in the Samnite House the *tablinum* has been blocked in by a partition wall, which reduces the opening to a window, in this house the *tablinum* is blocked off from the sight-line of the visitor by the splendid wooden structure that gives the house its name: the wooden screen. The survival of wood, carbonized or semi-carbonized, is one of the distinctive glories of this site, and this beautifully made screen, with its two sliding doors that allow access to the *tablinum* to be opened and closed at will, is a rare and precious find. But the truth is that it cuts off the *tablinum* as effectively as the low wall in the Samnite House. It can be related to a phenomenon well attested in both Vesuvian cities: the tendency, starting around the early first century BC, to shift the focus of the house to the peristyle garden, to ensure that principal reception rooms opened on the garden rather than the atrium, and to reduce the atrium to a sort of entrance parlour. The House of the Wooden Screen acquired for itself, probably by buying up the house behind it, a fine peristyle garden, and by the time the wooden screen was built, the space looked out primarily on this garden. In a word, what we see is not a classic illustration of Vitruvian architecture, but of that architecture *undergoing a slow process of transformation*.

We started by looking at the 'standard' housing units of the town, which are typically horizontal strips opening on the side roads, the *cardines*. It requires a considerable stretch of the imagination to house the richest elite of the town in these. They are 'middling' houses, which does not make the 'middle class' but middle wealth. Perhaps the most striking feature of them is their extraordinary variety, even in architectural terms. There is, as we have seen, the House of the Corinthian Atrium. Instead of the atrium–peristyle sequence (for which there is no room), it has an atrium which, with its six-columned peristyle and charming central garden,

*Archival photograph of the Wooden Screen.*

looks for all the world like a garden peristyle. This was a solution used in houses all over the Roman empire, to substitute the atrium with the peristyle as its core space. This is an early example, and done in miniature. The rooms around this atrium/peristyle space are nearly all decorated with modest elegance. Whether Vitruvius would have recognized a 'Corinthian' atrium here is to be doubted.

Back to back with it is the House of Neptune and Amphitrite. It has a Tuscan atrium, but the small plot leaves no room for a garden. Instead, the *tablinum* opens on a tiny courtyard area. Originally decorated with garden paintings, it was evidently intended to evoke a proper garden. Then, with the arrival of the aqueduct, they inserted a water cistern in this narrow space. Making a virtue of necessity, they decorated the structure for the cistern with mosaics, with an eye-catching background of blue glass chips of a type made popular by the fashion for blue glass, which came from Alexandria in Egypt. Most important, they inserted a central mosaic panel on the axis of the entrance, so that every visitor could see it, framed by the door and window of the *tablinum*. Neptune stands magnificently, resting on his trident; beside him a lady, taken to be his wife, the nymph Amphitrite. In terms of workmanship, it is one of the most noticeable sights of the town, yet the plot size tells us the owner was not among the super-rich, and Maiuri took him for a trader, one whose ships, protected by the sea god Neptune, plied the trading route to Alexandria. Maybe.

Just to the south of this house is another, of almost identical size, known as the House of the Carbonized Furniture. In fact, carbonized furniture of various sorts was found in several houses on the site, and Herculaneum offers our best opportunity for studying wooden furniture in the Roman world. The wooden frames of beds survived in several houses, wooden cupboards and shrines in others, sometimes tables and stools, and in one case a baby's cot. What distinguishes this particular house is the

survival of what was, at the time of excavation, an exceptionally well-preserved specimen of a wooden couch, together with a round table with three legs. Romans reclined to eat as well as to sleep, and dining couches, especially those with legs and supports in decorative bronzework, could be spectacular objects of luxury. The survival of a wooden couch is valuable for its rarity. Fashions in reclining changed through time, and the original models came from the Greek east, where couches had low supports at one end for the diner to rest their left arm on, while eating with the right. In the second half of the first century AD, a new fashion came in for couches surrounded on three sides with upright elements: these assume you will prop your arm on a cushion. Our house therefore not only offered a rare example of a wooden couch, but one that was up to date with the fashion of the day. Alas, the decision to leave it on show in the house as a tourist attraction, combined with the lack of maintenance work, has led to its almost complete disintegration.

Like the House of Neptune and Amphitrite, that of the Carbonized Furniture was organized around a tight atrium with a tiny garden area behind. With

*Plan of the House and Shop of Neptune and Amphitrite.*

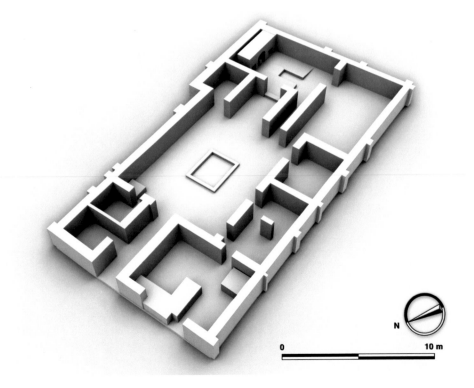

*Examples of carbonized wooden furniture from Herculaneum: a three-legged stool, provenance uncertain (far left, above); a small table with inlaid top from the House of the Two Atria (left, above); a baby's cradle from the House of Granianus (left, below); a small cupboard, provenance uncertain (right).*

an effect similar to that of the eye-catching mosaic of Neptune and Amphitrite, this house placed a shrine in the form of a little temple, with a niche decorated with shells, on the axis of view from the front door. A second angle of view was from the reception room that opens on the garden: lying on the wooden couch, you could see through the broad window to the garden and its shrine. There are plenty of other signs of aspirations to elegance in this house: the wall-decoration in this garden room, in the *tablinum*, and in the *triclinium* with its still-life scenes, a cock with cherries, a spread of fruit, nuts and a mushroom. The sleeping quarters were presumably upstairs, accessed by the two sets of stairs.

This house is one of the rare cases where we can put a name to the proprietors, and catch an idea

*Mosaic decoration of the back courtyard of the House of Neptune and Amphitrite. Hunting scenes around a small fountain, or* nymphaeum *(above); the sea god Neptune with his wife Amphitrite (above right); detail of the head of Amphitrite (below).*

of their social status. On the façade of the house, a marble plaque has been hung from an iron fixing (one of Maiuri's reconstructions, of course). Fixed at the boundary point between this house and its neighbour to the south, each side names its owner and declares their rights in perpetuity: on one side Julia, on the other M(arcus) Nonius M(arci) l(ibertus) Dama. Here is one of the innumerable bearers of the name of Marcus Nonius, explicitly a freedman, though one cannot tell whether the owner was a member of Balbus' blood family or one of the family's freedmen. Roman legal texts are full of neighbours squabbling over boundaries, and indeed, having a shared (or 'party') wall, as in this case, between two properties was discouraged because it generated so many disputes. There was probably a legal case, as so many

recorded in the wooden tablets of Herculaneum, which had to be resolved in front of an arbitrator. A parallel, in a more rural context, would be the argument between Cominius Primus and the owner of the neighbouring estate, Lucius Appuleius Proculus, over the removal by Cominius of 306 fencing poles, which the arbitrator Tiberius Crassius Firmus had to hold till the dispute was resolved. We cannot reconstruct what it was that made Nonius Dama and Julia argue over their boundary, but at least it reveals the identity of the owners on the two sides, a freedman belonging to the biggest family in town, and a woman whose imperial name implies that she too was from a family of imperial freedmen. Who owned which side (and if the plaque has been put back in the right position), we cannot tell.

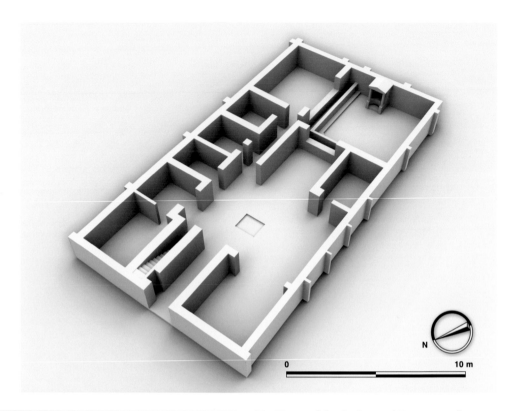

*The House of the Carbonized Furniture: plan (above), archival view of the room with bed and three-legged table on display (left); recent photograph of the bed in critical condition (above right).*

*Left: Marble plaque marking the boundary between the wall ('private in perpetuity') of Marcus Nonius Dama, freedman of Marcus, and (on the opposite side) Julia Paris.*

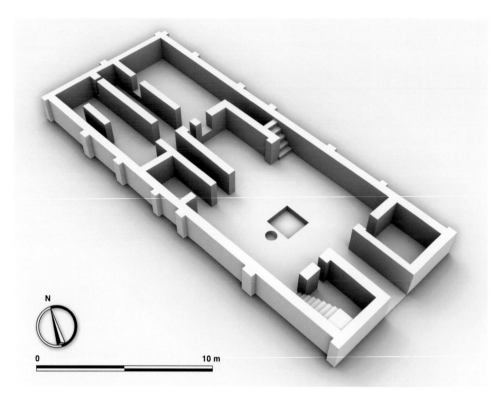

*House of the Wooden Shrine: plan (above left), the shrine (above right); archival photograph of the shrine in situ, revealing bronze statuettes and other objects found inside (opposite).*

For a final example of a 'standard' plot, we can briefly look at the House of the Wooden Shrine, which backs on that of the Carbonized Furniture, with its front door on Cardo V, to the south of the Corinthian Atrium. Slightly narrower than its neighbours, it represents the most stripped-down form of an atrium house: one room one either side of the entrance passage leads into a small atrium with central *impluvium* and no side rooms; beyond it, a central *tablinum*, with stairs up on one side, and on the other a small room and a narrow passage to a back space. Scarcely any decoration remains, and it looks as if the house had been little remodelled since its original construction, possibly in the second century BC. What gives it its interest is a single piece of furniture, found in the small room to the right of the door, though it compensates by its extraordinary quality. This is a wooden container, its upper part in the form of a tiny temple, with elaborately carved wooden columns with Corinthian capitals in ivory, and doors opening on an interior. Below is a simpler cupboard structure. Its identification as a 'wooden shrine' depends on the temple-like form and the presence of an elegant bronze statuette of Hercules, standing naked with a lion's skin

over his left arm. What the excavation diaries show is that this Hercules was not in the upper 'temple' but the bottom cupboard, along with an assortment of terracotta lamps, glass jars, bone dice and astragals, and a bronze stamp with the name Lucius Autronius Euthymus. Again the name takes us into the world of freedmen. If this was Euthymus' house, he does not seem to have been using his fine piece of wooden furniture as a shrine for his household gods, but as a general storage cupboard.

Some of the standard plots, then, could be very attractive, and often modern visitors catch themselves thinking, 'Now *here* is a house I could live in'. Others are more run down. Yet others, as we will see in the next chapter, formed commercial premises. The old housing stock that went back to the original layout of these blocks in the 'Samnite' period could be adapted and transformed in numerous ways: the old formula of construction round the partially open space of an atrium allowed for endless variations on a theme, with plenty of opportunity for improvisation. But for an understanding of how the richer households lived, we need to move upmarket, to the Decumanus Maximus and the spectacular houses overlooking the sea.

*The House of the Corinthian Atrium, view towards the west.*

# 8
# HIGH LIFE

However much the little houses on standard plots may charm the modern visitor, especially as enhanced by Maiuri's restorations, it is no good looking for the grandees of the town in them. We are much better off looking at the main drag of the Decumanus Maximus. Busy shopping streets in city centres may not appeal much to the modern powerful and wealthy, but in antiquity it was a normal place to find them. The ruling elite expressed their domination through the holding of political office, the local annual magistracies. These involved being at the heart of the community – being known to the voters, taking part, indeed officiating, at the local festivals, and adjudicating the endless local squabbles, for example between people who disagreed over boundary walls or tore down their neighbours' fencing poles, or who challenged whether a slave girl was a runaway or maybe not a slave at all. Living close to the heart of the town was seen as a political advantage, an issue on which Cicero, who spent so much of his life in the Forum, whether in the law courts or at senate meetings, was anxious to stress. The house of a politician should put him on display to the voters, framed in the view from the open front door as he conducted his business.

What is more, the figure of the magistrate was closely associated with the grand atrium, and it is in the houses along the Decumanus Maximus that we find some of the grandest. The Augustan architect Vitruvius, whose typology, as we have seen, Maiuri was so keen to illustrate, is particularly explicit on the linkage between high social standing and architectural form. The architect had to build houses suitable for the rank and profession of the owner. People of

common fortune, he says quite explicitly, had no need of magnificent vestibules or *tablina* or *atria*, because they went round 'paying court' to others, not being paid court to. The Latin word is *ambire* (root of our word 'ambition'), meaning 'go around', but our expression 'pay court' has the advantage of evoking the physical space, the 'court' which characterized the residences of early modern princes. How you shape a house, what your standing is, and how people treat you are all interlinked. The 'atrium' was the court of the Roman world, in which the mighty were literally courted.

That said, we may pause in surprise to note that the houses of our standard plots also had 'atria'. Did the owners expect visitors to court them? Partly, the answer is about 'trickle down': how the mighty lived created an image of success that was reproduced in miniature by the less mighty. But another answer may be that Vitruvius would have laughed in our faces to hear us speak of these tiny entrance halls as 'atria' just because they had rainwater basins in the middle. What he was thinking of, especially when he speaks of '*magnificent* atria', are central spaces with ample dimensions, and surely also with the classic cruciform pattern generated by having 'wings' on both sides and *tablina* with wide openings in the centre. Our standard houses, as we have seen, struggle to manage open space on either side, and are frequently found closing up their *tablina* to become rooms looking over the garden.

The House of the Bicentenary, excavated in 1938, at the height of the Fascist excavations, on the anniversary of two centuries of exploration of the site, ticks far more of Vitruvius' boxes than any house

*The House of the Black Saloon: view from atrium through tablinum to peristyle.*

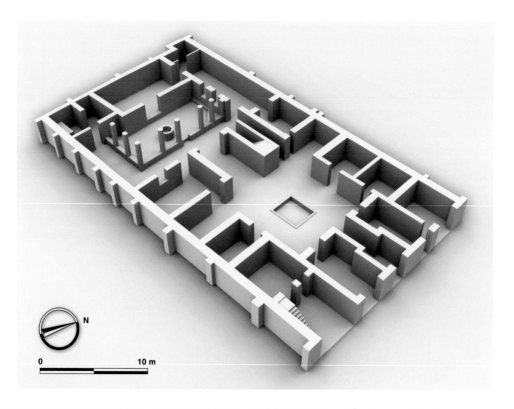

*The House of the Bicentenary: plan (above); façade with upper floors (left); view of the atrium towards the entrance (right).*

we have considered so far. That is made possible by scale: with a plot 18.6 metres (63 Roman feet) wide, and exactly twice that depth, and covering nearly 700 square metres, it is more than three times the size of a standard plot. It is not clear whether the block was originally laid out like this, or whether the house expanded over time, swallowing up smaller neighbours, but in Pompeii too we can see a pattern whereby the end plots that fronted on the main streets were privileged over the smaller plots along the side roads. A social division is implicit in this layout. The house maximizes its chances to present an appearance of a textbook grand house: an enormous 'Tuscan' atrium, with two *alae* and a *tablinum*, and beyond, a peristyle garden surrounded by colonnades, all framed in the view from the entrance. Small details enhance this

'classic' aspect. The side *alae* have marble thresholds that mark off spaces for display, the one on the right with wooden sliding doors in position, in which it would be nice to imagine that the images of the ancestors were displayed according to the Roman noble tradition, except that unfortunately not a single house has produced evidence of this type of ancestral image. (Those we do meet, as in the House of the Bronze Herm, another 'standard' plot, tend to be on stands by the side of the *tablinum*.)

But the House of the Bicentenary has some surprises that rather undermine this grand image. The first is the presence of the dossier concerning Petronia Justa, with its exotic cast of freedmen at loggerheads over an issue of free birth. The dossier was found in a basket in an upper room overlooking the peristyle. It does not follow that anybody mentioned in the dossier owned the house as a whole: Petronius Stephanus and his wife Calatoria Themis might have been the owners or the principal residents, but the very fact that Stephanus declared he had only one slave tells against his being a rich man. It is hard too to imagine a rich man, or his widow, going all the way to the praetor in Rome to dispute the status of a single slave girl. Possibly, then, they were tenants of part of the house.

More careful examination of the house plan reveals that it was composed of numerous units, on both ground floor and upper floors. A series of shops were built into the frontage: moving east to west, at no. 17, there is a shop with two ground-floor rooms, and stairs up to an apartment above (which may or may not have been occupied by the shopkeeper); then at no. 16 is another, single-roomed shop, but with stairs up to an apartment that stretched with a balcony across most of the façade, with as many as six or seven rooms; then after the main entrance to the house at no. 15, two more single-room shops at nos 14 and 13. There was at least one further upstairs apartment, probably two, accessible by a stairway from the peristyle garden. There seems to have been a third floor, so possibly another unit of habitation.

Maiuri, who saw freedmen as a sort of regrettable wave of immigrants, read this as the disintegration of a grand old house in the hands of freedmen upstarts. Of course, houses did change their social profiles over the course of time, and there is no doubt that the density of freedmen in AD 79 was a phenomenon of the early empire. We would expect a very different picture, say, in the second century BC. But this is a house constructed in its present form in the early empire, probably under Augustus, and it was built in the full expectation of precisely the pattern of shops and apartments that we meet in its final years. We should not underestimate the extent to which a grand house was compatible with revenue-generating activities, and indeed the extent to which

grandeur was a show, a bluff designed to impress the visitor awed by the scale of the atrium, and blind to the busy units of work and habitation hidden from sight by its imposing walls. This house illustrates vividly the difficulties of drawing inferences about the social standing of inhabitants from architecture. Its position and form made it suitable enough for the family of one of the local ruling elite, irrespective of the number of shops and flats. On the other hand, it is quite conceivable that its inhabitants in AD 79 were indeed freedmen.

The House of the Bicentenary is one of a number of large and imposing houses that open on the Decumanus Maximus. In the next *insula* to the west, the House of the Black Saloon is not much smaller, at around 600 square metres. We can safely assume that the three shops incorporated into its façade, one with rooms above, formed part of the same property. In Roman law, ownership went vertically with ownership of the ground, and units on different floors could not be sold off separately. Again, this is a grand town house that draws profit from its high street position. One of the shops was in fact the workshop of a metal worker, a *plumbarius* (the origin of our word

*The House of the Black Saloon: plan (below); entrance with paintings of priest and wine jugs (right).*

*Inside: Panoramic view of the peristyle.*

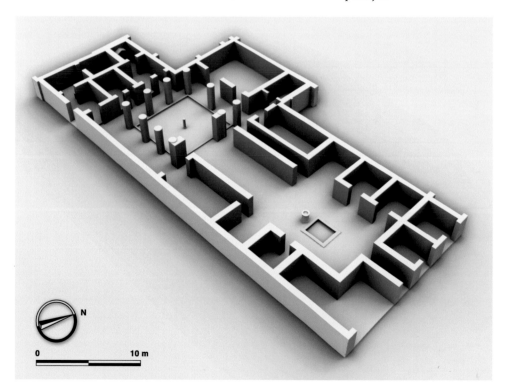

'plumber', from when pipes were in lead). The front part has the classic layout of a Tuscan atrium, with *alae* on both sides, and a generously proportioned *tablinum*. It is hard to recapture the feel of this imposing atrium in its present ruinous condition, but what makes the house impressive is the peristyle area behind. It is clear that the house has absorbed at least one property to its rear, causing its irregular outline. The peristyle has colonnades on all four sides, and round this cluster the most important rooms, most notably the unusually large reception room (the 'Black Saloon'), elegantly decorated in the style of the last decades of the city with a black background that was fashionable in similar large rooms in others of the finest houses in town, including the House of

the Stags and the House of the Mosaic Atrium. The bedrooms to the south of the peristyle, by contrast, have a white background, with delicate monochrome designs in shades of brown. This kind of monochrome brown is also met in the bedroom to one side of the 'Black Saloon' and is one of the characteristics of the decorative schemes of Flavian Herculaneum. It is usually assimilated to Pompeian 'Fourth Style', but one of the interesting things about Herculaneum is that it had its own distinctive fashions, variations on the themes met in Pompeii.

We have already met the owner of the basket of tablets found in an upper room overlooking the peristyle, Lucius Venidius Ennychus, and the story of his promotion from Latin to Roman citizen and

*The House of the Black Saloon: exterior with carbonized wooden beams supporting the roof (above); detail of entrance (right).*

*Overleaf: The mosaic wall panel of the sea god Neptune and his consort, from the House of the Neptune and Amphitrite.*

*The House of the Black
Saloon: large room decorated
in black (above left); detail of
decoration (above right).*

eventually *augustalis*. It is striking that in publishing this house, Maiuri says
nothing of this dossier, and its possible implications for ownership of the house.
He instinctively rejected the idea of a freedman owning a house this grand. It does
not follow from the discovery of the dossier that Ennychus either was or was not
the owner. This house, like that of the Bicentenary, has room for independent flats,
and indeed there are back-stairs from a back entrance that could well lead to the
room in which the dossier was kept. In Pompeii, where there is a strong tendency
to name houses after any potential owner, however slim the evidence, this would
surely have been called the 'House of Venidius Ennychus'. We must not press the
evidence for certainties, but rather be alive to a range of possibilities.

The neighbouring house to the west, that of the Tuscan Colonnade, has much
in common with the Black Saloon, despite its rather smaller extent (around 400
square metres). Its irregular, L-shaped plan is due to expansion into the properties to the rear, so acquiring the space for the colonnaded garden that gives the
house its name. It too has three shops incorporated in its façade. One of the signs
of the fluidity with which the front rooms of such a house could be assigned to
commercial use at will is the handsome decoration, including the representation
of a sacrifice to Hercules, found in shop no. 16, which presumably goes back to
its earlier use as a bedroom, accessible only from within the house. Its Tuscan
atrium is narrower than its neighbour's, and there is only room for one side wing,
and this is a well-decorated reception room, rather than a standard *ala*, including
a mythological scene of a Maenad and Pan, probably going back to a remodel-
ling of the house in the Augustan period. The climax is reserved for the peristyle
area reached down a narrow corridor, which obscures the 90-degree change in

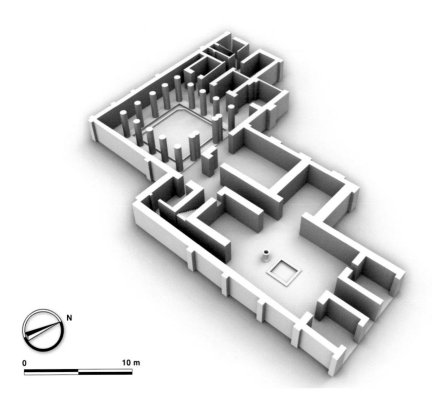

*The House of the Tuscan Colonnade: plan (above); details of decoration from the shop showing Hercules sacrificing (below left), and the main reception room (below right).*

orientation of this garden space. On one side is a large dining room, with elaborate decoration of the final years of the town, including the figures of Bacchus and Apollo. At the end are bedrooms, one with an alcove for the bed with its own lowered ceiling. There is enough in the house for the gracious entertainment of guests, a necessity whether you were a member of the local council or a rich freedman. At the same time, it conceals in the background shops and an upper apartment, reached from a side street (even now, it is hard to realize that the two parts are linked).

The Decumanus Maximus, then, has its fair share of houses that were grand enough for members of the elite. Yet, despite the discovery of dossiers of documents, we cannot be sure of the ownership of any of them. If we are looking for the sort of person we might imagine would be a local magistrate, the most plausible candidate would be Lucius Cominius Primus. We have met him as a landowner, uprooting stakes from his neighbour's boundary; we have met him repaying a loan to the slave of the Emperor Trajan's aunt; we have met him buying a slave girl, Olympias. In other documents, he lends sums of money to various parties – on two occasions, accepting slave girls as security. He is evidently a landowner and man of affairs about town. Yet his dossier is found in an upper room above a shop next to the House

of the Bicentenary, a far world from these gracious residences. The landowning elite slips through our fingers, just when we hope to pin them down.

The grandest of all the houses on the Decumanus Maximus lies unexcavated, on the north side of the road under the escarpment. Its ambitious scale can be seen not only in the impressive brickwork colonnade that runs along its frontage, supporting rooms and balconies above, and in the well-preserved wooden shutters on the windows, but in the breadth of its entrance door. Vitruvius speaks of the *vestibulum* as the first space you reach in a grand Roman house, as a sort of outer lobby where visitors could await admission. Yet, despite the occurrence of benches set on the pavement outside front doors (there is a good example outside the House of the Wooden Screen), no house

to date excavated in Pompeii or Herculaneum has a distinct 'vestibulum'. Only in the case of the nameless house north of the Decumanus Maximus can we see a wide entrance lobby, with benches on either side, leading to the front door – all that is visible of this are the wooden door posts on either side. Maybe if this house is explored one day, a genuine member of the elite may emerge, one of the many we can name as having held the office of duumvir, like Marcus Rufellius Robia and Aulus Tetteius Severus, the magistrates responsible for posting the notice on the opposite side of the street banning people from dumping rubbish near to the water supply, on pain of a fine (for the free) or a flogging (for the slave).

Just as the houses fronting the Decumanus Maximus are a whole league ahead of the ones on

*The House of the Tuscan Colonnade: panoramic view of the peristyle and main reception room.*

standard plots in the side streets, so we move again into a different league with the houses looking out over the town wall towards the south and west, and the incomparable view of the Bay of Naples. All these houses belong, as we have seen, to the period of the transformation of the town under Augustus, so closely associated with the name of Nonius Balbus. What his fellow citizens praised him for was his rebuilding of walls and gates; and yet, what the evidence shows is a comprehensive abandonment of the defensive function of the walls, permitting householders to extend their holdings, demolish the parapets, and gain access to the view. Town walls were naturally public property, as was the strip of land behind them. Here, just as at Pompeii, where houses like that of Fabius Rufus were terraced out to the west and south, swallowing

the town walls within their luxurious structures, such a transformation cannot have taken place without public decisions by the *decuriones* meeting in council. It took a figure like Balbus to pull off such a transformation, and it is not hard to imagine that those private individuals who profited from the sudden availability of public land were *decuriones* themselves, with Balbus and his allies at their head.

Stretching from the south-eastern to the south-western extremities of the town, a zone defined by the two rivers described by Sisenna, runs an unbroken succession of houses which in scale and luxury outrank all others. The most familiar are the two houses, set side by side, the House of the Stags and that of the Mosaic Atrium, which are among the most visited in the modern site. Each exceeds 1,000 square metres in ground plan. The House of the Stags marks itself apart in layout, in richness of decoration and in its collection of statuary. The layout, evidently profiting from the demolition of previous 'standard' plots to the south, as well as the acquisition of the public land of the wall, is dominated by its garden. The open space is over 200 square metres, the size of a standard plot. This is surrounded by a covered colonnade or cloister, minimizing the number of usable rooms, and concentrating the enclosed space on a series of magnificent rooms looking out to sea. The cloister is enhanced by a striking series of still lives, scenes of fruit in baskets, or in transparent glass jars, as well of scenes of cupids; these are now partly in the Naples Museum, partly left on site, where the Bourbon excavators missed them. In total, 375

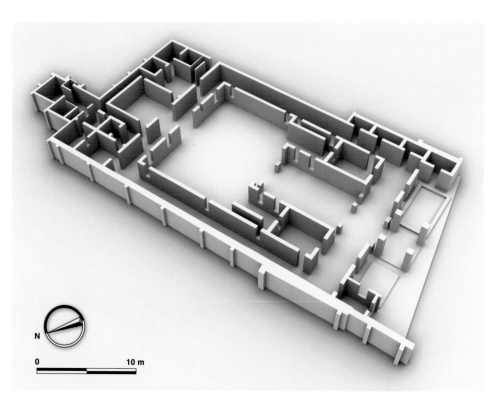

N

0        10 m

*The House of the Stags: plan (above); gazebo built over the town wall (left); garden decorated with marble statues of stags hunted down by dogs (right).*

square metres are sacrificed to non-living space, in a way reminiscent of the much earlier House of the Faun at Pompeii, with its vast peristyles and scarce rooms. But the trade-off for all this airy spaciousness towards the sea is a dense clustering of rooms towards the back of the house, in the area around the kitchen, which cuts jaggedly into a neighbouring house-plot. The service quarters and the service personnel are crowded to the back.

The prestige of the house is concentrated around the garden. Both the reception rooms looking out to sea, and the great reception room that stands on the central axis of the garden, are richly decorated, with frescoed walls (notably the black-ground walls of the main reception room, so much finer than those of the Black Saloon), and above all in the pavements, patterned with colour marble inlay (or 'opus sectile') of outstanding quality. Such *opus sectile* is one of the features that marks Herculaneum as in another league of quality from Pompeii. Expensively imported coloured marble cost far more than frescoes or mosaics (except the very finest). It is exceptional in Pompeii (the House of the Ephebe offers a rare example there). In Herculaneum, it is a mark of the most prestigious houses. Closely linked to the use of coloured marble is the occurrence of white marble sculptures of high quality. The House of the Stags is distinguished by four pieces – the two stags hunted down by dogs, and the drunken pair of a satyr pouring wine from a skin (the sign of Bacchic excess) and the patron of the town, Hercules, much the worse for wear and relieving himself.

The House of the Stags: testudinate atrium (left); still life from decoration of peristyle (below).

Right: Archival view of the main reception room with statue of boy with a wine skin (found in the garden).

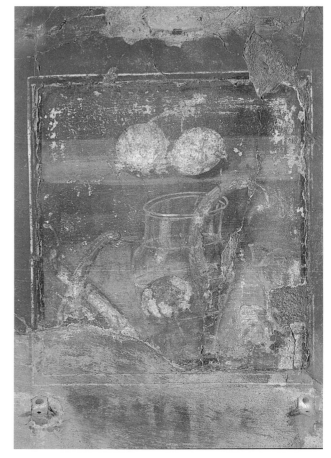

The layout of the house shows an almost complete shift of emphasis from atrium to peristyle as the core of the house. The entrance, which gave Maiuri his rare but surprising example of a 'testudinate' atrium (see page 204) is evidently no more than an entrance lobby, a circulation space which offers access on one side to the upper rooms, on the other to the eye-catching sequence of reception rooms visible 'en filade' through their aligned doors. It is the antithesis of the Samnite House, in the lofty Tuscan atrium of which Maiuri saw the values of the patriciate of the old days. But if Vitruvius could scarcely have approved, the House of the Stags has more in common with the layout of the majority of the luxurious houses of the imperial period.

Who then lived here? It was not until some forty years after Maiuri's excavation of the house that close study of the archives of the Bourbon excavations revealed this house as the source of one of the most famous finds of the site: the carbonized loaf of bread, long held in the Museum in Naples, on which are legible the letters of a stamp: CELERIS Q GRANI VERI SER: 'of Celer, slave of Quintus Granius Verus'. Granius Verus is known to have been a magistrate of the town in the 50s or early 60s AD, and his name appears as high-ranking witness on several of the wax tablets. A Quintus Granius, freedman of Quintus, Celer also appears on the great album of the town, one of the names inserted at the end, presumably close to the time of the eruption. If, as seems likely, it is the same Celer, he must have achieved

his freedom and citizenship shortly before the eruption. Yet the bread must have been more recent than the inscription. One might have expected it to have been one of the first things a freedman would change, to have a bronze stamp with his new name and status. It is slightly puzzling. Like the dossiers of wax tablets, these are prima facie evidence for ownership, and the House of the Stags might therefore belong to Quintus Granius Verus, one of the leading local citizens. We could be more confident if we understood better why people had these bronze stamps made What, apart from loaves of bread, did they stamp with them? Indeed, why should anyone think of putting their name on a loaf of bread in the first place? Because they had baked it? Because they were going to eat it in their own homes? Or because, like Gaius Julius Polybius of Pompeii, who was praised for his *panem bonum* (his 'good bread'), he intended to give it away free to others?

The House of the Mosaic Atrium is virtually the twin of the Stags, occupying a plot of the same shape and advantages, although, thanks to the diagonal course of the town walls at this point, even larger (1,200 square metres). The similarities leap to the eye: the enormous proportion dedicated to a peristyle garden, occupying even more open space (250 square metres), and the string of richly decorated rooms looking out to sea. But there are also significant contrasts, which show how dangerous it is to generalize from one house about changing fashions. Far from reducing the atrium to an entrance lobby, this house dedicated the entire area of what had once been a standard plot to an enormous atrium, made the more conspicuous by its fine mosaic floor. The undulations now visible in it are, of course, the consequence of the eruption, but what they reveal are the blurred outlines of the rooms of an earlier house buried beneath.

This atrium is far from standard. Rather than following an *alae* and *tablinum* arrangement, it culminates in a tall room, architecturally unparalleled in Vesuvian houses, which surely copies a

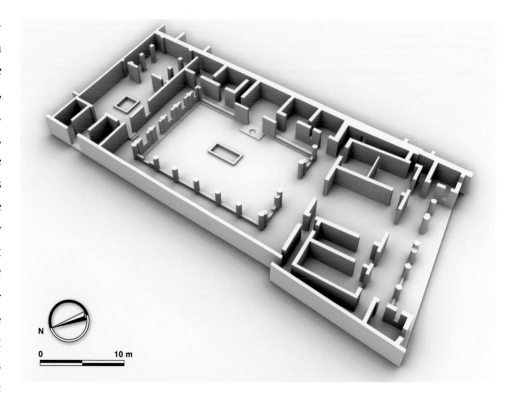

N

0   10 m

*The House of the Mosaic Atrium: plan (above); view from atrium to 'Egyptian oecus' (right, above); view of room overlooking garden (right, below).*

*Left: Carbonized loaf of bread found in the House of the Stags, stamped with the name of Celer, slave of Quintus Granius, possible owner of the house.*

public basilica (its shape, and especially its clerestory, make it feel very church-like to us). Since Vitruvius happens to specify that the room he calls an *Egyptian oecus* was like a basilica, this may well be the right label for it. But it does not follow that this was a standard Roman recipe. It is the sequence of atrium and basilica in place of *tablinum* that makes this space distinctive and impressive. The garden area is still where the main reception rooms open, including the central reception space decorated in blue, with mythological scenes in brown monochrome, in the

Top: *The House of the Mosaic Atrium, view of 'Egyptian oecus'.*

Above: *The House of the Gem: kitchen and latrine.*

Opposite: *Corridor leading to marbled room at lower level of the House of the Telephus Relief.*

idiom favoured in Herculaneum. The richest houses, then, experimented with the sort of architectural formulas we meet in Vitruvius' prescriptions, taking into account the shape and potential of the plot and its previous history. Two houses, which at first sight appear very similar, prove to have different solutions which produce unique effects.

Further east, the Insula Orientalis I provides yet another example of an innovative solution to a particular combination of plot shape and background. As we have seen, the ground to the east of Cardo V once sloped steeply downwards. The excavation of the Vicolo Meridionale, the side lane running just north of these houses, shows the lane dropping down towards the river-harbour below. Like the Palaestra, the houses here are terraced out, to gain the advantage of the terrain. What by the eruption had become two separate houses, today called the House of the Telephus Relief and the House of the Gem, were originally developed, in the Augustan period, as a single large property. They occupied the space of a string of previous standard plots; and the two atria, that became the separate atria of these houses, reflected the orientation, and partly used the wall foundations, of the older standard plots. To have two atria side by side in a single house is a well-known pattern in Pompeii, going back to the second century BC, as in the House of the Faun. But this property was developed in the Augustan period, and it is noteworthy that the double atrium plan was still a valid solution. If the House of the Stags minimizes its atrium, and the Mosaic Atrium maximizes it, this house makes double use of it.

The house also has a very different solution to the placing of the peristyle garden. Rather than using the strip overlooking the town wall towards the sea, it builds out a terrace for a peristyle that can look both out to sea, like the others, or down to the river and harbour. This enables a spectacular succession of rooms with different orientations at different levels. The excavations have revealed the string of rooms to the south of the garden at the ground level. Though

*The House of the Telephus Relief: view of tower and edge of excavations (left); marble panelling in the upper marbled room (above).*

ruinous, their coloured marble *opus sectile* pavements show their quality. Below them, still unexcavated, was another level of rooms. We can see from the excavated edges that they were richly decorated and had wide marble thresholds and windows. In front of them was a portico, the columns of which were tossed like matchsticks by the violence of the surges to the beach below. Below them was yet another level of rooms beneath concrete vaults. The edges of a *triclinium* couch, just visible in the unexcavated rock, show that these too were places of leisure.

A sequence of rooms on three levels, going down to the shore itself, was something that the House of the Stags and the House of the Mosaic Atrium could not boast. We can only speculate as to what must have

been on the eastern side of the peristyle garden, now disappearing into the high escarpment, on top of which runs the access road constructed by Maiuri. Here too the terracing must have offered the opportunity for rooms with views, terraced down to the port. What is, however, visible is the most unusual architectural feature of the house: the tower-like structure built out over the shore on what we now know to be four levels, the bottom one of which had to be abandoned as the sea rose. This tower is only conceivable in the context of Nonius Balbus' transformation of the town walls. Protruding southwards beyond the line of the walls, it gives the appearance of a defensive structure, and it may be that it replaced an original tower or bastion of the defences. But it is built for pure pleasure. From

the eastern side, it presents a series of half-columns, engaged in the walls, with between them either arches, or, higher up, rectangular openings, though these have been progressively blocked in or reduced as the structure took the full force of the incoming sea.

At each level will have been a string of three of four rooms, but it is the rooms at the end with the sea view that were the focus. On the top two levels, these rooms are decorated with *opus sectile* marble floors of the highest quality, and in both cases, the lower part of the walls are also clad in coloured marble. The room at the top level has especially lavish cladding, columns with delicate spiral fluting dividing carefully selected panels of large plaques of varied marble, the yellow-orange of Numidian marble from Chemtou, the white and red 'pavonazzetto' of Phrygia, with its peacock display of purples, and green 'cipollino' marble (with its onion-like cross-section) from Greek Karystos. The style is of the third quarter of the first century AD, which shows that the owners continued to improve the property after its Augustan construction.

Whoever built this house had the resources not merely to remodel the layout of an urban block, but also to remodel the landscape of the south-eastern edge of the town, with major engineering works. Who was responsible? Maiuri pointed to Nonius Balbus. There is no documentary

*The upper marbled room of the House of the Telephus Relief, with opus sectile floor and marble panelling.*

evidence. The argument depends on the proximity of the funerary altar and commemorative statue of Balbus on its terrace to the Suburban Baths, and the close interconnection of the baths to the great tower of the Telephus Relief house. These links suggest that all three areas were architecturally connected. The development of the baths is now better understood. They start as a smaller structure, with only *frigidarium*, *tepidarum* and *calidarium* in the Augustan period; the eastern part, with its vast 'samovar' hot bath, is built half a century later, and in doing so cuts into the Telephus Relief tower, causing its west-facing windows to be blocked off. It may also have caused the partial isolation of the lower floors from the rest of the house. The baths therefore cannot have been extended without the consent of the owner of the house. But in the original, Augustan, version, the baths were no obstacle, so it does not follow that one man built everything.

What makes so attractive the idea that Nonius Balbus was the builder is the intimate connection between the restructuring of the house and the restructuring of the town walls. Taken together, the operation literally changes the face of Herculaneum, at least as seen from the sea. Instead of presenting itself as a challenge to attackers, the *phrourion* or 'garrison' described by Strabo, it transforms its defences into a display of luxury. Rich houses occupy the place of the garrison and the tower protruding over the shore, and the rooms faced with porticoes terraced down to the sea give the appearance of one of those rich villas captured in the landscape paintings of the time. In

*The lower marbled room of the House of the Telephus Relief.*

place of military force, Augustan peace and prosperity is on display. It is exactly the sort of message this loyal supporter of the emperor wanted to give, and it makes sense that his own property played part of it. And, as if in confirmation, the marble relief which gives its name to the house, showing Achilles consulting the oracle at Delphi before going to heal the wound of Telephus, proves to have its closest parallel in a tondo from the Basilica Noniana. Balbus, whether in his building operations or his home life, shows the interdependence of the private and the public.

We have looked in detail at the easternmost of the grand houses overlooking the sea. But we should not underestimate the size and richness of the others to the west, even though their early excavation in the nineteenth century means that there is less to see now. The House of the Hotel (Albergo) derives its name from its vast size, twice that of the House of the Stags. It has two separate peristyle areas, the larger of which, covering 500 square metres, is by itself the size of a large house. It offers an unique example of a sunken garden, now planted sympathetically but not authentically with quince trees, set a metre below the surrounding colonnade, to protect it from the salt breezes of the sea. This house also offers the one surviving example of a private bath suite in Herculaneum (the House of the Stags had only a large bronze bathtub). On the other side of the street from this is what once must have been an impressive property. The House of Argus is only partially excavated, but the large peristyle area caught the imagination of the visitors in the early nineteenth century, when it was the 'show house' of the town.

The most tantalizing reflection, however, is that what may well have been the largest private property in the town lies in the unexcavated western part of the town. The maps drawn by the Bourbon engineers indicate that between Cardo I and II lay an enormous property, occupying the entire *insula*, and covering a potential footprint of over 5,000 square metres. The plans show what seems to be a gigantic peristyle, with dimensions of 40 × 70 metres (2,800 square metres). The only part that can now be verified is the portion that came down to the shore, and was exposed by the trench dug in pursuit of the Villa of the Papyri. The excavators did not anticipate that the edge of the town would protrude this far south, and discovered to their dismay a very substantial building that blocked their proposed drainage channel. The most interesting feature of this is a sort of pavilion with an arcaded façade, reminiscent of the tower of the Telephus Relief house. And just as the Telephus Relief house

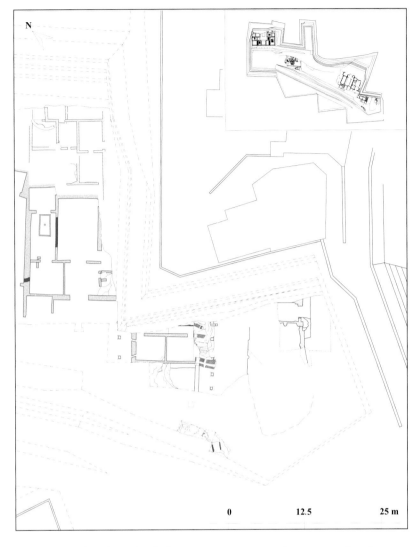

*Above: Plan of the lower level of a gigantic property on the western edge of Herculaneum, partly exposed by recent excavations.*

*Overleaf: Garden of the House of the Hotel (Albergo), today planted with quince trees.*

had a Greek marble relief fine enough to inspire its modern name, so the south-western mansion had two fine Greek marble reliefs, of similar proportions, discovered by recent excavations.

We can say virtually nothing about house and owner, but the most interesting result is the implication for the appearance of the seafront of the town. At both western and eastern corners were large private properties with tower- or pavilion-like structures that defined the limits of the town. In both cases, public baths with 'samovar' pools lay immediately adjacent. And in both cases, lower floors had to be abandoned as the sea rose. There is a striking symmetry about the 'new image' of the town Nonius Balbus engineered.

# 9
# LOW LIFE

Rich and poor, we have seen, did not live in glorious isolation in Herculaneum. Quite apart from the slaves and dependants under their own roofs, the rich had neighbours. To point out that there was a strip of grand houses looking out over the sea may create the impression of some sort of wealthy enclave. Yet study the street patterns and you swiftly appreciate that even when two grand houses lay alongside, like those of the Stags and the Mosaic Atrium, the inhabitants could not reach each other's houses to call or attend a dinner without making their way up the side street, along the lower Decumanus, and back down the next side street, passing a whole cluster of much humbler dwellings. In this little community, rich and poor,

mighty and humble, must have got to know each other quite rapidly.

We can go a step further. It is not just that grand houses happen to be next door to humble ones: they seem positively to attract them. Insula IV is a good example. The Stags and the Mosaic Atrium take up more than half the block, but their neighbours are a run-down lot. The House of the Alcove, immediately north of the Mosaic Atrium, is the one other house with pretensions. Occupying two 'standard' plots, it has a residential quarter with a large *triclinium* with a marble pavement, and the room with an alcove or apse that gives the house its name. But that apart, the remaining units have a distinctly commercial flavour. The House of the

*Left: Shop and upper apartment at the north-east corner of Insula V. The dossier of Cominius Primus was found in the upper apartment.*

*Right: Plan of Insula IV, showing smaller properties at the back of larger houses.*

*Overleaf: Shop on the north-east corner of Insula IV. The deep terracotta containers were for dry food, not for hot food as is often claimed.*

Fullery, occupying a standard plot, operated, at least in its final years, as a laundry. The House of the Painted Papyrus is a small strip forming a string of unassuming rooms. Oddly enough, its decoration included a painting of a papyrus, with the name of the Greek poet Eutychus, described as 'choriambic' (a *recherché* form of metre), a far from obvious choice of author – unless the owner was another Eutychus. It also contained a graffito referring to shipping, at both Puteoli and Herculaneum. Next to it is one of two *tabernae* that stretch along the north of the *insula*, with sales counters at the two corners. Then another *taberna*, named after the Priapus with an enormous phallus decorating the area behind the sales counter. Finally the House of the Fabric (Stoffa), named after a piece of cloth preserved there, is a multiple-occupancy dwelling, with two superimposed sets of wooden stairs leading to the two floors above.

We can only speculate about the relationship between the grand properties and their more modest neighbours. In the original layout of the plots in the pre-Roman period, each plot may have been an independent property. But it is also possible that the big houses, made by swallowing up several smaller ones, also owned some or all of their neighbours. The jagged property boundaries imply a complex set of transactions: the kitchens of the House of the Stags jut into the back of the House of the Alcove, while the House of the Alcove juts into the House of the Fabric. The latrine of the House of the Fabric discharges into the drains of the House of the Stags. Maybe the House of the Stags owned that of the Fabric, and traded a portion of that property with the House of the Alcove in exchange for what became the kitchen area. This is pure speculation: the essential point is that there existed close neighbourly relations between them.

Whether or not there was cause and effect in terms of property ownership, the smartest houses are frequently neighbours of the less smart. The group

of houses around the House of the Bicentenary are an interestingly mixed bag. To the west is the small but surprisingly elegant House of Apollo the Lyre-player (Citharoedus), named recently after a painting; its atrium and *tablinum* with handsome marble paving rank it with the more elegant 'standard' plots. Behind it is the most unusual House of the Beautiful Courtyard, dominated on its ground floor by an enormous room overlooking the 'beautiful' courtyard. The layout is not of a domestic space, and we may speculate that it functioned as a *collegium* or meeting place for a trade society. (This is the room Maiuri used as an on-site museum.) The presence of a blocked door between this and the peristyle of the House of the Bicentenary suggests one was formerly owned by the other. Stairs lead up around the courtyard to lodgings above.

*Above: Panoramic view of the House of the Beautiful Courtyard.*

*Right: The decorated tablinum of the House of Apollo the Lyre-player.*

To the east of the Bicentenary is a sequence of square plots. In each case, the frontages are occupied by shops, while the rooms behind them have the minimum of decoration; but stairs lead to lodgings above, where in at least one case there is elegant decoration, in the room where the archive of Cominius Primus was found. It is these units, with commercial premises below and rentable lodgings above, that begin to point to the pattern of living that is so familiar from Rome and Ostia of the imperial period. At Pompeii, which scarcely survives above the level of the ground floor, it is easier to forget that a substantial part of the population will have lived, in these cities too, in upper apartments. Herculaneum, thanks not only to the depth of its preservation, but the survival of wooden elements such as stairs, cupboards and beds, gives a reality to such upper lodgings that not even Ostia can match.

Let us look in detail at two contrasting examples. One is the transformation of a traditional house plot; the other involves the building of a new type of multi-storey construction that was to prove of major importance in the metropolitan context of Rome. The House 'a Graticcio' or 'of Wattlework' owes its name to another of Maiuri's illustrations of the text of Vitruvius. Situated just south of the

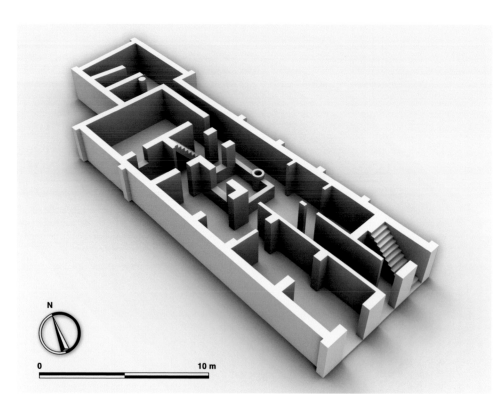

The House of Wattlework (*a Graticcio*): plan of ground floor (above); central court (below).

House of the Wooden Screen, it occupies a standard plot of typical size, some 150 square metres, though the addition of a space carved from the back of the House of the Skeleton, and the balcony suspended on pilasters over the pavement, increase the plan of its upper floor to just under 200 square metres. The feature that caught Maiuri's eye was its wooden frame construction. Although some pillars in brick and block work ensure structural stability at critical points, most of the partition walls are of timber framework, with a rubble infill. As Maiuri was swift to point out, there were few places in the Roman world apart from Herculaneum where construction based on timber could survive, and although this is by no means the only place in Herculaneum in which it was found (he lamented the nineteenth-century demolition of the upper storey of the House of Argus, built with similar technique), it is the most extensive example excavated.

The reference to *opus craticium*, however, may be felt to complicate matters. *Crates*, 'wattles', were used to make sheep pens and flimsy partitions. *Opus craticium* should be partitioning made of reeds or thin withies, much like the traditional English 'wattle and daub' technique. Vitruvius only mentions it to lament its existence, contrasting it with mud-brick, which he regards as durable if properly protected. This technique, by contrast, could only be disastrous, since it was like a torch to the flames. Fires were a major problem in Rome when Vitruvius was writing, and there was doubtless plenty of experience of this technique, with its high proportion of combustible material, representing a real fire risk. But it is hard to imagine that Vitruvius meant to describe the timber frame construction in general. There is just one wall in this house where the plasterwork shows the clear traces of reeds, which were used as a key for plaster on walls and ceilings. Where Maiuri was right was to point out that this house opens our eyes to the Roman use of lighter partition work, with the use of wood. Whether Vitruvius would have accepted this

*The House of Wattlework (a Graticcio): upper rooms with imprint of reeds in plaster (incannucciata) (above); plan showing relation of upper to lower floor (right).*

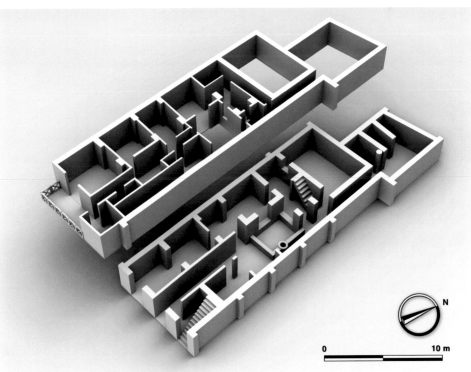

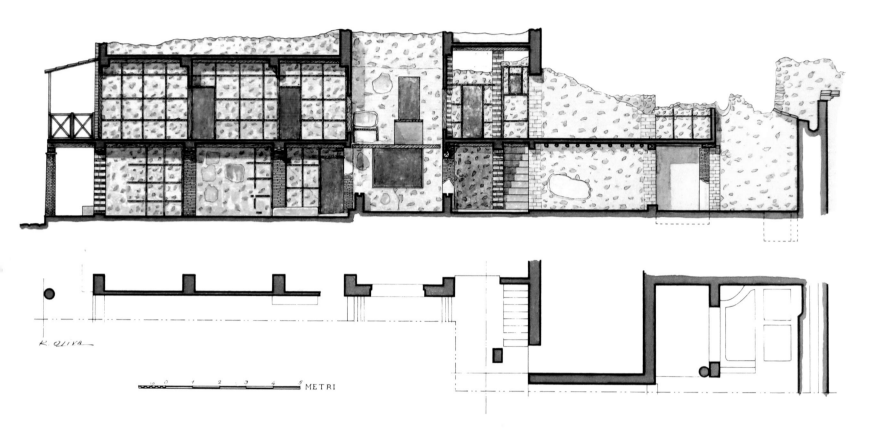

CASA A GRATICCIO - SEZIONE LONGITUDINALE

R. OLIVA

METRI

*The House of Wattlework (a Graticcio): east–west section showing timber-frame construction (above); wooden bed in the upper apartment (left); windlass and rope from the well in the courtyard (right above); decorative wooden element portraying a female head found in the house (right below).*

house as an example of *opus craticium* is not so certain, and after all, he might have been impressed by the success of the timber framing, which is known elsewhere for its resistance to earthquakes, in surviving the trauma of the eruption.

Timber framework is quite likely to have been used extensively for upper floors, with the advantage of lightness. To this extent, our House 'a Graticcio' offers a window on upstairs apartments invisible elsewhere. The house consists of at least three, possibly four, units of habitation. The ground floor has a shop and string of rooms behind. It was easy, with light partitions, to separate this off from the rest of the ground floor, accessible down a corridor that leads to a courtyard. The courtyard is the equivalent of an atrium, with an *impluvium* to catch the water. A wooden winch found near by with a long coil of rope gives a rare illustration of how water was fetched up. A number of ill-lit and undecorated rooms open off the courtyard. A set of wooden stairs leads up to an apartment that seems in every way more desirable than the ground floor. Two surviving rooms, lit by windows on the courtyard, have quite elaborate decoration in the style of the final years. But what makes an impression is the survival of furniture – two beds and a cupboard in one room, one bed and a cupboard in the other. One of these wooden cupboards was full of objects. As the excavation diaries describe it, on 9 November 1928 a thunderstorm caused part of a wooden cupboard found in this room to break, and there emerged a bronze statuette of Jupiter holding a thunderbolt (how appropriate that he emerged in a storm!), and others of 'Abundantia' (perhaps the Egyptian Isis), Aesculapius and Diana the Huntress. A week later, on 17 November, the rest of the cupboard was broken open in the presence of the Superintendent (Maiuri). There emerged more bronze statuettes: a matching pair of Lares, one with its right hand, the other with its left, raised to hold aloft drinking horns; another 'Abundantia' with the horn of plenty (she is more likely to be Fortuna, then); a Minerva; and the Egyptian god Harpocrates. It is surely right to see this impressive line-up of divinities, including two Lares, as belonging to the household shrine, or *lararium* (contrast the House of the Wooden Shrine with its one or two statuettes, page 218), but it is worth noting that plenty of other material was stored in the cupboard, including a bronze weight, several bronze coins, a glass plate, a pottery plate, and several glass paste beads. The household gods were good at keeping their eye on valued objects.

*Left: Bronze statuettes from a shrine in the House of Wattlework (a Graticcio), representing Jupiter, a household god (Lar) and Fortuna.*

*Below: View from the balcony of the upper apartment of the House of Wattlework (a Graticcio).*

*Inside: Subterranean view of the piscina of the Palaestra.*

The second flat was accessible directly from the street, and had rather more rooms, though those in the middle were ill-lit. The most pleasant rooms were at the end of the corridor, looking out onto the balcony above the street. Here too is decoration and furniture: two beds, one adult, one for a child, and the wooden pediment of another cupboard or shrine, though the contents were missing. Among the finds in this flat were two objects of marble: one a statue base, apparently inscribed 'Philadelphia daughter of Gnaeus Octavius' (the nomenclature is odd, since a daughter of Octavius should be called Octavia), and the other the lower half of a marble *oscillum*, a half-moon plaque carved on both sides, designed to rotate in the wind.

We may share Maiuri's satisfaction in the close-grained insight into the life of the inhabitants of these flats. But we may also sound a small note of caution before accepting the assumption that inhabitants of such flats were necessarily of low social status. We have already met the puzzle of the dossier of Cominius Primus, a freeborn landowner and moneylender, kept in a small flat above a shop on the high street. Equally, there is something strange about the best collection of bronze statuettes of gods from the site coming from a small flat. All sorts of people might use flats, including those passing through, like the heroes of Petronius' *Satyrica* when they reach Puteoli, or those who required no more than a *pied-à-terre* in this particular town. Even the Emperor Vitellius is said by the biographer Suetonius to have let his house and lodged his family in a rented flat when he left for his province – though this was a sign that his fortunes were at a low ebb. A rental notice from Pompeii offered apartments suitable for people of equestrian status, *cenacula equestria*. Again, without specific evidence, it is dangerous to guess who lived where.

Flats were certainly to be found in houses across the site, and we can use the example of the House of Wattlework (a Graticcio) to help us imagine less visible situations. In the many cases where stairs lead upstairs directly from the street, we can be confident that these were apartments to let (and not to purchase). The standard date on which to start a let was 1 July – as for Trimalchio's friend Diogenes, but also in an explicit notice from Pompeii, where Gnaeus Alleius Nigidius Maius advertised in his Insula Arriana Polliana 'shops with upper rooms [*pergulae*], high-class apartments suitable for knights [*cenacula equestria*] and houses for rent from 1 July, contact the slave Primus'. Nor should we exclude the possibility that people took in lodgers in rooms within their houses. Internal stairs might not be so convenient or so conducive to privacy as external stairs, but lodgers within the house have been a normal practice in many societies. All these situations, however, involve the adaptation of the existing housing stock for rental purposes. What makes the block of apartments next to the Palaestra, the Insula Orientalis II, so different is that it is purpose-built to this end.

*Views of upper apartment, from outside (below) and inside (bottom).*

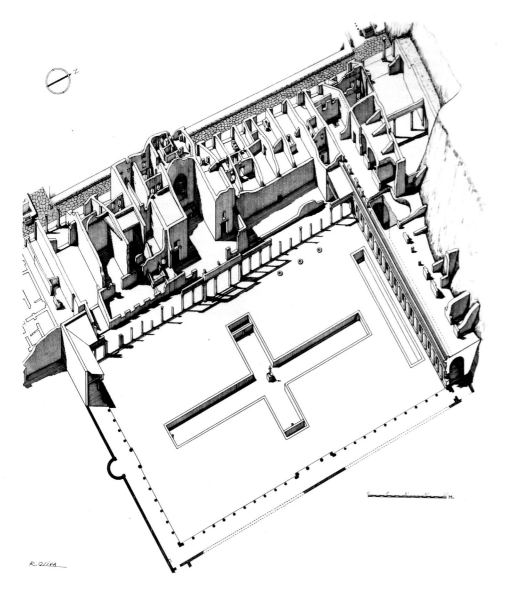

The importance of the Palaestra block is fairly evident. Surviving at least partially to three floors, plus the sewer below ground, it represents not only the sole example in Pompeii and Herculaneum of a particular type of multi-storey, multi-unit block which is familiar from Rome and Ostia, but the only case where, unlike Rome and Ostia, the finds were preserved in such a way as to cast unambiguous light on the nature of the activities within them. Given how much discussion there has been of this *insula* type in Rome and Ostia, we might have expected rather more interest in the light the artefactual record here in Herculaneum could cast. But a proper study of the block including finds has never been published, partly because Maiuri never got round to the second volume of his great publication which would have covered the finds. Even so, a widespread impression has been given that we know the finds, because of the way Maiuri both drew on them in his text to evoke a vivid picture of the life of the block and actually displayed them to the public on site. Alas, his presentation is, at least in part, significantly misleading.

*Apartment block by Palaestra: axonometric reconstruction by Maiuri (R. Oliva) (above left); archival view of excavation from north (top); view of block from south (above).*

*R. OLIVA*

*Reconstruction drawing of block by Maiuri (R. Oliva).*

The structure of the block is anything but usual. Large buildings are usually conceived as positive masses, making the air around them a negative shape. This block is conceived, at least on one side, as a negative, adapting itself to the requirements of the Palaestra to its side. In the middle, corresponding to the axis of the great cruciform pool at the centre of the Palaestra, an *exhedra*, a large hall-like area open on one side to the portico, runs up to the full, three-storey height of the building. To its sides are two reception rooms. The north end of the block is determined by the junction with the earlier north wing of the Palaestra, where originally a set of steps came down to its level. The south end is defined by the grand new entrance, replacing the steps. Our block of shops and flats has to occupy the left-over spaces, and especially around the Palaestra *exhedra*, the apartments have to follow the contours, perched perilously high above the level of the pool. This negative/positive relationship to the public space makes clear that the construction of the block is a public initiative, a decision presumably taken by the *decuriones*, even if financed by a private benefactor. Just as at Pompeii where public baths like the Stabian Baths were constructed to incorporate shops in their street frontages, this transformation of the Palaestra gives the added bonus of rental space.

*Apartment block by Palaestra: viewed from the south (above); north and south sections of the block by Maiuri (R. Oliva) (left); excavation of latrine on the second floor (right).*

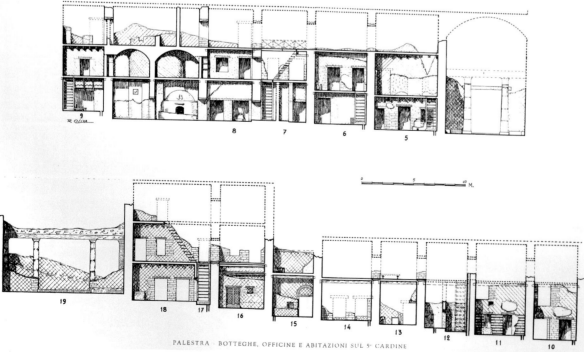

PALESTRA – BOTTEGHE, OFFICINE E ABITAZIONI SUL 5° CARDINE

The land runs fairly steeply downhill along the east of Cardo V. There is a steep drop in two directions, both north–south and east–west: if you stand down in the Palaestra itself, you understand that the buildings of the Aula to the north and of the *insula* to the west are a full storey higher. This all makes better sense when you consider the original contours of the site: we are on the very edge of the platform on which the town is built, before it drops off into the ravine below, where presumably the main ancient harbour lies. The Palaestra was only built by levelling the terrain with substructures; the natural lie of the land is a steep slope. At the same time, there is a north–south downhill slope, such that if you enter the complex from the top of the road at the Aula, you are on the upper level, if by the monumental gateway halfway down the road, you are only slightly above the lower level. The *insula* construction thus forms part of an ambitious engineering operation to re-contour the eastern edge of the town, an operation that can now be dated by a recent trench at the south end of the block to the mid-first century, a few decades later than Maiuri's Augustan dating. The Augustan phase is limited to the top end of the Palaestra.

The block is effectively split into three separate units: one on the corner, to the south of the monumental entrance to the Palaestra; one to its north, up to the great *exhedra* of the Palaestra, which rises to the full height of the block without upper floors; and one further uphill, as far as no. 14 (see section, left), the limit of the new sewer. No. 15, though later converted into a shop, originally led to a stairway down to the Palaestra. This is the limit of the new Claudian construction, and the Augustan part is to its north. The ground floor consists of a series of ten shop units, many of which had internal stairs to their own upper floors; in addition, each of the three sections had separate entrances with stairs rising to the two or more upper floors. The rooms on the first floor follow roughly the same plan and layout as the ground floor; generally, the first floor rooms are associated with the shop rooms below them. The second floor is the least well preserved, though the robust construction of the Palaestra *exhedra* seems to have kept the central section more intact. It is here that we can trace the layout of at least one flat, with several rooms around a central space. The entrance seems to have been from the wooden balcony that ran across the façade. By a bit of luck, Maiuri's men in 1933 failed to complete their clearance of these rooms, and it was possible in 2006 to excavate the final layers of the latrine of the apartment, together with its downpipe dropping down to the sewer below. To reach the latrine from the flat, you had to go out onto the balcony.

Despite the good evidence for the upper floors, Maiuri's publication focuses on the ground level (though his architect Oliva's superb elevations and axonometric drawings made up for his silence). The story he tells about the commercial life of a block is a lively one, corresponding closely to his presentation to the public. Down at the bottom, door 1A leads to a bakery, with an oven and the familiar flour mills, plus the bonus of a donkey's skeleton discovered beside the mills, rather than in the stable behind. Round the corner, *taberna* no.1 is a shop, maybe the baker's sales point, with a latrine in the corner and stairs to an apartment above. No. 3 is a tiny shop, but also with a latrine in the room behind. *Taberna* no. 5 is a dye-shop, *officina tinctoria*, with a great *dolium* or storage jar walled into position for the dye-vat, and a latrine in the corner. No. 6 is a shop with a sales counter with four *dolia* built into it, and a number of amphorae stacked in the backroom, one carrying the address label 'M. Livi Alcimi Herclani', Marcus Livius Alcimus of Herculaneum. No. 8 is another bakery, with two mills, identified by a bronze stamp as that of Sex(tus) Patulcius Felix. The oven is particularly well preserved, in the tiny room behind the great wall of the Palaestra *exhedra*; no less than three good luck phalli give additional interest. Patulcius' bakery is given closer characterization (and differentiation from that at no. 1A), thanks to the presence of a couple of dozen circular bronze dishes, originally displayed to the viewing public by hanging them on the back wall of the backroom, in clear view from the road outside. These bronze dishes, in a complete range of sizes from large to small, led to the characterization of the baker as a *pistor placentarius*, maker of *placentae* or 'focacce'. Maiuri cheerfully glosses him as 'un vero e proprio pizzaiuolo': a real pizza man; anything less, on the Bay of Naples, would be a disappointment.

Moving on, we find next door at No. 9 a wine shop, *taberna vinaria*, complete with a large stack of amphorae, a mezzanine with an amphora rack beneath it and address labels that identify the wine merchant as L.R. Antigonus; in the back shop is a bed. Next, no. 10 is the shop of a *gemmarius*, a gem-cutter identified by a large haul of gems, partly cut and partly roughed out. However, the emotional climax of the house is the room of the embroidery girl, the *ricamatrice*, whose teenage skeleton was

*Opposite: Archival line drawing of the bakery of Patulcius.*

*Top right: Stamp naming (in reverse) Sextus Patulcius Felix.*

*Above left: Drawing of the oven from the bakery, decorated with phalluses.*

*Above right: Series of bronze dishes of graded sizes.*

*Far left: Shop no. 13, with wares displayed on counter.*

*Left: Watercolour reconstruction of the wine shop of Antigonus by Maiuri (R. Oliva).*

found lying on the bed, 'adolescente vittima, chissà, di quale crudele o angoscioso abbandono' ('adolescent victim of who knows what cruel or anguishing abandonment'); by her bed is her embroidery frame and a little inlaid stool, as well as a bronze candelabrum and a marble table. The interconnected shop, No. 11, is shown by its vats to be another *tinctoria*. Then comes shop No. 13, its sales counter found with a large quantity of carbonized grain, beans and chickpeas, which are duly displayed to the public in glass cases. No. 14 is a blank, with no finds.

One has to admire Maiuri's ability to conjure up life, and indeed his ability to display it to the public. But careful examination of the actual excavation records for summer 1936 suggests that by the time, twenty years later, he was writing this all up for publication, he had either lost track of the actual records or ceased to care, and was more interested in publishing the 'open museum' he had so ingeniously constructed. One major fraud has been mentioned above (page 83). The little weaving girl is, alas, pure myth. The excavation diaries do indeed record a skeleton on the bed, but it is that of a young man (*giovanotto*). But this apart, there were no finds: *nessun ritrovamento*. The wooden stool came from the house opposite, the loom and candelabrum from heaven knows where. It looked great for the public. Of course, what could not be displayed was the story of the gem-cutter, since the valuable gems were taken off to the Museum in Naples. But the diaries also reveal that the rest of house was a treasure trove, with far more objects than in any other unit in the block: numerous lamps, pots, bronze vessels, a strigil, glass perfume bottles, a bronze balance, an interesting little terracotta altar inscribed HERCULIS, a marble bust of Bacchus and an elegant marble portrait bust of a man with an Augustan hairstyle, with red paint in its hair. No sign of gem-cutting equipment, but that is no argument against him being a gem-cutter. The portrait is more likely to be the gem-cutter's patron than himself: the hairstyle is too early, harking back to the Augustan age, and an almost identical portrait was found in Pompeii. That would make our man, as one might anticipate, a freedman. He either became wealthy on gem cutting and was able to afford far more objects than his neighbours, or his gems were part of his wealth; it is interesting to note that a substantial collection of gems was also found in a chest on the upper floor of a different flat. The discovery (below) of further gems in the sewer raise the question of whether these too derive from the gem-cutter.

*Right: Objects found in the shop of the gem-cutter: a bronze saucepan (top); a ceramic beaker (centre); a marble bust of Bacchus from wine shop no 9 (bottom).*

*Opposite: Marble portrait of a man with an Augustan hairstyle, perhaps the patron of the gem-cutter.*

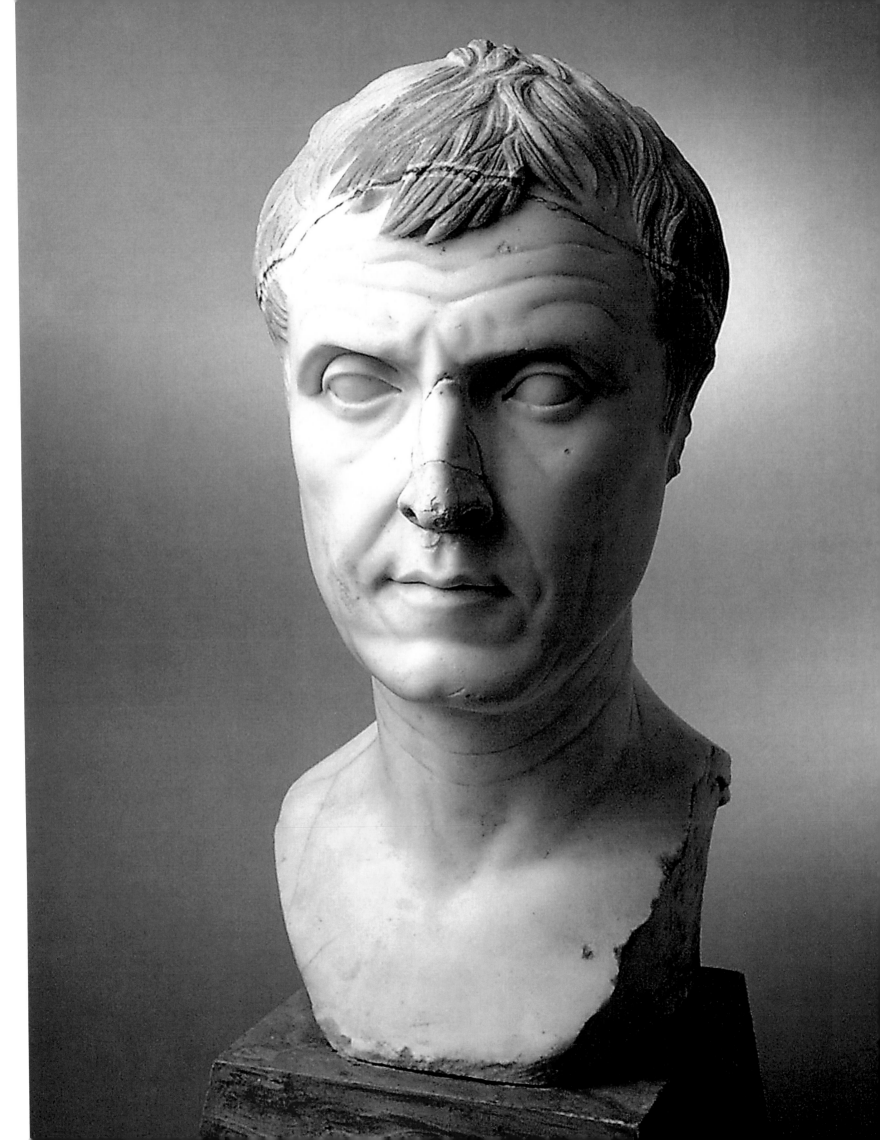

Ironically, though we must deprive shop No. 10 of its weaving girl, we can restore to it a great deal else of interest. The finds are rich. It is also interesting that they correlate so closely with the sort of material found in the sewers, and these links will bear detailed investigation. As for the other shops, here too the excavation diaries show up Maiuri as less than meticulous. Take the 'pizzaiuolo'. Unfortunately, the bronze pizza dishes were not found in the shop, but in an upper apartment unconnected to it. In any case, a set of dishes, each different in size, neatly graded, are not the obvious containers for someone trying to sell food in standard sizes at standard prices. In any case, what pizza man ever used a bronze dish?

Then the wine amphora bearing the name of L.R. Antigonus was not found in the wine merchant's shop, no. 9, but actually in the shop of the *gemmarius*, no. 10, along with no less than four other amphora necks with the initials L.R.A. We can even be specific about the wine they contained, since one also has the Greek name Teuponos, a known producer of the sweet Lyttian wine from Crete. It was a wine particularly recommended to women, who were not supposed to get drunk on ordinary red wine: instead they tippled this sherry. On this showing, Antigonus is the name of the *gemmarius*, not the *vinarius*, and some loans had to be made from one space to the other to kit it up as a convincing wine shop. Doubts fall too on the carbonized grain, beans and chickpeas found in the *dolia* in the counter of shop no. 13. The excavation diaries say nothing of these finds, but do mention amphorae full of similar carbonized material found in the upper floor of a nearby flat.

Maiuri's reconstruction of a string of commercial units must be taken as unreliable. It isn't just that he moved stuff around to make up stories. He completely failed to analyse the upper floors, which included, as we have seen, bronze dishes, amphorae full of foodstuffs, and a chest full of gemstones. This work needs to be done again. But we now have the advantage of the excavation of the great sewer that runs under the block, which has the potential to tell us much else about the inhabitants. Maiuri explored and mapped this sewer, but, realizing that it was full of organic material, left it only partially excavated. In the course of trying to provide an effective drainage system for the site, in 2005–6 the Herculaneum Conservation Project reopened the sewer and completed its excavation.

The first point to strike us, as it had Maiuri, was how intimately the sewer was connected to the construction of the block above it. The sewer had two branches, both robustly constructed: one running north–south along the length of the street, but set inside the outer wall of the *insula*; the second, of over 40 metres length, cutting west–east under the Palaestra itself. Throughout there are downpipes feeding into it from above, coming from either individual shops and apartments, or clusters of them. The construction was all of a single phase, except that at the north end there was a clear junction with an earlier phase. The sewer was designed from the first to service the *insula* in its entirety.

It was not, however, designed as a drain, to remove everything that descended into it and take it out to sea. On the contrary, the sewer was firmly end-stopped at its southernmost point. It became clear that it was rather an enormous cess pit, designed for the accumulation of all the waste of the block, which could compost and rot away until it eventually needed digging out. Drainage water from the street did indeed enter, but the function was not as a drain but as a trap to avoid foul odours rising up the drains, sealed off beneath water. What was a disadvantage for our aim to drain the site of water became an archaeological advantage. Though Maiuri had completely cleared the first few metres, he left most of the north–south branch only partially explored, including a layer of ancient waste material that varied from a few centimetres to

*Sewer beneath the Palaestra block: plan showing sewer (below); excavation of the sewer (right).*

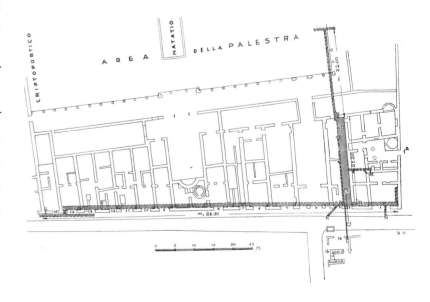

*Sewer after excavation, looking south.*

over a metre in depth. It was evident that this material was completely full of broken rubbish as well as waste.

The Herculaneum Conservation Project's lead archaeologist, Domenico Camardo, therefore adopted an excavation strategy that divided the sewer into 1-metre lengths. Each section was excavated stratigraphically, and it was indeed possible to distinguish up to three strata in each deposit, divided by fine sandy layers that seemed to result from occasional flooding of the sewer. The earth, rich with organic remains, was carefully separated from the remarkable quantity of non-organic materials, broken pots, lamps etc., which found their way down the drains. Everything was carefully bagged up with reference to the context number to allow association with specific deposits. The non-organic material filled some 177 trays. Finds include: a large number of lamps, some discarded because broken, others apparently intact; numerous small containers, never as large as a full amphora, though with some it is surprising they could travel down the drain intact; vessels, including red-glazed wares from South Gaul (famously a crate of these was found

in Pompeii, and is now in Naples Museum, but these were arriving some time before the eruption in not insignificant quantities, to be used, broken and disposed of); bronze vessels, heavily corroded by the acidic context but recognizable; glass perfume jars; a range of oddities, like a terracotta antefix, a small terracotta statuette of a mother-and-child figure; and a range of jewellery, especially rings with bronze stamps, gold rings, and semi-precious gemstones.

At this point we called in Mark Robinson from Oxford, an environmental archae-ologist whose experience with Pompeian cesspits, latrines and waste material went back to the late 1990s. He confirmed that the deposit was indeed rich in organic waste material, including fishbones, eggshells, pips and seeds, and that it would be worth analysing systematically. Since the waste tended to heap beneath individual downpipes, it would be worth looking at the material, not as one vast deposit, but as a series of separable deposits associated with individual households. Given the rich variety of commercial and other activities in the units above, it would be the more interesting to establish whether there were different patterns of consumption

*Above left: Exploration of a branch of the sewer.*

*Top: Bags containing organic remains.*

*Above: Corroded rings and coins.*

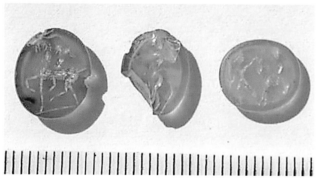

*Top left: Mark Robinson examines the results of flotation.*

*Top right: Painting of game birds and mushrooms, from the House of the Stags.*

*Above: Gems and a gold ring.*

and waste disposal. Robinson's group took a selective sample from the 774 bags that have been set aside, both to try to ensure coverage of all sections of the sewer, and so that plenty of untouched material remains for cross-checking. Seventy-six bags, or a 10 per cent sample, were examined. These were then separated by wet-sieving through a series of meshes, so separating out material by size. A remarkable quantity of the coarser material consisted of building materials, including small lumps of concrete, broken pottery and tile, small iron objects like nails, lumps of rusty, black, glassy slag-like material, etc. There was also a rich harvest of small finds, beads, gaming counters, hairpins, hinges, a gaming die, and no less than three engraved gemstones. It is evident, since we are only looking at a 10 per cent sample, that a significant number of gems found their way down the drains, and when we look at the material excavated above ground, there are obvious potential associations.

The Oxford team also found a great variety of biological material. Some has evidently not passed through the gastric tract, and is kitchen waste from the cooking process (we may be struck by how undifferentiated their waste was, with everything from broken household rubbish through kitchen waste to human waste passing down the same outlets). Large quantities of charcoal, chopped animal bone and seashells were found, as well as large quantities of eggshell. Other bones could more easily have passed through the digestive system, copious fish bones and small bird bones. Sea urchin also seems to have been popular. What

*Above left: Fish bones. Above right: Fig pips.*

*Centre right: Fragments of cloth.*

*Below right: Snail shells and carbonized olive pits.*

have certainly been digested are the coprolites (these containing fish bones), mineralized fig pips, a grape pip and a mulberry pip. But what strikes one immediately, especially since this is the sewer of a block of 'commercial' units and apartments, not one of the rich houses of town, is the evident variety and health of their diet, with plenty of fish and seafood, poultry, eggs and fruit. The much repeated story that working Romans lived on a dreary diet of pulses and porridge will need some modification.

The lesson that comes very clearly out of a re-examination of this block is that we should not underestimate those who lived in such surroundings. The temptation is to see the rich restricted to their grand houses, and the other inhabitants as being, to a great or lesser extent, poor. Yet, just as when we look more carefully in the flats of the House of Wattlework (a Graticcio) and find good decoration, well-made furniture, bronze household gods and pieces of marble reliefs, so the Insula Orientalis II proves to be full of objects, many of which suggest a level well above poverty (marble busts, gemstones and good quality bronze-ware), while its sewers point to a varied and healthy diet. The imagined 'low life' of this Roman town at least is something altogether more complex.

# 10
# THE TALE OF
# TWO CITIES

On Tuesday 14 June 1740, just eighteen months after the Bourbon explorations of Herculaneum began, Horace Walpole, son of Prime Minister Robert Walpole, author and collector of antiquities, visited the site in company with Thomas Gray, future author of the famous 'Elegy'. He wrote enthusiastically to his friend, Richard West, of the special importance of these discoveries, accurately anticipating their future potential:

> There might certainly be collected great light from this reservoir of antiquities, if a man of learning had the inspection of it; if he directed the working, and would make a journal of the discoveries. But I believe there is no judicious choice made of directors. There is nothing of the kind known in the world; I mean a Roman city entire of that age, and that has not been corrupted with modern repairs. Besides scrutinizing this very carefully, I should be inclined to search for the remains of the other towns that were partners with this in the general ruin. 'Tis certainly an advantage to the learned world, that this has been laid up so long. Most of the discoveries in Rome were made in a barbarous age, where they only ransacked the ruins in quest of treasure, and had no regard to the form and being of the building; or to any circumstances that might give light into its use and history.

*(Horace Walpole, Correspondence with Thomas Gray, Richard West and Thomas Ashton Vol. 13)*

It would be nearly a decade before Pompeii emerged to fulfil his prediction. His assessment was completely accurate. The Roman world was indeed known from numerous remains, more of which would continue to emerge. The importance of the Vesuvian cities lies in their not having suffered the corruption of modern repairs, in the sense of a city like Rome itself, constantly adapted and recycled through time, and ransacked by barbarians (let alone papal families). But he also rightly anticipated the dangers. These ruins were precious

*Left: Detail of marble opus sectile flooring from the house of the Telephus Relief.*

*Opposite: Casts of skeletons from Pompeii.*

*Panoramic view of the shop in the House of Neptune and Amphitrite.*

and irreplaceable, and needed to be excavated judiciously, by 'men of learning' who would keep proper records. The Bourbon records, though better than nothing, are fragmentary and inadequate. Worse, even in the twentieth century, when a great 'man of learning', Amedeo Maiuri, was in charge, the records kept were still patently inadequate, and not even fully consulted by the excavator when he came to publish. Moreover, he did precisely what Walpole did not want, and left it 'corrupted with modern repairs'. The combination of heavy restoration and inadequate documentation means that what we are left with is not the remains of an ancient city, but an interpretation or presentation of those remains. Only too often the above chapters have had to question Maiuri.

The other issue to which Walpole rightly drew attention was the desirability of exploring more than one ancient city. It is not just a matter of accumulating more evidence. Each place is unique, quite specific to its individual location and historical development. Of course, any one site may be taken as representative, to some extent, of the Roman world and Roman civilization in general. But seeing from the viewpoint of a single site brings a loss of perspective. It is like looking with one eye. Put Pompeii and Herculaneum together, and it is like looking through two eyes. They may be close together, but that is enough to restore a sense of depth. It is because they are both similar and different that they give us a more three-dimensional view.

The geographer Strabo treated Herculaneum and Pompeii as if they had the same history: 'The Oscans held both this town and the one next to it, Pompaia, past which the river Sarnus flows, then the Tyrrhenians and the Pelasgians . . .' The fate of these cities which shared a common end is to be treated like identical twins, joined together at birth. And because they are taken to be identical, Herculaneum is systematically overlooked. Each

year, the publishing industry brings out a new spate of books on Pompeii. Those on Herculaneum can be counted on the fingers of one hand.

What, then, makes Herculaneum different and special enough to give us this depth of perspective? It is precisely the tiny differences that change a flat view into a three-dimensional one. Only 10 miles separate the two cities, yet in terms of the mechanics of a volcanic eruption, that is enough to make a profound difference, between burial under the ash-fall of *lapilli* and under the hot clouds of a pyroclastic flow. A small difference in distance translates into a difference in temperature, which brings with it enormous consequences for the preservation of materials. At 400–500°C, flesh evaporates: the consequence is that the skeletons of Herculaneum and Pompeii are wholly different. Fiorelli's casts at Pompeii, which preserve the outline of the body and even of its clothing, are not possible at Herculaneum, but though one kind of drama is lost,

another is gained, and it is Herculaneum's skeletons that offer the best hope for future analysis. At the same high temperature, organic materials carbonize: the wooden elements of Herculaneum, beams, beds, cupboards, winches, and writing tablets, along with the foodstuffs, grain, beans, fruit, nuts, even loaves of bread, and the occasional pieces of fabric, including above all rolls of papyrus, containing both literary texts and business documents, all these give the evidence of Herculaneum a quality absent from Pompeii.

The differences lie not only in the consequences of heat. The sheer depth of the cover left by the pyroclastic flows, at points three or four times greater than at Pompeii, ensures the preservation of upper floors, without which the understanding of the working of a house must be necessarily partial. Combined with the capacity of carbonization to preserve flimsy structures like timber frame-work, often characteristic of upper floors, let alone balconies and wooden mezzanines, this means the preservation of vital evidence invisible at Pompeii. How many shops does the visitor to Pompeii pass with counters containing terracotta jars, labelled, with characteristic indifference to the evidence or physical possibilities, as *thermopolia* or hot food shops? (You cannot heat, or even keep warm, food in a terracotta container set in a counter; nor can you keep it clean and prevent a deadly accumulation of bacteria.) It is from Herculaneum that we can see the sort of dry foods these counters were designed to serve. And it is at Herculaneum that we can reconstruct the complex woodwork that turned bare masonry structures into a working shop – the shelving and wine-racks, the screens for working areas, the lofts for storage. Put just one shop from Herculaneum, the one in the front of the House of Neptune and Amphitrite, alongside the dozens from Pompeii, densely distributed round the city, and the world of small-scale commerce begins to come into focus.

The difference is not only of means of preservation but of scale. Herculaneum, as we have seen, was a much smaller place than Pompeii, a quarter the size or less. Communities change with scale. The urbanization of Italy in the first century AD was dense, with the number of 'cities' running into hundreds. The elder Pliny, writing not long before the eruption, lists just short of 400 cities in Italy, of which 46 were *coloniae*. The distinction between a *colonia*, like Pompeii, and a *municipium*, like Herculaneum, was more a matter of historical origins than of legal status or size. A *colonia* was a community of Roman citizens, subject to the laws of Rome, but with its own local magistrates, elected by the assembly of citizens, and its council (the *decuriones*, meeting in the *curia*), on the model of Rome. What distinguished colonies is that they were deliberately created as communities by Rome, even if displacing a former community, by sending out its own existing citizens, typically army veterans. Augustus founded no less than twenty-eight colonies in Italy, in most cases by confiscating

the lands of existing towns and assigning them to his colonists, the land-hungry veterans who had fought the civil wars.

A *municipium* was in origin an independent, self-governing community, in alliance with Rome, and providing Rome with certain obligations (*munera*), above all the supply of contingents of troops or ships for war. The area round Naples had been conquered by Rome at the turn of the fourth and third centuries BC, and Naples was an important source of ships for the Roman navy, which was soon to challenge and defeat the Carthaginians, a naval power from the start. Herculaneum, with its idyllic harbour, may also have been a supplier of ships. The Social War of 91–89 BC, when numerous Italian allies rebelled again Rome, radically changed their status. Pompeii and Herculaneum were among the rebels, and were defeated by force. Pompeii was punished by the confiscation of lands and the imposition of a colony. Herculaneum remained a *municipium*, except that under the Lex Julia of 90 BC all its citizens became Roman citizens. In effect, the biggest distinction between a colony and a *municipium* – that its citizens were Roman citizens – had now disappeared. By the time of Cicero, the phrase 'the *coloniae* and *municipia* of Italy' became a way of saying, 'all the cities and towns of Italy'. Even so, a *colonia* was seen as 'ranking higher' than a *municipium*, for historical rather than legal reasons, and in the first two centuries of empire, there was a stream of *municipia* petitioning for 'promotion' to the status of *colonia*. When the Emperor Hadrian's home town in Spain, Italica, asked this favour of their most famous son, he questioned whether it was a promotion at all. But self-evidently, it was perceived to be so, and therefore it was so.

Herculaneum, consequently, was not merely smaller than Pompeii, but had a different legal status, one that was seen as making it less important. This has the advantage of allowing us to see from the contrasting perspectives of the two principal types of Roman urban community. How do the differences show? One very striking contrast between the two sites is the frequency of electoral advertisements or *programmata* in Pompeii, and their absence in Herculaneum. The Pompeian *programmata* take a standardized form. A candidate's name is recommended for one of the magistracies, the senior duumvirate (equivalent to the consulship at Rome), and the junior aedileship (Rome too had junior magistracies of this title) by an individual or group of people, with the abbreviated recommendation 'OVF', 'oro vos faciatis', 'I beg you to make him'. Of these many thousands survive from Pompeii, painted on the plaster of the exterior walls of houses, with a heavy concentration on the main streets. Some candidates score hundreds of recommendations. They may be painted over earlier recommendations, thus providing a vital clue for the sequence of elections and the dating of the magistrates, which cluster in the last thirty years of the town's life. The names of those making the recommendations are also a rich source, both as possible indications of the names of house owners (at least in some cases, the coincidence with names on address labels on amphorae inside the houses confirms this hypothesis), and of the sort of trades and other groupings which could form (ranging from the bakers, barbers, dyers, feltmakers, fruitsellers, goldsmiths, innkeepers, muledrivers, porters, perfumers, to the followers of Isis, or simply neighbours, to the evidently satyrical 'petty thieves', 'toastmasters' and 'late drinkers').

This entire lively scene is almost completely absent from Herculaneum. To date just one such potential *programma* has been claimed, on the brick portico of a house on the north side of the Decumanus Maximus, bearing the name of Marcus Caecilius Potitus. But it is not written in the clear, large, capital letters typical of Pompeian advertisements, it lacks the letters 'OVF', and the name of the magistracy, 'quaestor', does not correspond to the two standard magistracies of the *municipium*,

*Painted announcements from Herculaneum: the magistrates Marcus Rufellius Robia and Aulus Tetteius ban the dumping of rubbish in the vicinity of the water-tower (above); shop sign 'Ad Cucumas' (At the Cooking Pots), with the name of the city of Nola below (right).*

the duumvirate and the aedileship. So maybe it served some other function. Otherwise there is no trace of *programmata*. It is not for lack of plastered façades on which to paint the advertisements. Even if the side streets, the *cardines*, were too minor, the Decumanus Maximus should be, if the Pompeian distribution pattern is anything to go by, a hot spot for *programmata*.

Nor can we suggest that the levels of literacy were so much lower at Herculaneum than at Pompeii that the written word had no impact: apart from numerous graffiti, we can point to the evidence of the wooden tablets, which suggests the literacy not only of those involved in the transactions (the exceptional illiterates were identified as such, and others wrote for them), but also of the hundreds of locals who witnessed the documents. Painted messages do indeed occur on the streets, especially the Decumanus Maximus. We have met the edict of the aediles, Rufellius Robia and Tetteius Severus, against dumping rubbish by the public water supply. Then there are shops, like the wine shop 'ad cucumas', 'At the Kettles', which advertised the prices of different wines. But election advertisements are lacking, along with another conspicuous type of public announcement in Pompeii, namely announcements of forthcoming gladiatorial fights: these were principal ways in which the local elite made their names visible and their presence felt in Pompeii.

The silence of Herculaneum ought therefore to reflect a real difference. It cannot be a difference in social structure. Herculaneum had a ruling elite of members of the *ordo decurionum* just like Pompeii, and membership was defined by winning public office. The numerous statues celebrating these people in public places, and the celebration of acts of public benefaction, like the erection of buildings or the distribution of largesse, show this elite to be in a similar 'euergetic' relationship, where generosities buy public support. The vote had to count in

Herculaneum too. What explains the difference is not at all clear. Maybe Herculaneum, being a smaller, 'face-to-face' community, depended less on written communication: it was enough to stand up and harangue your fellow citizens. But possibly too there was something about the rhythm of political life in a *municipium* that was less aggressively competitive than in a *colonia*. The important point is that the contrast with Herculaneum warns us against generalizing from Pompeii about *all* Roman cities.

This contrast goes hand-in-hand with the impression that Herculaneum was altogether a quieter place. The account above of 'low life' at Herculaneum is considerably less colourful than a similar account of Pompeii could be. It is tempting to suggest that Pompeii had a livelier commercial life, and that its position at the mouth of the Sarno river did indeed give it, as Strabo suggests, a bigger role as the place of exchange between the hinterland upstream and the overseas network to which the Bay of Naples offered access. Pompeii, unlike Herculaneum, can lay claim to the production of commodities that travelled far and wide. The fish sauce, *garum*, made by the family of Umbricius Scaurus, certainly travelled as far as Spain. Pompeian wines, to judge by the elder Pliny, had a good reputation beyond local boundaries, even if the amphorae found in the city suggest extensive imports from the eastern Mediterranean. It is frustrating that we cannot say more about the wool trade of Pompeii: its position on the Sarno made it an ideal place for exporting woollen goods derived from the flocks of the Monti Lattari to the south and the Monti Irpini to the east. Attempts to turn Pompeii into an industrialized centre of a wool industry have proved overambitious, and the ubiquitous fullers have been demoted from key players in an industry of wool production to neighbourhood laundries. Even so, it is the contrast with Herculaneum, with its solitary, and very minor, fullery, and its two *tinctoriae* or dye shops, that suggests there is indeed something special about the fulleries of Pompeii, and that such

*Above left: Carbonized foodstuffs from Herculaneum: a loaf of bread, eggshells, walnuts, chickpeas and figs.*

*Above right: A fresco showing figs and bread from the House of the Stags.*

*Right: Carbonized figs.*

activity there may have gone beyond the famous definition by Lewis Mumford of a city that lives by 'taking in the neighbours' washing'.

Herculaneum, then, surely did have commerce, but a much better case can be made for the shops here serving a purely local function, so putting Pompeii in a perspective more interesting for the economic historian. The farms round Herculaneum were evidently productive, and the local wine had a value, otherwise Quintus Junius Theophilus would not have needed to make such a careful agreement with Aulus Tetteius Severus about the fruits of the farm, the *fundus Blandianus*, he had recently purchased from the latter, allowing Tetteius Severus to continue to store the new vintage in the vats until the following 1 August. Figs, of which a good number have been found carbonized on site, were a local speciality, and the elder Pliny mentions the 'Herculanean fig' as a specific variety to be found in Italy (*Natural History* 15.70). Several other tablets revolve around purchases of farms, like the *fundus Linisianus*, for which Cominius Primus paid the not insignificant sum of 295,000 sesterces. There are references to both vineyards (*vineae*) and woods (*silvae*), and the woods on the middle slopes of Vesuvius were regarded by the Romans as a resource quite as valuable as vineyards. The German sociologist Max Weber (1864–1920),

Far left: Scene of a satyr discovering Hermaphroditus from the House of the Carbonized Furniture.

Top left: Graffiti: 'Diogenes the Cynic philosopher, seeing a woman swept away by a river, said: "Let one bad thing carry off another".'

Middle left: 'Apollinaris doctor of the Emperor Titus here crapped well.'

Bottom left: View of the latrine in the House of the Gem where Apollinaris left his comment.

Below: Paving of a street without ruts.

followed by Moses Finley, argued that the function of an ancient city was to consume the produce of its hinterland. This model, that of the 'consumer city', works rather more convincingly for Herculaneum than Pompeii. In Herculaneum, the visible signs of ostentatious consumption, of costly public buildings, rich decoration in private houses, and prosperous material culture, outweigh the visible signs of any form of urban productivity. The same is not quite so true of Pompeii.

One sign of commercial activity that always strikes visitors to Pompeii is the presence of wheel ruts in the hard stone paving of the streets. Because most Roman carts had the same axle-span, each cart tended to cut down the same parallel tracks, and despite the hardness of the volcanic lava used to pave the streets, the ruts can be several inches deep. What is more, they are so consistent, carts taking corners in one direction not another, and wearing down the stone curbs on one side of a bend not another, that

Right: Bronze tintinnabulum
in the form of a flying phallus
with bells suspended beneath.

Far right: Ceramic double-
volute lamp with erotic
scene on the disc (both from
Herculaneum, provenance not
recorded).

it has been possible to suggest that Pompeii had an organized traffic system, with one-way streets and other zones closed to commercial traffic. The streets of Herculaneum have similar paving, but the ruts are rare and unremarkable. The conclusion seems inescapable: fewer carts plied their way along its streets.

Just as the commercial pace of Herculaneum seems to have been quieter than that of Pompeii, so other signs of 'low life' seem to be less evident. A familiar aspect of Pompeii is the frequency of a range of features that can be described as 'pornographic'. The 'great brothel' of Pompeii has become a major tourist destination, and though the casual identification of every house that contains scenes of a sexual nature as another brothel is unjustified, it is evident that there were a good number of establishments, including taverns, in which sex was for sale. Prostitution was an important source of profit in a slave-owning society, and Pompeii, between structures focused entirely on beds, and paintings

explicitly representing a variety of sexual acts, and hundreds of graffiti either advertising prices of prostitutes or celebrating the satisfaction of their clients, is a place where prostitution leaves its unmistakable mark. Not so Herculaneum. No space here has been identified as a brothel. Sexually explicit scenes are absent, unless one counts a version of the standard scene of a satyr surprising Hermaphroditus at rest, or the rare *tintinnabulum* or lamp with sexual scenes..

In Pompeii, Matteo della Corte was able to decipher numerous graffiti of an erotic nature. His harvest in Herculaneum was poor indeed. In the peristyle of the House of the Gem he deciphered 'Bombycion fellat': the name of this fellator is to be corrected to Bombylion. On the ramp to the sea beneath Cardo IV he saw in charcoal letters the nonsense sequence, 'sala . . . glabe rusiunnae lavinia futui', of which only the last word, 'fucked', can be understood. But for unmistakable sexual activity, we have to make do with a small group of graffiti in a

*Bronze gladiatorial parade helmet, embossed with scenes from the fall of Troy (Naples Museum, from Herculaneum, provenance not recorded).*

of times in Pompeii, *futuo*: 'I fuck'. Apelles Mus, an imperial chamberlain, and his 'brother' Dexter 'dined here most pleasantly and fucked together', and again with greater precision, 'we pleasantly fucked two each twice'. Another two companions 'were here and since they long had a servant bad at everything, by name of Epaphroditus, with difficulty late in the day they chucked him out; they spent most pleasantly, when they fucked, 105½ sesterces'. Finally we find a recommendation to a prostitute (or 'mistress') to seek him out at home: 'Hermeros to his mistress Primigenia: come to Puteoli to the Timnian quarter and ask at Messius the moneychanger for Hermeros the slave of Phoebus'.

All the characters here identifiable are slaves, or possibly imperial freedmen. Their world is recognizably that of Petronius' *Satyrica* (see pages 199–201), right down to the useless servant. It may be significant that they are visitors from outside, from the imperial household or Puteoli and not locals. Another visitor left his mark in the latrine of the House of the Gem: 'Apollinaris, doctor of the Emperor Titus, here crapped well'. References to shitting, *cacare*, are common in Pompeii, including painted signs aimed to deter people from fouling the vicinity. But good bowel movements were important to ancient medicine, and Apollinaris as a doctor is celebrating an act of good health, in a way reminiscent of the Baths of the Seven Sages at Ostia, where the sages offer good, if manifestly humorous, advice on the subject. Titus became emperor on the death of his father, Vespasian, on 23 June 79, only a few months before the eruption, so if he really was emperor when Apollinaris wrote, it was within weeks of the eruption. On the other hand, Titus shared the title 'imperator' with his father from 70 onwards, so we cannot be that precise.

Again, the contrast between Pompeii and Herculaneum serves to put Pompeii in perspective. It is a caution against 'normalizing' Pompeii. The sort of sexual activity met in Pompeii may indeed

backroom of the Suburban Baths (public baths were frequently associated with sexual activity, as we see in the Suburban Baths of Pompeii, where the 'Kama Sutra' series of numbered sexual scenes, whether humorous or not, make explicit the sexual associations, and the Stabian Baths, the back door of which leads to the town's largest concentration of places of sale of sex). Here a cluster of graffiti make up for rarity with social and topographical precision, and raises Herculaneum's score of a word found hundreds have been characteristic of a Roman society in which slavery made the sale of sexual services, even to other slaves, a constant fact of life. It is hard to imagine that we would not meet the same in Puteoli, a far larger port city. Herculaneum has more the air of a small town, where neighbours know each other too well for such vulgarities to be flaunted.

Less sex, but also less violence. Pompeii is one of the best places in the Roman world to study gladiatorial games. Its amphitheatre is the earliest known specimen of the new architectural form to survive. Its activities were conspicuous enough to enter the historical narrative, and the great riot that broke out there in AD 59, when the Pompeians and Nucerians came to blows, with much shedding of blood, led to a debate in the Roman senate, resulting in a ten-year ban on gladiatorial *ludi* and the exile of the senator, Livineius Regulus, who had been responsible for these particular games (Tacitus, *Annals* 14.17). The same event is depicted in a familiar painting, which shows not only the riot, but the advertisements for games of Lucretius Satrius Valens. Advertisements for *ludi* are common on the walls of Pompeii, as are graffiti of gladiators and records of their victories. Then there are the gladiatorial barracks, discovered in the 1760s, with their spectacular collection of gladiatorial equipment. Finally, there are the depictions from various tombs of gladiators fighting, which remind us of the continuing importance of the fights at funerary games, from which the tradition originated.

Against this, Herculaneum has next to nothing to offer: no amphitheatre, no advertisements or graffiti, no painted tombs. Just once, inside a private house, that of the Corinthian Atrium, we find an advertisement for the ten pairs of gladiators of Numisius Genialis that will fight at Herculaneum on 22 February. If it were not for the discovery in the Bourbon excavations of several gladiatorial helmets, beautifully embossed with scenes from the Trojan War, one might almost imagine Herculaneum was innocent of such games. Again, scale and status make a palpable difference. There is a good argument that it was precisely Pompeii's status as a colony for Sulla's veterans that encouraged the early building there of an amphitheatre: games were meant to be good for martial mettle, *virtus*. Herculaneum's population, by contrast, may have been felt to be too small to fill an amphitheatre, though amphitheatres have been found in smaller settlements, like the little market centre of Forum Novum (modern Vescovio in the Sabina).

The relative absence of pornography, scatology and gladiatorial violence may make Herculaneum seem less 'vulgar' and hence more 'up market' than Pompeii. This impression is misleading. It is simply quieter. One of the notable features of Pompeian graffiti is their wit and learning, which extends to the ability both to cite passages of Latin verse and to improvise on a theme, even if the verses do not always scan perfectly or obey the rules of grammar. If Herculaneum had a better-educated population than Pompeii, it might be expected to have even more of these learned graffiti; but here too it has little to offer. There is one example of one of the standard verse tags of Pompeii, the archetypal visitor's graffito: 'venimus hoc cupidi, multo magis ire cupimus', 'we came here keenly, and are even keener to go'. Then there are two verse maxims, in the same House of the Gem where Apollinaris made his mark, of the type made popular by the early imperial mime-writer, Publilius Syrus: 'qui se tutari nescit, nescit vivere', 'he who does not know how to defend himself, does not know how to live', and, rather more wisely, 'minimum malum fit contemnando maximum', 'neglect of the smallest problem makes it the biggest one'. (The motto would do well for the problem of archaeological conservation.) In the Palaestra, some joker has twice written 'May the bears eat me!': the same exclamation is attested in Pompeii. Finally, we may note a long graffito in Greek found in a backroom of the bar on the corner of Cardo V and the lower Decumanus, which says more for the writer's knowledge of popular philosophy than his respect for women: 'Diogenes the Cynic philosopher, seeing a woman swept away by a river, said: "Let one bad thing carry off another"'. The Cynics were notorious for their 'street-corner' philosophy, and this disagreeable saying of Diogenes, which is attested by other sources, fully fits the bill.

While these few graffiti are enough to show that there was awareness of both verse and street philosophy in Herculaneum, they are certainly not enough to make the population seem better educated than that of Pompeii. There is a total absence of Virgil, constantly cited at Pompeii, of Ovid and the erotic poets, even of the philosophic Lucretius. While the Villa of the Papyri may have the largest known collection of Epicurean texts, it was in Pompeii, in the House of Fabius Rufus looking out over the sea, that someone scratched the Lucretian citation, 'suave mari magno': 'sweet it is in a great storm'. The full thought is that it is sweet in a storm to watch others in trouble and know that you are

*Left: 'First-style' false marbling from the entrance of the Samnite House.*

*Right: Examples of inlaid colour marble: the House of the Stags (top left); the House of Apollo the Lyre-player (middle left); the House of the Telephus Relief (bottom left); the House of the Bicentenary (top right); the House of the Corinthian Atrium (bottom right).*

*Detail of monochrome decoration from the House of the Black Saloon.*

has the same range from very grand houses built over the city wall, effectively urban villas, through grand town houses of a traditional sort, to a range of middling houses and small units of shops and workshops. The underlying architectural grammar, so to speak, is the same, and Vitruvius proves a useful commentary in both cities. But for all that, Herculaneum is different: less repetitive and more experimental. The standard size houses display great cunning in seeming to offer more than their modest plot-size would suggest: the House of the Corinthian Atrium, with its charming peristyle-atrium, and the House of Neptune and Amphitrite, with its spectacular mosaic *nymphaeum*, offer two examples within the same block of imaginative uses of a small plot, hard to parallel at Pompeii. At the other extreme, the House of the Mosaic Atrium, with its unique atrium-basilica sequence, and the House of the Stags, with its unassuming covered atrium leading to a spectacular suite of rooms facing the garden, are two completely different, and equally un-Pompeian, solutions to the use of a large plot of land.

It is frustrating that we know so little about what housing in Rome itself looked like at this period. Would we find Herculaneum closer to the metropolis in its range of innovative solutions and variants on the old atrium formula? Or was it the influence of nearby Neapolis at work? Or was it simply a different set of builders and architects working in this town to give it its distinctive character? One argument in favour of closeness to metropolitan Roman fashion is the Palaestra block. This is so similar to the brick and concrete blocks familiar from Ostia and the capital itself (a fine example survives at the foot of the Capitoline hill), and so unlike anything in Pompeii, that it is tempting to point to Rome as the model. Another possible, and closer, source is Puteoli, at this period the most important port city in the western Mediterranean. As its architecture gradually emerges from the demolition of Rione Terra, we may find the most convincing model there.

safe, a state to which Epicurean philosophy would take you. Instead of citing high verse, the people of Herculaneum mostly used their writing for banalities like names, numbers and lists: 'wine received from the master, 7 April'.

The impression that Herculaneum is no carbon copy of Pompeii is strongly reinforced when we consider its architecture and decoration. In many ways, as we have seen, the housing stock of Herculaneum is comparable to that of Pompeii: it

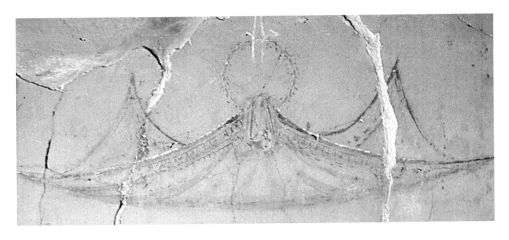

*Details of blue-ground decoration from the House of the Mosaic Atrium (top and bottom left) and the House of the Grand Portal (top and bottom right).*

Decoration too at Herculaneum is quite distinctive. What leaps at once to the eye is the use of polychrome marbles for flooring in a breathtaking variety of patterns. This use of *opus sectile* depended on a regular supply of marble from quarries in Africa, Egypt, Greece and Asia Minor (Turkey). The port of Puteoli must have been a major terminus for the marble trade. However, to ship the cut and polished veneers from Puteoli to Pompeii will have cost no more than the trip to Herculaneum. Yet in Pompeii, the use of *opus sectile* is very rare. The grandest room in the House of Fabius Rufus at Pompeii, comparable in wealth and size to the House of the Stags at Herculaneum, indeed had a marble veneer floor; and though the slabs of marble have been robbed out, it is evident from the impressions left in the mortar that they formed a very simple pattern, not approaching the complex geometry of the equivalent in Herculaneum. The main room of the House of the Stags had flooring composed of 368 separate pieces of marble. Among the 240 that survive, there are 82 different motifs, of which 68 are unique. This is not like rolling out patterned carpet; it is original craftsmanship at the highest level. Polychrome marble floors are found repeatedly across Herculaneum, whether in public buildings (the so-called College of the Augustales and the Palaestra), grand houses (like those of the Stags, the Mosaic Atrium, the Telephus Relief, the Bicentenary, the Tuscan Colonnade), or even medium-sized houses like that of the Skeleton, and (with one of the most beautiful examples) the House of Apollo the Lyre-player. Mosaic flooring, more standard in Pompeii, exists in Herculaneum too, alongside the marble, sometimes, as in the House of the Corinthian Atrium, combined to great effect in a single design.

Marble in Herculaneum is not limited to floors. Just as was the case in grand houses in imperial Rome, marble panels could be used to clad the lower parts of walls. This is what we find used to dramatic effect in the two storeys of the tower building of the House of the Telephus Relief. Again, Pompeii has no parallels. Equally, a special feature of Herculaneum is the insertion in domestic walls of white marble panels carved in low relief. The scene of Achilles healing the wound of Telephus is one of two such reliefs from this house. As we have seen, the even grander house of the south-western corner of the town likewise displayed two reliefs in one of its rooms. Carved in the style of classic Athenian sculpture, they probably, rather like the versions of the Amazon head, were intended if not as 'reproductions of Greek art' (an idea that has fallen out of fashion among modern art historians), at least as bravura performances in a classical tradition.

All these decorative contrasts point to Herculaneum as a place of greater wealth and sophistication than Pompeii. Even the wall painting is different. The standard account points to the four styles of Pompeian painting as if they were universal in the Roman world. The first is false marbling, the second introduces architectural perspective, the third depends on panels separated by more delicate decorative elements, and the fourth returns to a use of architectural perspectives, though more fantastical than those of the second style. There is indeed some truth in this, and wall decoration found elsewhere in Italy, and even in France or Germany, at least when it belongs to the first centuries BC and AD, can be related to the four 'Pompeian' styles. But the same story of gradual evolution of fashion could not have been told starting from Herculaneum. Surviving decoration from the second or even first century BC is exceptional in Herculaneum. The Samnite House preserves a fine example of the 'false marble' idiom of the First Style in its entrance corridor, but only there. Otherwise we are reduced to looking for a faded fragment in the House of the Wooden Shrine. The Second Style, with its architectural perspectives, is amply attested in a good number of Pompeian houses, as well as the villas outside the walls (the Villas of the Mysteries, Oplontis and Boscoreale). At Herculaneum too the Villa of the Papyri with its mid-first century date has the same style, but within the town, examples are limited to the baths of the House of the Hotel (Albergo), and a fragment in the ruinous House with Garden. The rarity of these earlier styles is an effect of chronology. Either the houses of Herculaneum were more extensively redecorated in the first century AD than those of Pompeii, or, just possibly, real wealth did not reach Herculaneum till later, with Nonius Balbus' revival of the town's fortunes in the Augustan age.

The decorative styles of the Early Empire, Third and Fourth, are rather harder to distinguish from each other, even for experts. The classic contrast offered for Pompeii is that in the Third Style walls are more 'closed', with architectural elements reduced to delicate details, whereas the Fourth Style uses architectural perspectives to 'open' the vista of the wall. This contrast does not work so well at Herculaneum, where even the architectural perspectives of the Fourth Style tend to be reduced to delicate detail. There are cases, as in the House of the Black Saloon, the Wooden Screen, the

*White marble plaque with drawing of five girls playing knuckle-bones (astragaloi), found in the House of Neptune and Amphitrite.*

room is occupied by what looks like a curtain in a theatre, against which are represented masks and other details. We can happily attribute this room's decoration to the Fourth Style, but would struggle to find anything quite like it in Pompeii. Another exceptional decorative scheme is that of the lower 'room of the marbles' in the tower of the House of the Telephus Relief. Here, a red background is enriched by layer after layer of decorative borders. The individual elements can be paralleled in other Fourth Style schemes, used as borders to panels. What is unusual is their superimposition. The style is more one of a piece of woven fabric or carpet, and maybe it is meant to evoke a wall hung with cloth. The loss of woven cloth and tapestries is one of the biggest blind spots in our appreciation of ancient material culture.

Where does this leave Herculaneum? The town has picked up something of the reputation of a small south-coast resort, populated by rich holiday-makers and retired civil servants, a Weymouth perhaps or a Key West, Florida. But this too may be inappropriate and misleading. It is true that the Bay of Naples attracted large numbers of the Roman rich, who lined the crescent of the bay from Misenum to the shrine of Athena at the point of the Sorrentine peninsula, as Strabo describes it, with a continuous line of villas. You can reasonably look for the metropolitan wealthy, for the retired and convalescent, in villas like that of the Papyri or at Oplontis. Baiae, the bathing spa on the north of the bay, comes much closer to the image of the resort of the idle rich. Herculaneum is altogether more modest and down to earth. Its lists of names, both on the marble inscription and the witness lists of the wooden tablets, suggest that part at least of the population originated from elsewhere, including no less than Nonius Balbus from Nuceria. Others included the Marci Stlaccii from Puteoli, Gaius Nasennius probably from Capua, the Gnaei Octavii from Neapolis, and so on. But the presence of such

Carbonized Furniture and the Grand Portal, where we have to speak of 'transition' between the two styles: they fall securely into neither one category nor the other.

All this is quite technical. But from the viewpoint of the visitor, the walls of Herculaneum have a different *feel*. One notable feature, met in a series of houses, is the use of a monochrome background, in black, blue or white, against which decorative details are picked out in subtle shades of brown and white. The effect can be magical, as in the black backgrounds of the House of the Black Saloon or the light blue backgrounds of the grand House of the Mosaic Atrium or the tiny House of the Grand Portal. In the latter house we meet another feature that seems special to Herculaneum: the representation of fabrics. The middle zone of one entire *incolae*, or residents, is far from making it a retirement village, and rather illustrates a general mobility at the local level. Indeed, the relative scarcity of freeborn men suggests that slavery was far more important a route for immigration than retirement.

It is in those lists of names that we have the best chance of grasping the social realities of Herculaneum, at least as we see it in its final two decades. There is still much to be understood about these lists, and much potential insight to be derived about the composition of the society of the town in this period. Given that the 500 or so names that survive on fragments represent at most a half of the thousand and more names that the full document originally carried, we must hope that future excavations will restore further fragments, and give us for the first time a full view of the free, adult male inhabitants of a Roman community and their different statuses. But even the half of the inscription that survives says much about this community. On the one hand, it illustrates, as we have seen, the geographical mobility of the inhabitants of the towns of the area. This is why Herculaneum can never make sense as a place apart, but only as an element in a system. Communities of different characters fruitfully interconnected: the great Roman colony and port of Puteoli, centre of a network of trade spreading across the entire Mediterranean, and its counterpart, the Greek colony of Neapolis (modern Naples), nurtured by emperors who welcomed its continued use of Greek language and social institutions, like the *ephebeia*, the physical and intellectual training of pubertal males, and promoted its character as a western centre of Greek culture by instituting a cultural festival of Olympic status, the lists of winners in which have recently emerged in the excavation of the new metro line. Further inland there was Capua, once the city that dominated the Campanian plain, and still famed in Cicero's day for its urban amenities, and a centre of bronze production. Then inland up the Sarno valley was Nuceria, the old Oscan town which was in constant contact with Pompeii, riotously visiting its amphitheatre and supplying some of its most famed prostitutes. Finally, there was the Roman imperial fleet at Misenum, and nearby the luxury spa of Baiae. They make a set of communities more conspicuous for their variety than their similarity, and in their context the diversity of Pompeii and Herculaneum should not surprise us.

But though to some extent people flowed round the Bay of Naples, we can also see them in the Herculaneum lists putting down their roots. It is striking how often the same family names recur. By now, what marks family links is the combination of *praenomen* and *nomen*: thus, Marcus Nonius. The older tradition was for the first name, *praenomen*, to be the element that distinguished an individual in a family. Marcus Tullius Cicero might have his father's first name, and pass it to his son, but his brother was a Quintus, and that distinguished him within his generation. The third name, *cognomen*, was so far from being his distinctive name by the old Roman tradition that the man we call Cicero was referred to in the senate as 'Marcus Tullius'. But this tradition changed in the early empire, and increasingly the *praenomen* became a fossilized element, and the *cognomen* distinguished people. This is what we see at work in the Herculaneum tablets.

Partly this is driven by the phenomenon of freedmen who took their master's *praenomen* and passed it on to their children, almost as a badge of honour. Thus, of the twenty-six men named Nonius named on the list, all but one is a Marcus. The exception, Quintus Nonius, freedman of Quintus, Faustillus, might be the freedman of a descendant of the great Marcus Nonius who was still, like Cicero's family, using the *praenomen* to distinguish brothers. Of the others, only one is freeborn, Marcus Nonius Fuscus, and he like all the freedmen preserves the most famous and familiar combination. In general, the freeborn men on the list are extremely tenacious of the fixed *praenomen-nomen* combination. Of the forty *ingenui* whose first names are preserved on the list, not one single one has a different first name from that of his father. Some at least must have been second sons, and if the old convention was being respected, at least a proportion should have *praenomina* different from that of their fathers. This is the more noticeable when, as happens from time to time, two freeborn men with the same family names are listed one after the other: Gnaeus Lusienus, son of Gnaeus, Justus and Gnaeus Lusienus, son of Gnaeus, Probus, or, on the same list Sextus Caecilius, son of Sextus, Proculus and Sextus Caecilius, son of Sextus, Astus. This happens for five pairs, a quarter of the names. To judge by these lists, your third name, *cognomen*, was the way to distinguish the individual for this population, whether freeborn or slave-born. It may mark a change of fashion, and may be a clue of how many of the freeborn are themselves descendants of freedmen.

Another pattern we may notice is how frequently the same combination of family names occurs in all three social categories, the *ingenui*, the *liberti*, and the strange class that is neither the one nor the other. Of the 500 or so names preserved, about a fifth have unique *praenomen-nomen* combinations. The rest have at least two with the same combination, half have three or more with the same combination, and more than a fifth have five or more individuals with the same combination. Again and again, where there are numerous individuals with the same combination, they are found in more than one category, and not infrequently in all three. So those with the Marcus Calatorius combination (a family which produced the Marcus Calatorius Quartio who was honoured with a fine bronze statue) include one freeborn member, Acceptus, five freedmen, Fortunatus, Januarius, Menophilus, Pierus and Salvius, and three in the neither-nor category, Acratus, Crescens and Diodorus. This is a pattern that repeats itself even on a modest scale: so of the four bearers of the combination Tiberius Acutius, one is freeborn, Spendon, one is a freedman, Adauctus, and two are neither-nor, Barbula and Paterculus.

The strong impression that arises from this is of a closely interlinked community. They may be distinguished in the hierarchy of status, but there is a great deal of overlap between each of the three categories, and a high proportion belonged to a relatively limited number of 'families'. This underlines what is perhaps the most striking characteristic of Herculaneum, which is a function of its small scale: it is what we can call a 'face-to-face' society, one

*Marble list of names of citizens.*

in which people could mostly know each other personally, and many had complex personal links. This is something that comes out of the case of the so-called Petronia Justa, the woman whose dispute over her status took a little group of people to Rome. Gaius Petronius Stephanus, who gave Justa's mother Vitalis her freedom, was one of a well-attested family: on the great list of names, we meet the freeborn Gaius Petronius Justus (did his name influence Justa's choice of *cognomen*?), freedmen called Celsus and Stephanus, and neither-nors called Cominianus (which on the face of it implies adoption from the family of Cominius) and (again) Stephanus. His wife, Calatoria Themis, belongs to the 'family' of Marcus Calatorius, and indeed Marcus Calatorius Speudon is one of those who stood bail for Petronia Justa, while the illiterate Marcus Calatorius Marullus was one who was confident that the girl in question was in fact a freedwoman. Calatoria Themis had a tutor, Gaius Petronius Telesphorus, a necessary figure in Roman law for one who no longer had a husband, though he managed to take the stand against his pupil. Gradually the network extends from those who are interlinked by name or friendship to the many witnesses who signed the documents, and draws into the picture more and more members of the community.

Perhaps because documentation of the same quality does not survive for Pompeii, but surely also because it was a larger community, though there are evidently multiple connections there too, the impression is of a society with more players, a larger and more competitive elite. The fact that it was so easy to know each other evidently did not stop the inhabitants of Herculaneum from quarrelling with each other, though in their nature legal documents tend to bring out disputes. Nor would we want to characterize the community of Herculaneum as inbred. Both the throughput of outsider residents (*incolae*) and the high levels of recruitment though slavery must have ensured that the gene pool was constantly refreshed. Nevertheless, it was a community within which a level of intimacy was possible. Where Pompeii can seem promiscuous, Herculaneum seems intimate, perhaps because the quality of the evidence allows us to get to know its population so well.

# 11
# THE FUTURE
# OF THE PAST

Herculaneum offers a window on the past of unique and irreplaceable value. But it is also fragmentary, fragile, at constant risk of loss. It is fragmentary, as the chapters above have stressed, both in the sense that the site is only partly excavated and, more importantly, in the sense that even what has been excavated is partial, the surviving pieces of the violent trauma of a volcanic eruption, then pieced together in a process of 'restoration' that both creates a misleading impression about the nature of the evidence and risks putting the values of tourist appeal above those of truth to the evidence. But even this concoction of surviving remains and restoration remains fragile and at risk.

The evidence is before the eyes of every passing tourist. Each house that is barred to public access is in a critical state: collapsed roofing, water dripping over delicate surfaces, frescoes faded and losing their pigment in flakes, plasterwork constantly disintegrating and falling off, mosaic floors blistering up and dissolving into their component *tesserae*, carbonized wood crumbling to dust, ceilings crashing to the floor, walls too long exposed to the elements unprotected finally slumping to the ground. Even the passer-by can see this much, and the weeds growing not only on floors but on rooftops, and pigeons, despite the deterrence of a regime of falcons, obstinately roosting in the site's

*Left: Tourists crowd the shop on the north-east corner of Insula IV.*

*Right: Damaged frescoes from the House of the Gem, with black paint faded to white (left) and from the new excavations in the south-west of the site (right).*

*Inside: The atrium of the House of the Bicentenary before conservation.*

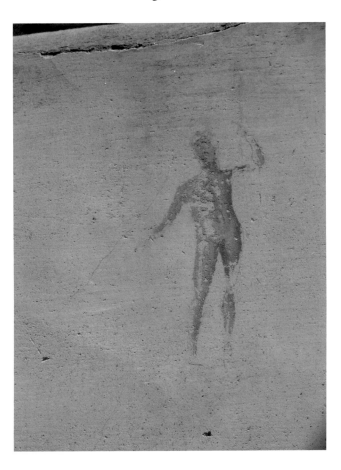

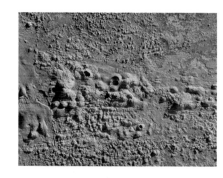

*Top: Frescoes damaged by salts.*

*Middle left: A mosaic floor in the House of the Stags damaged by standing water.*

*Middle right: Hawks struggle to keep the pigeons at bay.*

*Bottom: Standing water soaks a frescoed wall.*

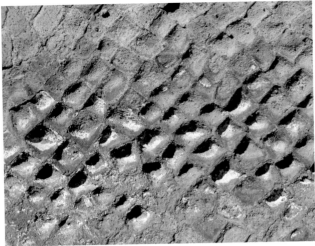

Top left: Detail of a disintegrating mosaic.

Top right: Wall eroded by salts.

Above: A carbonized wooden beam disintegrates as wax protection drips off.

abundant nooks and crannies. Not even the finest houses on the site, and most interesting to tourists, are spared this agony: the House of the Bicentenary, with its magnificent atrium and rare upper floor, is still closed after years: the room once made famous by the discovery of the mark of the cross in the plasterwork, which long attracted attention as potential evidence for early Christianity, though more recent scholarship reinterpreted the cross as the trace left by the support brackets for a cupboard, unusual and important though it was, lost its floor and no longer exists, while the roundels of satyrs and bacchants that decorated the *tablinum* have seen their brightly coloured paintwork flake off year by year.

Why? It is right to be angry, and natural to look for someone to blame. But nearly a decade's experience of a project designed to help to remedy these problems – the Herculaneum Conservation Project – suggests that the problems are highly complex, existing at numerous levels, defying any hope of a quick fix, and rendering it impossible to point the finger of blame in any one direction. Those who wish to preserve the site must face a daunting concatenation of seemingly intractable problems: the iron laws of physics that make decay inescapable, the difficulty of reconciling the demands of access to visitors with those of conservation, the management problems faced by the country blessed and cursed by what is often claimed to be the world's greatest concentration

*The House of the Bicentenary in archival photographs before the damage. The atrium (left) and the upper room with cupboard and supposed Christian cross (above).*

of heritage, and the profound social, economic and political problems that have haunted the Italian south for centuries. No problem can be solved at any one level without attending to the others.

The immediate and visible problems are physical. Change, not stability, is the natural order of the physical world: no structure and no object can remain untouched and unaltered over time unless energy is continuously injected into keeping it so, and even then we can only delay or slow down the process of change, which we see as decay. Conservators today no longer aspire to *stopping* decay, only to *minimizing* or *retarding* it. Seneca, whom we met in Chapter 1, with his understanding of the inherently

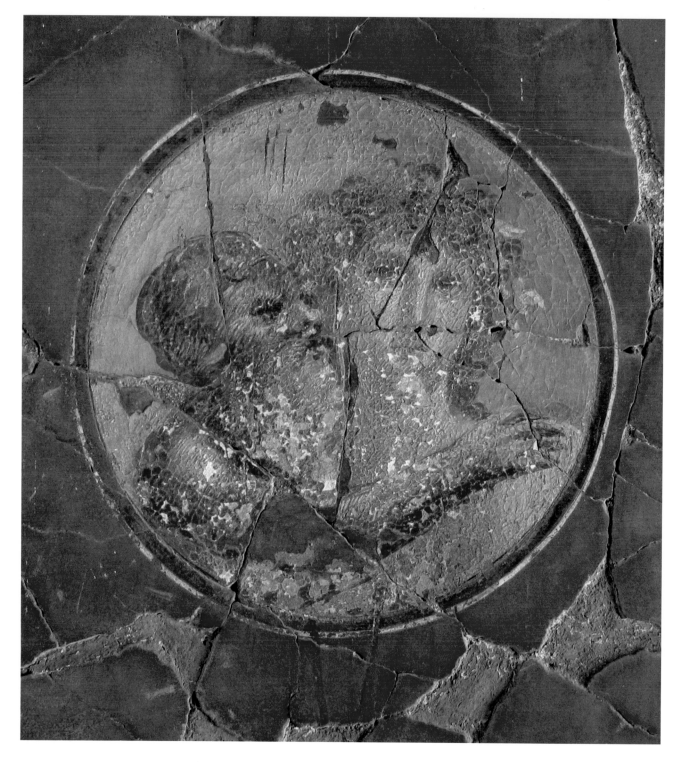

*Detail of the decoration from the tablinum of the House of the Bicentenary, satyr and maenad, with the upper layer of paintwork peeling off.*

unstable nature of the earth, already grasped the underlying philosophy. We understand better today the processes of geological change, the shifting of continental plates that remodels the earth's crust, and the longer processes of erosion by wind and water and changes of heat that constantly modify it. If time can make and remove mountains, what chance has a delicate archaeological site? To stand under the shadow of Vesuvius and demand permanence and stability is evidently unreasonable.

But it won't do to cite the second law of thermodynamics, point to entropy, and give up on conservation as an impossible goal. The conservation of archaeological remains is a problem that we create by the very act of excavating, and if we excavate, we must take responsibility for the consequences. In a famous scene in Fellini's *Roma*, the mechanical digger drilling a new metro line reveals a room full of frescoes, vivid with images of Roman life. But as rapidly as they are revealed, the frescoes fade and crumble, to the sound of whistling wind. It is an accurate, if accelerated, representation of the consequence of all archaeological excavation. If not before our eyes, then in the course of time, visible to anyone who observes over the course of years, frescoes fade and perish.

The earliest visitors to the Bourbon excavations in Herculaneum recognized this problem. So Horace Walpole in 1740:

> I forgot to tell you, that in several places the beams of the houses remain, but burnt to char-coal; so little damaged that they retain visibly the grain of the wood, but upon touching crumble to ashes.

It is precisely because the difficulties of preserving such fragile traces of the past have always been apparent that the history of the site is one of a long, and seemingly losing, battle against decay. Not infrequently, the attempts to preserve have added further to the damage. The early Bourbon policy of removing frescoes and mosaics, like statues and small finds, from their archaeological context, although we now dismiss it as treasure-hunting, was at the same time a strategy of conservation. We may disagree with it because of the damage caused to the archaeological context, yet the frescoes taken up to the Royal Palace at Portici, and later transferred to the Naples Museum, have generally survived a great deal better than those left *in situ*. The moment a fresco is exposed but left in place, in a new atmosphere drier than its old volcanic cladding, a thermodynamic imbalance is created and entropy indeed does its work. The moisture in the wall behind the fresco is drawn out, depositing the salts in the stone or the mortar on the face of the fresco. A fine white coat is formed, which rapidly hardens, causing permanent damage to the surface.

The frustration of seeing salts form and colours fade has led to a long history of physical interventions, from the varnishes applied by the Bourbons, to the wax and paraffin mixtures of the nineteenth and early twentieth centuries, to the paraloids favoured by restorers in the second half of the twentieth century. Each solution is in its own way damaging. Anything that forms a new and non-porous crust on the painted surface displaces rather than removes the problem. The moisture unable to breathe through the outer surface creates tensions between the outer layer and the careful build-up of layers of plaster below, causing the layer of paint to blister and flake off. A short-term gain and the fleeting opportunity of glamorous 'before and after' photographs leads in the end to irreparable damage. The search for a better chemical preparation to apply to the surface is misplaced. The winning strategy is to create the equilibrium of temperature and moisture that avoids the underlying problem. Interestingly enough, the removal of the fresco from the original context is one way in which to achieve a new equilibrium.

The specific conservation problems that the site faces are the direct consequence of decisions made about presentation. The early Bourbon solution of removal was driven not by conservation, but by the desire to make the palace and its new 'Herculanense Museum' the essential place of display. As we have seen, the new policy of leaving material *in situ* and making the site, especially that of Pompeii, the focus of the visitor experience was a response to the complaints and requests of the visitors. It was not accompanied by a corresponding policy of providing shelters on site, and the damage done in this period was perhaps the most rapid and irreversible of all phases of decay of the sites. By the late nineteenth century, a policy of reconstructing roofs enormously improved the situation; but it was partial and driven as much by the desire to provide the visitor with a more vivid and convincing experience.

Amedeo Maiuri took this approach to its most advanced expression. The 'living museum' he created at Herculaneum allowed a visitor experience of a quality never achieved before, with extensive reconstruction of roofs *ad identicum*, 'exactly like the original', and even display of objects in what appeared to be, but often was not, the original context. His display solution was also a conservation solution. He was deeply shocked by the speed of decay and destruction of the nineteenth-century excavations, and wished to avoid the same errors, employing the best technologies of his day. But the reinforced concrete he used for beams above doors and windows and solid flat roofs proved to have its own conservation problems: within half a century, penetration of damp caused the iron reinforcement bars to rust, expanding and causing the outer layer of cement to crack off and fall. To span the vast space of an atrium in what was supposed to look like the original fashion, concrete beams of vast weight were inserted, putting new stresses on the structures below. As they have decayed, a new problem has emerged. In theory, the best solution is to substitute them with wooden beams. Yet solid wooden beams of these dimensions are rarely known to modern carpentry, hard to source, and difficult to transport on site. The alternative of laminated wood was fashionable in the 1980s and 1990s, but laminated wood has its own problems in situations of damp, and the removal of large concrete beams is a difficult and traumatic process.

The success of Maiuri's solution in terms of visitor experience has its cost in terms of conservation problems. The more extensive and sophisticated the reconstruction of these Roman house-museums, the more demanding they are in terms of maintenance. When these solutions were adopted at the heyday of Fascist investment in archaeology, little thought was given to the cost implications for the future. Maiuri kept on site a team of dozens of skilled craftsmen (*maestranze*), who not only restored the houses as they emerged but provided the ongoing maintenance squad. Many of the conservation solutions of reconstruction *ad identicum*, the recreation of

a living house, are only possible if they go hand in hand with a maintenance regime such as a house would have enjoyed in antiquity: a hoard of slaves to keep the floors swept, the gardens weeded, the drains unblocked, the missing roof tiles replaced. Maiuri's squad was able to keep on top of the problems for a time, but they would be needed forever, or rather so long as the site survives in that state. The reduction of the maintenance team started immediately with his retirement, and continued in an ineluctable downward line until its complete elimination by the beginning of the twenty-first century. The authorities had enough of a struggle on their hands keeping up the team of custodians to police the behaviour of visitors, and maintenance went by the board.

A new generation of conservation solutions was already on its way. The conservation community by the late twentieth century was giving considerable thought to the problems of roofing archaeological sites. Reconstruction *ad identicum* was becoming deeply unfashionable, and the lack of authenticity of the very sites that tried hardest to be authentic, like Pompeii or Knossos, brought the traditional approach into disrepute. Archaeological 'shelters', which spanned the site on independent supports and made no pretence to reproduce the original situation, became increasingly popular. They also provided opportunities for the sort of metal-frame architecture which was in vogue in non-archaeological contexts like airports. Not all experiments were successful. A segment of the brand new shelter over Akrotiri on Thera, the Minoan site preserved by a volcanic eruption a millennium and a half before the Vesuvian cities, collapsed, killing a visitor and leading to the indefinite closure of the site. The ambitious tensile structure over the 'Hanghäuser' of Ephesus has proved to create new problems of heat, and has had a questionable aesthetic impact on the rest of the site. Less ambitious experiments were made at Pompeii, and the simple scaffolding roof over the new excavations of the House of the Chaste Lovers provided

both an unparalleled degree of protection against the elements and a visitor experience which, rather than presenting the house as if immediately before the moment of its destruction, made visible the process of destruction itself, and even the process of archaeological exploration. But this solution in turn created maintenance problems, as the brittle and inaccessible corrugated plastic roofing sheets broke and let in water. The same problems tormented the temporary shelter over the new excavations at the Villa of the Papyri, and new roofing in more robust material has been recently installed. Its success, like the success of all previous solutions, can only be judged against the test of time.

Perhaps the hardest challenge in conservation is to get the balance right between major interventions, at high cost but one-off capital investments, and less ambitious but annually or periodically repeating continuous care regimes. There are extraneous political and economic reasons for favouring major, one-off interventions. In Italy, as in many countries, it is easier to find occasional, one-off funding for such major projects than the steady revenue stream which continuous care requires. In particular, the arrival of what is regarded as windfall funding, notably in the form of grants from the European Union, favours such ambitious projects which deliver conspicuous results. But these have often proved too hasty in their planning, and too inflexible in their execution, trapped in an endless sequence of bureaucratic structures and processes. And, whether they acknowledge it or not, the major interventions generate a legacy of maintenance needs.

Whose problem is all this anyway? The Italian State, the local area, or the entire gamut of 'stakeholders', those to whom the site has importance, including the local tourist industry, the visitors themselves, and the international community of scholars? The answer in law is clear. The Italian constitution defines all heritage as the responsibility of the Italian State. A wise provision makes

*Above: The atrium of the House of the Gem in 2001, with collapsed roof tiles.*

*Overleaf left: The House of the Gem before (above) and after (below) conservation work.*

*Overleaf right: The upper terrace of the Palaestra before conservation work.*

illegal the sale of heritage outside the country. All archaeological heritage is regarded as the property of the State and inalienable. The responsibility for the protection (*tutela*) of this heritage is delegated to the Ministry of Culture, which organizes the country into regions, each with its own director, and within the regions into superintendencies. 'Pompei', which includes Herculaneum and all the archaeological sites buried by the eruption of AD 79, became in 1980 a superintendency in its own right, separate from Naples. In 1997, an important reform assigned it partial autonomy, the most important feature of which was a degree of financial autonomy, in particular the control of the revenues generated by ticket sales, and the ability to raise money by sales (e.g. from the bookshop) and by sponsorship deals, including the rental to one of the most prominent wine producers in Campania of the plots within Pompeii where vines had grown in antiquity. As part of this financial independence, the superintendency was given its own financial administrator or 'City Manager', on a par with the superintendent responsible for archaeology. This arrangement persisted until 2008, when Pompeii and Naples were reunited, and the anomaly of the financial administrator not reporting to the superintendent was eliminated. The united superintendency retained the special status of financial autonomy previously restricted to Pompei. Further reforms, however, are imminent.

Because the Italian State assumes responsibility for *tutela*, it follows that any failure in the protection and maintenance of the site is technically its failing, and that of the officials to whom responsibility is delegated locally. In a laudable display of candour, the superintendent for the last fifteen years, 1995–2009, Professor Pietro Giovanni Guzzo, drew the attention of the Ministry, the public, and the international scholarly community to the crushing difficulties he faced in delivering what was imposed on him by law. The bureaucracy of the superintendency, in his analysis, was not fit for purpose. The personnel was unbalanced, with a dearth of the sort of professional support the site required and a long tail of under-qualified staff enjoying job protection in roles that were marginal (an excess, for instance, of librarians). The effectiveness of the staff, he argued, was stifled by an excess of bureaucratic procedures, diverting effort into formalities. Above all, the laws which were set up to protect against fraud and corruption slowed down urgent interventions to a snail's pace. The law governing public works required contracts to be given to the lowest bidder satisfying stated criteria, and thereby generated endless legal appeals, and resulting perversely in the award of contracts to underqualified firms unscrupulous enough to underbid, and compensate by bad quality work.

Guzzo's analysis, building on that on the distinguished economist, Luca Zan, never made explicit the political dimension of the problem, the perennial distortion of public administration by political clientelism, the corrosive trade of jobs for votes and political support. The role of 'City Manager', designed to bring healthy managerial experience to the administration of an archaeological site run by archaeologists, rapidly proved too tempting to politicians on both sides of the spectrum, who saw in the financial management of the site access to Pompeii's revenues, and to the lucrative contracts those would generate. At one point, resources amounting to tens of millions were diverted from the superintendency, allegedly to finance work in the northern city where the then Minister was standing as candidate. In any case, the division of powers between superintendent and administrator only led to stalemate, and the damaging delay of pressing conservation work.

The thing that Guzzo, beset by such problems, seized upon from the outset was the role of the international community in protecting and supporting the site. Launching an appeal to universities and learned bodies (such as the foreign academies) both in Italy and internationally, he stimulated a new generation of dozens of projects in Pompeii, particularly with

*The atrium of the House of the Gem after insertion of temporary roofing in 2006.*

the aim of documenting and publishing a still lamentably unpublished site. It is rare for archaeological projects to come with sufficient resource to permit conservation work, though even here documentation could provide the superintendency with the essential knowledge base for future conservation. It was fully in line with this spirit of international collaboration that when, in 2000, the Packard Humanities Institute expressed interest in a project in Herculaneum that would address some of the problems of conservation, Guzzo grasped a potential that went beyond financial resource. If, as he argued, the superintendency was clogged up by its own bureaucratic procedures and shortage of qualified technical staff, an externally financed and run conservation project could have the freedom to find the right experts and consultants, intervene without the impediments of red tape, experiment with new and more effective solutions, and produce new recipes for conservation that would eventually translate into a new set of more effective bureaucratic procedures. The project was set up with American philanthropic finance, a scientific committee composed of heritage experts of international standing, and a predominantly Italian team

*Below: Replacement of flat roofs in the Palaestra block.*

*Right: Temporary roof over the tower of the House of the Telephus Relief during (left) and after (right) construction.*

on the ground, chosen to pull together expertise in archaeology, architectural conservation, conservation of surfaces and artefacts, structural and hydraulic engineering, chemical analysis, archaeological surveying and IT management.

The standard model for a conservation project is to take a specific house or group of structures and attempt to address all problems comprehensively. The downside to large projects on isolated areas of a site is that they fail to address the needs of the site as a whole or see beyond the boundaries of the house or project in question. A roofing solution which considers only the house in question, and then, by throwing water on to a neighbouring house, creates new problems there, is merely moving the problem on, not solving it. Driven by these considerations, the Herculaneum Conservation Project, which had initially aimed to 'restore' one *insula*, the Insula Orientalis I (incluing the House of the Telephus Relief and the House of the Gem), comprehensively addressing all its conservation problems, shifted its priorities to site-wide infrastructural issues of three types.

The first, and most urgent, was to provide an adequate drainage network for the site as a whole, and this could be best done by reactivating, so far as possible, the ancient drainage system. Anyone who has witnessed the damage, across the entire site, caused by water standing pooled on ancient pavements, seeping though to the very rooms which have been protected by roofing, and creeping up the decorative surfaces causing paint to fade and plaster to collapse, understands how essential a basic drainage system is. The fact that the one the Romans provided was effective and extensive makes the intervention less traumatic to the site.

The next infrastructural issue was roofing. Damage to decorated surfaces correlates closely with damage to, or absence of, roofs. On the traditional model, a roof is only repaired in the context of a project on a house as a whole, and the snail-like progress of such projects left numerous roofs compromised. By constructing a project 'typologically', aimed at the repair of a series of different roofs in different locations that presented similar problems, it is possible to accelerate the process and dramatically slow down the damage.

The third and most important element is that of continuous care. It is not a substitute for big restoration projects, but something that must necessarily follow them if the good is to last. If the site cannot afford a standing maintenance team such as Maiuri built up, with an accumulation of transmitted knowledge about what the recurrent problems are, and how and when to address them, the alternative must be to draw up schedules which the managers of the site can implement effectively, analysing in detail the typology of problems that will recur, and providing tested and costed solutions. That in turn requires a continuity of monitoring. Mistakes are inevitable, but a site can learn from them. It is by periodically monitoring how successfully past solutions stand up to the test of time that they can be improved.

How much can international help achieve, and at what point is it better to leave the problems to local hands? The relations between the Pompeian authorities and the international community have had a difficult history. The international pressure on the Vesuvian sites is both a blessing and a curse. From the earliest visitors, like Horace Walpole and Thomas Gray, and even more

*Conservator-restorers at work stabilizing frescoes.*

markedly Johann Joachim Winckelmann, foreigners have felt that this is material of exceptional quality and interest for the international community, and that the perceived shortcomings of the local authorities should not be tolerated. The Bourbon kings learnt that their discoveries were a two-edged weapon: they brought a massive advantage in terms of international profile, along with a disadvantage in exposure to international criticism.

In 1860, the novelist Alexandre Dumas asked Garibaldi, in reward for his significant assistance, for two favours: a permit to hunt in the park of Capodimonte and the continuation of the excavations of Pompeii. As he wrote to Garibaldi:

> Do you wish all the papers, all the artists, all the painters, all the sculptors, all the architects to give a cry of joy? Then issue a decree couched in these terms: 'In the name of the artistic world, the excavations of Pompeii will be started again and continued without interruption once I am at Naples'.

Garibaldi granted Dumas part of his wish, in making him Honorary Director of the Museum and Excavations, but the appointment caused vigorous local protests, and eventually a riot demanding his dismissal. The figure who emerged from this confusion as the new excavator of Pompeii was, as we saw in Chapter 2, the great Giuseppe Fiorelli, but the episode had exposed the deep ambivalence of locals towards the wrong kind of international interest. Charles Waldstein encountered the same type of Italian hostility to his project for an international excavation of Herculaneum in the first decade of the twentieth century, and Giuseppe Maggi felt he was faced by something of the same in the resistance to his American-funded project in the 1980s. The foreign community, rather than resenting this, should bear in mind that, while in broad terms the sites may be 'world heritage' and the common property of mankind, in legal fact they are the inalienable property of the Italian State, and that morally the sites belong also to the local population, a fragment of whose tangled history they represent. International help can only work if actually wanted by local interests.

It is perhaps here that the crux of the problem lies. The relationship between local interests and the Vesuvian sites is ambivalent and complex. Beyond question, the sites are honeypots, attracting millions of visitors a year, and raising the international fame and profile of the area to levels that are the envy of other, less fortunate, regions. The profit that visitors bring to the area, to hotels, restaurants, bars, souvenir and other shops, agencies, tour guides, let alone employment on the sites themselves, is gigantic – the Regione Campania reckons its tourist industry in the area to generate a turnover of tens of billions. In an area whose economy and industry have still not recovered from the lopsided impact of the unification of Italy in 1860 under the most northerly of its kingdoms, Piedmont, this is all the more significant.

Yet profit does not flow into the hands of those who shoulder the burdens and costs. The Ministry itself is well aware of the potential of profiting from visitors, has introduced bookshops on site in both Pompeii and Herculaneum, and, rather late in the day, is beginning to realize the potential of sales of food and drink. Nevertheless, the real profits go off site, and especially in the case of Ercolano, well beyond local hands, to the hotels of Sorrento or Naples, to international tourist agencies and the shipping lines that run cruises. The 'Urban Herculaneum' project has seen a regeneration of local business, with the establishment of a luxury hotel, a string of bed-and-breakfast facilities, many in historic buildings, and a new growth of high-class restaurants. Nevertheless, for the locals the commonest type of tourist is 'mordi e fuggi', 'bite and run', descending on the site for a couple of hours, only to hurry off elsewhere. Inescapably, the result is a sense of alienation, a feeling that the archaeological site is a mere hole in the modern city, a wound in its fabric, run by the State without reference to local interests and visited by outsiders with equally little interest in its local context.

The danger of alienation of the local community is mirrored by the equal danger of alienation of the visitor. The proximity to the site of houses of the modern town, many in a ruinous condition, leads to the perception of the modern town as an incumbrance, one indeed that prevents the full excavation of the site. Nor is the experience of passing through the streets of one of the most crowded communities in Europe as welcoming as it might be. Add to that the distress caused by persistent problems with refuse collection, and the fear generated by the unseen but ever-present proximity of organized crime, and it is not surprising that many see the area as one to be entered with caution and left with haste. It takes time, a privilege of those working longer on site, to come to see the local context with different eyes: the rich historical fabric of the string of magnificent eighteenth-century villas spawned by the Bourbon court, strung along the main road of the Corso Resina, and the rich local colour of the clothing market that stretches up via Pugliano.

Modern Ercolano is caught between two worlds – of beauty and squalor, of cultural wealth and social degradation. The negative elements are there. The role of the Bay of Naples in the international drugs trade has led to the growth of powerful local Camorra clans (the Ascione and Birra are frequently named in local papers), though no visitor to the ancient site is likely to see any sign of them, for archaeology has never offered the quick and easy profits they look for, and the worst to be feared is extortion from construction and earth-moving firms. But against this should be set the widespread desire of the local population to improve and modernize their community, and the determination of the local authorities to promote the necessary urban regeneration. The local municipal authority (*comune*), which in 1969 sought to take advantage of the international reputation of the ancient site by changing its name from Resina to Ercolano, and by taking Hercules as its symbol, has continued to place the site at the heart of its strategy of regeneration. The creation of a new access route, coach park and entrance complex has transformed the accessibility of the site. Major grants have been successfully procured from the *regione* (ultimately from the European Community) for improving the juncture between

modern city and site, most recently through the reinforcement of the north escarpment and the creation of a new pedestrian access bridge.

It is only by pulling together and combining the efforts of the 'stakeholders' – the State, the local authorities and the international community – that real progress can be made. The desire on all three sides to do so led to the creation of the new body, the Associazione Herculaneum, and a new institute under its aegis, the International Centre for the Study of Herculaneum, with its mission to foster international and local interest in the site. By relaunching an old initiative of Amedeo Maiuri in the building which housed his study centre and which came to bear his name (the Villa Maiuri), it acknowledges the transformational impact which Maiuri's excavations had upon the modern city. Appropriately, then, two of the first initiatives of the centre have been to gather the oral history of memories of Maiuri's times, and to generate a new programme in local primary schools of awareness of the site.

When Maiuri retired in 1961, he left unfinished business, to which he rightly attached great importance. The focus of his excavations of the 1920s and 1930s had been determined by the relationship between the ancient and modern cities. He started with the south-eastern quarter of the ancient town because this was the part least impeded by modern housing. But gradually he bought up and demolished the houses that overlay the Decumanus Maximus. His major ambition in the 1950s was to push the excavations towards the heart of the ancient town to the north-west. This involved a massive campaign of expropriations and demolitions, financed by funds for the support of South Italy, the Cassa del Mezzogiorno. Archaeologically, Maiuri was driven by the desire to reach the monumental heart of the town and its trio of public buildings. But he was also deeply conscious of, and vocal in expressing, an obligation to the local community. The part of the modern city that overlapped the site was the

most run-down slum area. He sent in photographers to document, and their images leave no doubt of the poverty and degradation of the area, nor of the grotesque juxtaposition of these slums and the site. The programme he pioneered would bring a double benefit to the modern city: the demolition of these slums (together with the rehousing of the population) and the addition of a major new attraction to the ancient site. His retirement left this project suspended midway. While many houses had been demolished and the excavations advanced, a cluster of buildings above the Basilica and to the north of the site along what was once via dei Cortili were left as abandoned ruins. Some progressively collapsed into the road below, leading to the abandonment of via dei Cortili; some were illicitly reoccupied; some remained as gaunt skeletons, overhanging the site, especially the large block that came to be known as the Barbacane (Barbican) from its fortress-like appearance.

This situation persisted for over forty years, and in the meantime the social degradation of the area kept pace with its physical ruin, as drug-pushers moved in on it as a no-man's land. Visitors to the site were appalled by the spectacle of modern ruins overhanging ancient ones. The juxtaposition symbolized the unhealthy relationship of the two worlds, ancient and modern. As this emerged as one of the most urgent problems of the site to be addressed, and as the willingness of the Comune to collaborate became apparent, an alliance was formed of Comune, State and Conservation Project. The Packard Humanities Institute provided support for acquiring property on the edge of the site, the project provided technical support in resolving questions of legal ownership, and the Comune embarked, in the summer of 2006, on a major campaign of demolitions that finally cleared a swathe of land to the north and west of the site.

The demolitions have cleared the way for a new campaign of excavation, one which promises to bring to light the Basilica. But it is not a matter of returning to the days of Maiuri. At least as much of

*Left above: The Villa Maiuri, home to the International Centre for the Study of Herculaneum.*

*Left below: Hercules from the Villa Comunale of Ercolano, office of the mayor, celebrating the renaming of Resina as Ercolano in 1969.*

These pages and overleaf: Photographic campaign by the Soprintendenza of Pompei in the 1950s, before expropriation and demolition in 1955–61.

Herculaneum still lies buried as has been exposed, including the major part of the Villa of the Papyri. It is no longer a sustainable ambition to excavate the entire site. We cannot afford, and would have difficulty in justifying, the demolition of *all* modern buildings above the site. They represent the historical core of the modern settlement, going back to the Bourbon period and before, and have their own historical value. Even could we simply remove them and excavate, who would then sustain the burden of maintenance of a much larger site, when the already existing excavations prove so hard to maintain?

New excavation can best be justified in the context of a strategy that renders the site easier, not harder, to manage. The demolitions carried out in recent years have been of houses already in a ruinous condition. Many of the remaining houses overlooking the site are structurally sound and require upgrading (provision of modern services, etc.). The enviable views they afford over the site render them an ideal location for support services to the site – restaurants, bars, bed-and-breakfast establishments. Here, if anywhere, it can be demonstrated that archaeology can work to the advantage of the local economy. What is needed

*Below: Renewed campaign of demolitions by the Comune of Ercolano in 2007.*

*Overleaf: North-eastern corner of the site with view over the Palaestra to the access bridge.*

is not further enlargement of the site for its own sake, but the completion of unfinished business, the excavation of a major Roman building left partially exposed, and the definition of a new boundary to the site that allows it to sit comfortably within the envelope of the modern city.

Twenty-five years ago, Joseph Jay Deiss ended the revised version of his book, *Herculaneum: Italy's Buried Treasure*, with these words:

> So far as is known, nowhere else in all the world is such a time capsule waiting to be opened. Antiquity is Italy's greatest natural resource, Herculaneum the richest of all fields. It seems incredible and absurd to discover a buried treasure – and not to dig it up.

> But buried treasure lies secure for future generations. For our own generation, it is enough to appreciate the extraordinary value of the treasure that has already been dug up, to look after it as it merits, and to pass it on to future generations.

*Northern escarpment of the site with modern housing above.*

*Overleaf: Detail of the Samnite House.*

# FURTHER READING

## General Reading

Books devoted to Herculaneum have been rare. The principal modern publication is:

Amedeo MAIURI, *Ercolano. I nuovi scavi*, 2 vols (Rome 1958).

The same author produced more popular versions of his excavation results:

Amedeo MAIURI, *Ercolano* (Novara 1932), as well as his valuable guidebook in the series of 'Guidebooks to the Museums, Galleries and Monuments of Italy' published both in Italian and English between 1936 (first edition) and 1970 (seventh edition).

Modern guidebooks in Italian include:

Mario PAGANO, *Ercolano. Itinerario archeologico ragionato* (Naples 1997).

Mario PAGANO, *Gli Scavi di Ercolano* (Naples 2003).

Fabrizio PESANDO and Maria Paola GUIDOBALDI, *Pompei Oplontis Ercolano Stabiae* (Guide Archeologiche Laterza, Rome-Bari 2006).

Maria Paola GUIDOBALDI, *Ercolano: Guida agli Scavi* (Electa Napoli 2006).

The most significant books in English are:

Charles WALDSTEIN and Leonard SHOOBRIDGE, *Herculaneum: Past, Present & Future* (London 1908).

Joseph Jay DEISS, *Herculaneum. Italy's Buried Treasure* (first edition, New York 1966, revised edition 1985, reissued by the J. Paul Getty Museum 1989).

See also:

Ethel Ross BARKER, *Buried Herculaneum* (London 1908)

Among numerous general books principally on Pompeii, one which gives particular space to Herculaneum is:

Michael GRANT, *Cities of Vesuvius: Pompeii and Herculaneum* (London 1971).

Some of the most valuable recent publications have been in the form of exhibition catalogues:

Mario PAGANO (ed.), *Gli antichi Ercolanesi. Antopologia, Società, Economia* (Ercolano, 30 marzo–26 luglio 2000) (Naples 2000).

Antonio D'AMBROSIO, Marisa MASTROBERTO, Pietro Giovanni GUZZO (eds), *Storie da un'eruzione. Pompei, Ercolano, Oplontis* (Naples Museum, 20 March–31 August 2003) (Milan 2003).

Josef MÜHLENBROCK and Dieter RICHTER (eds), *Verschüttert vom Vesuv. Die letzten Stunden von Herculaneum* (Mainz am Rhein 2005).

Maria Paola GUIDOBALDI (ed), *Ercolano. Tre secoli di scoperte* (Naples Museum, 16 October 2008–13 April 2009) (Naples 2008).

## Chapter 1 Geology

Modern understanding of the eruption starts with:

Haraldur SIGURDSSON, S. CASHDOLLAR and S.R.J. SPARKS, 'The eruption of Vesuvius in AD 79: reconstruction from historical and volcanological evidence', *Amercian Journal of Archaeology* 88 (1982), 39–57; see also

Haraldur SIGURDSSON, S. CAREY and T. PESCATORE, 'The eruption of Vesuvius in AD 79', *National Geographic Research* 1 (1985), 332–87.

Haraldur SIGURDSSON and Stephen CAREY, 'The eruption of Vesuvius in AD 79' in *The Natural History of Pompeii*, edited by Wilhelmina Jashemski and Frederick G. Mayer (Cambridge 2002), 37–64.

Ernesto DE CAROLIS and Giuseppe PATRICELLI, *Vesuvius AD 79. The Destruction of Pompeii and Herculaneum* (Rome 2003).

On the excavations of the ancient shoreline in the 1980s, see:

Giuseppe MAGGI, *Ercolano: fine di una città* (Naples 1985).

On the dynamics of the destruction of humans, see:

Giuseppe MASTROLORENZO, Pier Paolo PETRONE et al, 'Herculaneum victims of Vesuvius in AD 79' in *Nature* 410 (2001), 769–70; see also:

Pier Paolo PETRONE and Francesco FEDELE, *Vesuvio 79 AD Vita e morte ad Ercolano. Mostra fotografica e di reperti archeologica* (catalogue of exhibition held at Napoli, Museo di Antropologia 13 maggio-13 luglio 2002).

On new evidence for bradyseism at Herculaneum, see:

Aldo CINQUE and Giolinda IROLLO, 'La paleogeografia dell'antica *Herculaneum* e le fluttuazioni, di origine bradisismica, della sua linea di costa' in *Nuove Ricerche archeologiche nell'area Vesuviana*, edited by P.G. Guzzo and M.P. Guidobaldi (Rome 2008) 425–38, with 'Lo scavo dell'Ala meridionale della Casa del Rilievo di Telefo' in the same volume, 421–3.

Aldo CINQUE, Linda IROLLO & Domenico CAMARDO, 'Antiche attività estrattive e cicli bradisismici sulla costa della antica Herculaneum: percorsi, esisti e prospettive di una ricerca geoarcheologica' in Antonella CORALINI (ed.), *Vesuviana: archeologie a confronto. Proceedings of the international conference, Bologna, 14–16 January 2008* (Bologna 2009), 261–76.

## Chapter 2 The Politics of Archaeology

On the history of the Bourbon excavations, the best account is:

Christopher C. PARSLOW, *Rediscovering Antiquity: Karl Weber and the Excavation of Herculaneum, Pompeii and Stabiae* (Cambridge 1995); see also:

Sergio PACE, *Herculaneum and European Culture between the Eighteenth and Nineteenth Centuries* (Naples 2000).

On the Bourbon Court, the classic account remains:

Harold ACTON, *The Bourbons of Naples, 1734–1825* (London 1974).

On the political background of excavations, see:

Agnes ALLROGGEN BEDEL, 'Gli scavi di Ercolano nella politica culturale dei Borboni' in *Ercolano 1738–1988. 250 anni di ricerca archeologica*, edited by L. Franchi Dell'Orto (Rome 1993), 35–40.

On the Royal collection at Portici, see:

Renata CANTILENA and Annnalisa PORZIO (eds), *Herculanense Museum. Laboratorio sull'antico nella Reggia di Portici* (Naples 2008).

On the Prince d'Elbeuf, see:

Valerio PAPACCIO, *Marmi Ercolanesi in Francia. Storia di alcune distrazioni del Principe E.M. d'Elbeuf* (Naples 1995).

The principal eighteenth-century publications are:

Marcello VENUTI, *Descrizione delle prime scoperte dell'antica città d'Ercolano, ritrovata vicino a Portici, villa della Maestà del Re delle Due Sicilie* (Rome 1748).

Charles-Nicolas COCHIN and Jérôme-Charles BELLICARD, *Observations sur les antiquités d'Herculanum; suivies de Lettre sur les peintures d'Herculanum aujourd'hui Portici* (Paris 1751, reprinted Geneva 1971).

Ottavio Antonio BAYARDI (Accademia Ercolanese), *Le Antichità di Ercolano Esposte* 9 vols (Royal Press, Naples 1755–1792, available online at http://www.picure.l.u-tokyo.ac.jp/arc/ercolano/index.html

Thomas MARTYN and John LETTICE, *The Antiquities of Herculaneum* (London 1773).

Original documents of the eighteenth-century excavations were later published by:

Michele RUGGIERO, *Storia degli scavi di Ercolano ricomposta su' documenti superstiti* (Naples 1885), supplemented by:

U. PANNUTI, 'Il "Giornale degli Scavi" di Ercolano (1738–1756)' *Memorie Accademia Lincei, scienze morali* series 8 26 (1983) 143–410.

Mario PAGANO, *I diari di scavo di Pompei Ercolano e Stabiae di Francesco e Pietro La Vega (1764–1810)* (Rome 1997).

Mario PAGANO, *I primi anni degli scavi di Ercolano, Pompei e Stabiae. Raccolta e studio di documenti e disegni inediti* (Rome 2005).

Mario PAGANO e Raffaele PRISCIANDARO, *Studio sulle provenienze degli oggetti rinvenuti negli scavi borbonici del regno di Napoli. Una letteratura integrata, coordinata e commentata della documentazione* (Castellamare di Stabia 2006).

## Chapter 3 Ruins Restored

On Maiuri's excavations, the most valuable source is the *Giornali degli Scavi* held in the Superintendency, but now available in digital format. On his vision for Herculaneum, see particularly:

Domenico CAMARDO, 'Gli scavi ed I restauri di Amedeo Maiuri. Ercolano e l'esperimento di una città Museo' in *Ocnus. Quaderni della Scuola di Specializzazione in Archeologia di Bologna* 14 (2006), 69–81.

Maria Paola GUIDOBALDI, 'La bottega di un *gemmarius* (Ins.Or. II,10) e l'ingannevole "stanza della ricamatrice"' in *Storie da un'eruzione* (above), 102–119.

In general on Maiuri, see:

Giuseppe MAGGI, *Archeologia magica di Amedeo Maiuri* (Naples 1974).

Carlo BELLI (ed), *Amedeo Maiuri mestiere d'archeologo. Antologia di scritti* (Naples 1978).

Maiuri recalls his meeting with Waldstein in:

Amedeo MAIURI, *Dallo scavo di Ercolano allo svolgimento dei papiri: scritti e documenti inediti* (edited by Mario CAPASSO) (Naples 1991).

## Chapter 4 The Town in its Setting

For Campania, Naples and the Bay of Naples, see:

John D'ARMS, *The Romans on the Bay of Naples: A Social and Cultural Study of the Villas and their Owners from 150 BC to AD 400* (Cambridge, Mass. 1970).

Paul ARTHUR, *Naples, from Roman Town to City-State* (London 2002).

Martin FREDERIKSEN, *Campania*, edited with additions by Nicholas PURCELL (Rome 1984).

David RIDGWAY, *The First Western Greeks* (Cambridge 1992).

On the cult of Hercules, see:

Antonella CORALINI, *Hercules Domesticus. Immagini di Ercole nelle case della regione vesuviana (1 secolo a.C.–79 d.C.)* (Naples 2001).

Umberto PAPPALARDO, 'Le culte d'Héraklès à Herculanum', *Antike Kunst* 36 (1993), 140–1.

On the town plan, see:

John B. WARD-PERKINS, 'Note di topografia e urbanistica' in *Pompei 79* (edited by Fausto ZEVI) (Naples 1979), 25–39.

Werner JOHANNOWSKY, 'Problemi urbanistici di Ercolano', *Cronache Ercolanesi* 12 (1982), 145–9.

On the villa of the Papyri and its owners, see:

Domenico COMPARETTI and G DE PETRA, *La villa ercolanese dei Pisoni. I suoi monumenti e la sua biblioteca* (Turin 1883, reprinted Naples 1972).

Robin G.M. NISBET, *Cicero, In L. Calpurnium Pisonem Oratio*, edited with introduction and commentary (Oxford 1961) 183–7.

Marcello GIGANTE (ed), *La villa dei Papiri* (*Cronache Ercolanesi* 13, 1983).

R WOJCIK, *La Villa dei Papiri ad Ercolano* (Rome 1986).

Stefania ADAMO MUSCETTOLA, *La Villa dei Papiri ad Ercolano* (Naples 2000).

Antonio DE SIMONE and Fabrizio RUFFO, 'Ercolano 1996–1998. Lo scavo della Villa dei Papiri', *Cronache Ercolanesi* 32 (2002) 325–44.

Antonio DE SIMONE and Fabrizio RUFFO, 'Ercolano e la villa dei Papiri alla luce dei nuovi scavi' in *Cronache Ercolanesi* 33 (2003) 279–311.

Carol C. MATTUSCH, *The Villa dei Papiri at Herculaneum. Life and Afterlife of a Sculpture Collection* (Los Angeles 2005).

Valeria MOESCH, 'La Villa dei Papiri' in *Ercolano. Tre Secoli di scoperte*, 71–9.

Mantha ZARMOKOUPI (ed.), *The Villa of the Papyri at Herculaneum: Archaeology, Reception and Digital Reconstruction* (Berlin 2010).

On the Getty Villa:

Kenneth LAPATIN, *Guide to the Villa and its Gardens* (Los Angeles 2005).

Marion TRUE and Jorge SILVETTI, *The Getty Villa* (Los Angeles 2005).

On the south-western corner of the site:

Maria Paola GUIDOBALDI, Domenico ESPOSITO and Eleonora FORMISANO, 'L'insula I, l'insula nord-occidentale e la Villa dei Papiri di Ercolano: una sintesi delle conoscenze alla luce delle recent indagini archeologiche' in *Vesuviana* 1 (2009), 43–182.

## Chapter 5 Inhabitants

On the excavation of skeletons by the shore and their analysis, see:

Giuseppe MAGGI, 'Lo scavo dell'area suburbana meridionale di Ercolano' in *Rivista di Studi Pompeiani* 9 (1998), 167–72.

Sarah BISEL, 'Human bones at Herculaneum' in *Rivista di Studi Pompeiani* 1 (1987), 123–9.

Sarah BISEL and Jane BISEL, 'Health and nutrition at Herculaneum: an examination of human skeletal remains' in *The Natural History of Pompeii*, edited by Wilhelmina JASHEMSKI and Frederick G. MEYER (Cambridge 2002), 451–75.

Luigi CAPASSO, *I Fuggischi di Ercolano. Paleobiologia delle vittime dell'eruzione vesuviana* (Rome 2001).

Ernesto DE CAROLIS and Mario PAGANO in *Storie da un'eruzione* (2003), 124–49.

Pier Paolo PETRONE and Francesco FEDELE, *Vesuvio 79 AD: Vita e morte ad Ercolano* (catalogue of Naples, Museum of Anthropology exhibition of 13 May to 13 July 2002) (Naples 2002).

On the inscriptional evidence for the inhabitants of Herculaneum, the two principal sources of information are the waxed wooden tablets and the list ('Album') of names. Both await the completion of a fundamental study by Giuseppe Camodeca. In the mean time, on the waxed wooden tablets, see:

Giuseppe PUGLIESE CARRATELLI and Vincenzo ARANGIO RUIZ, 'Tabulae Herculanenses', Parola del Passato il 81946), 3 (1948), 6 (1951, 8 (1953), 9 (1954), 10 (1955), 12 81957), 16 (1961).

Giuseppe CAMODECA, 'Per una riedizione delle Tabulae Herculanenses. I' in Cronache Ercolanesi 23 (1993), 109–19.

_____, 'Per una riedizione delle tabulae Herculanenses. II. I nomina arcaria TH. 70 + 71 e TH. 74', Ostraka 2.2 (1993), 197–209.

_____, 'Riedizione del trittico ercolanese TH 77+78+80+53+92 del gennaio 69' in Cronache Ercolanesi 24 (1994), 137–46.

_____, 'La ricostruzione dell'élite municipale ercolanese degli anni 50–70 d.C.: problemi di metodo e risultati preliminari' in Cahiers Glotz 7 (1996), 167–78.

_____, 'Le tavolette cerate di Ercolano' in Gli antichi Ercolanesi (2000), 71–4.

_____, 'Per una riedizione dell'archivio ercolanese di L. Venidius Ennychus. I' in Cronache Ercolanesi 32 (2002), 257–80.

_____, 'I papiri documentari ercolanesi (PHERC. MAN): relazione preliminare' in Cronache Ercolanesi 32 (2002), 281–96.

_____, 'Une inedita THerc. E la corretta lezione di Tacito, Hist. IV 7.2: Cn. Sentius Saturninus, cos. 41, damnatus ex S.C. nel 66' in Zeitschrift für Papyrologie und Epigraphik 144 (2003), 235–8.

_____, 'Per una riedizione dell'archivio ercolanese di L. Venidius Ennychus. II' in Cronache Ercolanesi 36 (2006), 189–211.

_____, 'La società ercolanese alla luce della riedizione delle Tabulae Herculanenses. L'élite municipale fra Claudio e VespasianoI: un'oligarchia ritrovata' in Ostraka 15 (2006), 9–29.

_____, 'La popolazione degli ultimi decenni di Ercolano' in Ercolano. Tre Secoli di scoperte (2008), 86–103.

_____, 'Gli archivi privati di tabulae ceratae e di papiri documentari a Pompei ed Ercolano : case ambienti e modalità di conservazione' Vesuviana 1 (2009), 17–42.

On the lists of the so-called Augustales, see:

Giuseppe GUADAGNO, 'Frammenti inediti di albi degli Augustali' in Cronache Ercolanesi 7 (1977), 114–22.

Mario PAGANO, 'Nuovi frammenti di albi da Ercolano' in Cronache Ercolanesi 22 (1992), 189–95.

Paul WEAVER, 'Children of Junian Latins' in The Roman Family in Italy, edited by Beryl RAWSON and Paul WEAVER (Oxford 1997), 55–72.

Andrew WALLACE-HADRILL, 'Imaginary feasts: pictures of success on the Bay of Naples' in Journal of Roman Studies supplement 57 (2004), 109–26.

Henrik MOURITSEN, 'The album of Herculaneum and the nomenclature of Latini Iuniani' in Zeitschrift für Papyrologie und Epigraphik 161 (2007), 288–90.

Giuseppe CAMODECA, 'La populazione degli ultimi decenni di Ercolano' in Ercolano. Tre Secoli di scoperte (2008), 87–98.

## Chapter 6 The Public Face of the Town

The public buildings of Herculaneum have been the subject of prolonged and sometimes impenetrable debate. For a (not easy) overview, see:

Mario PAGANO, 'La nuova pianta della città e di alcuni edifici pubblici di Ercolano', Cronache Ercolanesi 26 (1996), 229–62.

On the theatre:

Francesco PIRANESI, Il teatro di Ercolano (Rome 1783).

Mario PAGANO, 'Il teatro di Ercolano', Cronache Ercolanesi 23 (1993), 121–56.

Alfredo BALASCO, 'L'architettura del teatro di Ercolano' in Gli Antichi Ercolanesi, 79–85.

Mario PAGANO and Alfredo BALASCO, The Ancient Theatre of Herculaneum (Naples 2000).

Agnes ALLROGGEN BEDEL, 'Il teatro' in Ercolano. Tre Secoli di scoperte, 25–32.

On the statues from the theatre:

Jens DAEHNER (ed.), The Herculaneum Women: history, context, identities (Los Angeles and Dresden 2007).

On the Area Sacra and Temple of Venus, see:

Alfredo BALASCO and Mario PAGANO, 'Indicazioni preliminari per un progetto di documentazione del tempio "della quattro divinità" dell'area acra di Ercolano', Rivista di Studi Pompeiani 15 (2004), 194–8.

Maria Paola GUIDOBALDI, 'L'area sacra suburbana' in Ercolano. Tre Secoli di scoperte, 55–8.

Giuseppe CAMODECA, 'Le iscrizioni di dedica del Tempio di Venere e delle imagines Caesarum ad opera di Vibidia Saturnina e di A. Furius Saturninus' in Ercolano. Tre Secoli di scoperte, 59–61.

On the terrace of Nonius Balbus and the Suburban baths, see:

Mario PAGANO, 'Iscrizione della statua di M. Nonio Balbo trovata davanti alle Terme Suburbane' in Rivista di Studi Pompeiani 2 (1988), 238–9.

Umberto PAPPALARDO, 'Nuove testimonianze su M.Nonio Balbo ad Ercolano' in Römische Mitteilungen 104 (1997), 285–97.

Maria Paola GUIDOBALDI, 'La terrazza di Marco Nonio Balbo' and 'Le Terme Suburbane' in Ercolano. Tre Secoli di scoperte, 63–9.

On the Basilica Noniana, see:

Agnes ALLROGGEN BEDEL, 'Das sogenannte Forum von Herculaneum und die borbonische Grabungen von 1739' in Cronache Ercolanesi 4 (1974), 97–109.

Stefania ADAMO MUSCETTOLA, 'Nuove letture borboniche. I Nonii Balbi e il Foro di Ercolano' in Prospettiva 28 (1982), 2–16.

Agnes ALLROGGEN BEDEL, 'Dokumente des 18. Jahrhunderts zur Topographie von Herkulaneum' in Cronache Ercolanesi 13 (1983), 139–58.

Mario PAGANO, 'Un ciclo di imprese di Ercole con iscrizioni greche ad Ercolano' in Römische Mitteilungen 97 (1990), 153–61.

Maria Paola GUIDOBALDI, 'Le ricerche archeologiche nell'area della Basilica Noniana (VII,16)' in Nuove Ricerche archeologiche nell'area vesuviana (2008), 410–13.

Valerie MOESCH, 'La testa femminile della Basilica Noniana' in Nuove Ricerche archeologiche nell'area vesuviana (2008), 413–5.

Agnes ALLROGGEN BEDEL, 'La Basilica Noniana' in Ercolano. Tre Secoli di scoperte 47–53.

On the 'So-called Basilica' or 'Augusteum' or 'Forum', see:

Mario TORELLI, 'La Basilica di Ercolano: una proposta di lettura' in Eidola. International Journal of Art History 1 (2004), 117–49, reprinted in Noctes Campanae. Studi in memoria di M. Frederiksen (Naples 2005), 105–40.

Mario TORELLI, 'Chalcidicum. Forma e semantica di un tipo edilizio antico' in *Ostaka* 12.2 (2003), 215–38.

Tina NAJBJERG, 'A reconstruction and reconsideration of the so-called Basilica in Herculaneum' in *Journal of Roman Archaeology* supplement 47 (Portsmouth 2002), 122–65.

Fabrizio PESANDO, 'Appunti sulla cosidetta basilica di Ercolano' in *Cronache Ercolanesi* 33 (2003), 331–7.

Agnes ALLROGGEN BEDEL, 'L'Augusteum' in *Ercolano. Tre Secoli di scoperte*, 35–45.

On the so-called 'College of the Augustales' or 'Curia', see:

Giuseppe GUADAGNO, 'Herculanensium Augustalium Aedes', *Cronache Ercolanesi* 13 (1983), 159–75.

Erich MOORMANN, 'Sulle pitture dell' Herculanensium Augustalium Aedes', *Cronache Ercolanesi* 13 (1983), 175–7.

Giuseppe GUADAGNO, 'I graffiti della Aedes Augustalium: documenti sull'accesso all'Augustalità' in *Cronache Ercolanesi* 18 (1988), 199–204.

Robert ETIENNE, 'A propos du cosidetto édifice des Augustales d'Herculanum' in *Ercolano 1738–1988* (1993), 345–9.

### Chapter 7 Standards of Living

On housing in Herculaneum, in addition to Maiuri's 1958 publication of his excavations, see:

John R. CLARKE, *The Houses of Roman Italy, 100 BC–AD 250. Ritual, Space and Decoration* (University of California 1991).

Andrew WALLACE-HADRILL, *Houses and Society in Pompeii and Herculaneum* (Princeton 1994).

Richard E.L.B. DE KIND, *Houses in Herculaneum. A New View of the Town Planning and the Building of Insulae III and IV* (Amsterdam 1998).

Fabrizio PESANDO and Maria Paola GUIDOBALDI, *Gli Ozi di Ercole. Residenze di lusso a Pompei ed Ercolano* (Rome 2006).

### Chapter 8 High Life

On the grander houses in Herculaneum, in addition to the books cited for Chapter 7, see:

Giuseppina CERULLI IRELLI, *La Casa del Colonnato Tuscanico* (Naples 1974).

Maria MANNI, *Le pitture della Casa del Colonnato Tuscanico* (Rome 1974).

Agnes ALLROGGEN BEDEL, 'Das Hausherr der "Casa dei Cervi" in Herculaneum' in *Cronache Ercolanesi* 5 (1975), 101–3.

Tran Tam TINH, *La Casa dei Cervi à Herculanum* (Rome 1988).

Giuseppina CERULLI IRELLI, *Le pitture della Casa dell'Atrio a Mosaico* (Rome 1971).

Maria Paola GUIDOBALDI, Domenico CAMARDO and Gionata RIZZI, 'L'Herculaneum Conservation Project e il progetto pilota dell'Insula Orientalis I' in *Nuove Ricerche archeologiche a Pompei ed Ercolano* (2005), 9–18.

Maria Paola GUIDOBALDI, 'La Casa del Rilievo di Telefo: considerazioni sulla storia edilizia di una *domus* aristocratica ercolanese' in *Ostraka* 15.1 (2006), 31–46.

### Chapter 9 Low Life

On Roman rental apartments, see:

Felix PIRSON, *Mietwohnungen in Pompeji und Herkulaneum. Untersuchungen zur Architektur, zum Wohnen und zur Sozial-uns Wortschaftsgeschichte der Vesuvstädte* (Munich 1999).

On commercial life, see:

Nicolas MONTEIX, 'Fouilles des de l'atelier de métallurgie du plomb (VI,12) et de la boutique VI,15 en façade de la Casa del Salone Nero à Herculanum, *Rivista di Studi Pompeiani* 16 (2005), 330–41.

Nicolas MONTEIX, 'Les boutiques et les ateliers de l'insula VI à Herculanum' in *Contributi di archeologia Vesuviana* 1 (2006).

On upper floors, see:

James N. ANDREWS, *The Use and Development of Upper Floors in Houses at Herculaneum* (University of Reading PhD thesis 2006).

On the Palaestra block and new excavations, see:

Fikret K. YEGUL, 'The Palaestra at Herculaneum as a new architectural type' in *Eius Virtutis Studiosi. Classical and Postclassical Studies in memory of F.E. Brown* (London 1993), 369–93.

Domenico CAMARDO, 'Lo scavo della fogna di Insula Orientalis II' in *Nuove ricerche archeologiche nell'area Vesuviana* (2008), 415–21.

### Chapter 10 The Tale of Two Cities

On wooden fittings from Herculaneum, see:

Tommasina BUDETTA and Mario PAGANO, *Ercolano: legni e piccoli bronzi. Testimonianze dell'arredo e delle suppellettili della casa romana*

(catalogue of exhibition at Rome, Castel sant'Angelo, 23–26 April 1988) (Rome 1988).

Stephan T.M. MOLS, *Wooden Furniture in Herculaneum. Form, Technique and Function* (Amsterdam 1999).

Stefan T.A.M. MOLS, 'Identification of the woods used in the furniture at Herculaneum' in *The Natural History of Pompeii* (2002), 225–34.

Peter I. KUNIHOLM, 'Dendrochronological investigations at Herculaneum and Pompeii' in *The Natural History of Pompeii* (2002), 235–9.

J.R. STEFFY, 'The Herculaneum boat: preliminary notes on hull construction' in *American Journal of Archaeology* 89 (1985), 519–21.

A.M. FERUCCI and Costantino MEUCCI, 'Prime osservazioni sulla barca di Ercolano: il ricupero e la costruzione navale' in *Il Restauro del Legno I*, edited by G. TAMPONE (Florence 1989), 105–12.

On the population as revealed by graffiti, see:

*CIL (Corpus Inscriptionum Latinarum)* IV, 10478–10913.

Heiki SOLIN, 'Die herkulanischen Wandinschriften: ein soziologischer Versuch' in *Cronache Ercolanesi* 3 81973), 97–103.

Giuseppe GUADAGNO, 'Supplemento epigrafico ercolanese (I)' in *Cronache Ercolanesi* 8 (1978), 132–55.

Giuseppe GUADAGNO, 'Supplemento epigrafico ercolanese (II)' in *Cronache Ercolanesi* 11 (1981), 129–64.

Mario PAGANO, 'Un'iscrizione elettorale da Ercolano' in *Cronache Ercolanesi* 17 (1987), 151–2.

Mario PAGANO, 'Semo Sancus in una insegna di bottega ad Ercolano' in *Cronache Ercolanesi* 18 (1988), 209–14.

### Chapter 11 The Future of the Past

On problems of conservation in the eighteenth century, see:

Maria Pia ROSSIGNANI, 'Saggio sui restauri settecenteschi ai dipinti di Ercolano e Pompei' in *Contributi dell'Istituto di Archeologia dell'Università Cattolica del S. Cuore*, series III, 1 (1967), 7ff.

P. D'ALCONZO, *Picturae excisae. Conservazione e restauro dei dipinti ercolanesi e pompeiani tra XVIII e XIX secolo* (Rome 2002).

Stefania ADAMO MUSCETTOLA, 'Problemi di tutela a Pompei nell'ottocento: il fallimento del progetto di esproprio murattiano' in *Pompei, Scienza e Società* (Milan 2001), 141–6.

On recent conservation problems, see:

Gionata RIZZI, *Ercolano. Capire un monumento allo stato di rudere* (Naples 2000).

Maria Paola GUIDOBALDI, 'L'Herculaneum Conservation Project: un programma di conservazione per salvare la città antica' in *Ocnus: Quaderni della Scuola di Specializzazione in Archeologia* 14 (2006) 135–42.

Andrew WALLACE-HADRILL, Domenico CAMARDO, Monica MARTELLI CASTALDI and Gionata RIZZI, 'L'Herculaneum Conservation Project' in *Oebalus* 1 (2006), 233–72.

Domenico CAMARDO, Monica MARTELLI CASTALDI and Jane THOMPSON, 'Water supply and drainage at Herculaneum' in *Cura Aquarum in Ephesus: Proceedings of the Twelfth International Congress on the History of Water Management and Hydraulic Engineering in the Mediterranean Region* (Babesch supplement 12, 2006), 183–92.

Andrew WALLACE-HADRILL, 'The Herculaneum Conservation Project: Introduction'; Jane THOMPSON, 'Conservation and management challenges in a public/private partnership for a large archaeological site (Herculaneum, Italy)';

Domenico CAMARDO, 'Archaeology and conservation at Herculaneum: from the Mairi campaign to the Herculaneum Conservation Project'; Paola PESARESI and Monica MARTELLI CASTALDI, 'Conservation measures for an archaeological site at risk (Herculaneum, Italy): from emergency to maintenance'; Paola PESARESI and Gionata RIZZI, 'New and existing forms of protective shelter at Herculaneum: towards improving the continuous care of the site', in *Conservation and Management of Archaeological Sites* 8.4 (2008), 187–252.

Maria Paola GUIDOBALDI, Andrew WALLACE-HADRILL *et al.* in Antonella CORALINI, (ed.) *Vesuviana: archeologie a confronto. Proceedings of the international conference, Bologna, 14–16 January 2008* (Bologna 2009), 199–288.

On management problems of the Superintendency of Pompeii, see:

Raffaele ORIANI, *Pompei: scene da un patrimonio* (Milan 1998).

Pier Giovanni GUZZO, 'Autonomia della Soprintendenza Archeologica di Pompei. Impostazione e strumenti' in *Pompei, Scienza e Società* (Milan 2001), 119–25 with the round table discussion at 164–80.

Pier Giovanni GUZZO, *Pompei 1998–2003. L'esperimento dell'autonomia* (Milan 2003).

On Garibaldi and Alexandre Dumas, see:

Ronald T. RIDLEY, 'Dumas père, Director of Excavations', *Pompeii Herculaneum Stabiae: Bollettino dell'Associazione Internazionale Amici di Pompei* 1 (1983), 259–88.

On the problems of the Camorra, see:

Roberto SAVIANO, *Gomorra. Italy's Other Mafia* (2007).

Raffaele CANTONE, *Solo per la Giustizia* (Milan 2008).

Gigi DI FIORE, *L'Impero. Traffici, stroie e segreti dell'occulta e potente mafia dei Casalesi* (Milan 2008).

*Marble relief depicting satyrs and a maenda from the north-western Insula I.*

# GLOSSARY

**aedile** *see* magistrate

**ala** *see* House Plan, below

**atrium** *see* House Plan, below. The central circulation space or hall of a traditional Roman house, normally with a central roof opening for light and water (*impluvium*). The entrance passage (*fauces*), normally led directly into this space. Various rooms, including smaller bedrooms (*cubicula*) and larger dining rooms (*triclinia*), may open off this space, but these always have doors. A distinctive feature of the Roman atrium is the addition of further spaces not separated by walls and doors: the 'side-wings' (*alae*) and the central reception space (*tablinum*), usually on the dominant axis.

**Augustalis** An order of dignity invented under Augustus, junior to senators and equestrians at Rome, and to decurions in provincial towns, typically granted by a decision of the local senate to rich citizens of slave origin (freedmen or *liberti*). The order appears to have had a semi-religious role in the imperial cult, but an Augustalis was not a priest of Augustus as such.

**Bourbons** The Spanish royal house (descended from the French royal family of Louis XIV) set up in 1734 to rule South Italy, known as the Kingdom of the Two Sicilies, and finally defeated by Garibaldi in 1860. In succession, the kings were Charles, son of Philip V of Spain, 1734–59 (later king Charles III of Spain), his son Ferdinand I (1759–1825), briefly deposed by the 'Parthenopean republic' of 1799, and then by Napoleon's brother, Joseph, 1801–8, followed by his brother-in-law Murat, (1808–15); Ferdinand's son Francis I (1825–30); his son, Ferdinand II (1830–59), known as 'King Bomba' for his bombardment of Messina; and his son Francis II (1859–60), forced to leave Naples on 6 September before Garibaldi entered the city on 7 September.

**bradyseism** The 'slow quaking' (Greek *bradys* = 'slow') caused by the movement upwards and downwards of the earth's crust in a volcanic area. This process, still visible today at Pozzuoli, may take place almost imperceptibly over decades.

**cardo** (plural: *cardines*) One of the relatively narrow 'vertical' streets that cut across the broader avenues or decumani in a Roman city. The literal meaning of the word is 'hinge'.

**Colonia** *see* magistrates

**consul** *see* magistrates

**cunicoli** An Italian term based on the Latin for 'rabbit holes' (*cunicula*) to describe the 'rabbit warren' of tunnels made by the early explorers of Herculaneum.

**decumani** The broader avenues that cut 'horizontally' across a Roman city. The main road is called the Decumanus Maximus.

**Decurio** *see* magistrates

**dolium** A large ceramic container or vat, used to store wine and other food products.

**domus** A residential building in a city, contrasted to the 'villa' in the country, but also to the multiple occupancy block in the city (*insula*).

**duumvir** *see* magistrates

**equestrian** An official order of dignity at Rome, junior to that of senator. The name derives from the older practice of awarding a horse for military and parade purposes to people of this rank.

**fundus** An agricultural estate.

**insula** Literally, 'island'. The term used by modern archaeologists to describe an urban block, normally described by four roads. The ancient term, rather confusingly, was applied to a block of property under a single owner, which could consist of several adjoining houses and shops, or as in the case of the property by the Palaestra, a complex of shops and apartments.

**lapilli** Small pebbles of pumice, produced by the expulsion of material by the eruptive column of a volcano into the upper atmosphere. This characteristically covered Pompeii in the early hours of the eruption of AD 79, but not Herculaneum.

**magistrates** Roman cities were administered by officers called magistrates, annually elected by the citizens from among the better-off citizens, with a mixture of judicial and executive functions. At Rome the two senior magistrates were the consuls; junior to them were praetors, aediles and quaestors. An exceptional magistracy was that of the ten tribunes, who championed the rights of the citizen body, and rather than enjoying active powers, served to intervene and block the actions of other magistrates in the interests of the people. The senate was composed of magistrates and ex-magistrates. In provincial towns, whether *coloniae* (colonies of Roman citizens) or *municipia* (self-governing townships), the local senate or curia was composed of 'decurions'. The senior magistrates were called *duumviri*, the junior ones aediles.

**municipium** *see* magistrates

**negotium** The Latin term for 'business', literally the negation of *otium*, or leisure. Traders and businessmen were called *negotiatores*.

**opus craticium** As described by the architect Vitruvius, this is a type of flimsy construction, perhaps like the English 'wattle and daub', making use of 'crates' or wattles. Taken by Amedeo Maiuri to apply to the House of Wattlework (a Graticcio), which is however of timber and rubble construction.

**opus reticulatum** A building technique in which an outer skin of regular blocks or 'teeth' is laid in a network pattern. The outer skins contain an inner core of concrete.

**opus sectile** Flooring made of different coloured marbles, cut into a variety of geometric patterns.

**opus signinum** The modern name for a style of flooring based on crushed pottery or brick and mortar, usually with a decorative pattern of white marble chips. The name is based on an apparent misinterpretation of a passage of the architect Vitruvius.

**otium** *see negotium*: the leisure that the Romans contrasted with business.

**peristyle** (Latin: *peristylium*) *see* House Plan. An open area in a house or villa surrounded by colonnades or porticos, and typically containing a decorative garden, sometimes with fountains and sculptures.

**plateiai** The broad, 'horizontal ' avenues of A Greek city, corresponding to the Latin *decumani*.

**portico** (Latin: *porticus*) Literally, 'porch'. A roofed walkway with a wall on one side and columns on the other. These may occur either singly, along the edges of buildings, or in a rectangle as a peristyle or cloister. The Latin *porticus* was often applied to public buildings with colonnaded walkways on four sides, whereas the same form in a house was called a *peristylium*.

**praetor** *see* magistrates.

**pyroclastic surge/flow** A burning cloud of hot gas, at temperatures up to 500°C, dense with ash, and travelling down the sides of a volcano at speeds up to 100kph, followed by 'flows' at lower speed but with more dense debris inclusions. Pyroclastic surges take place in a secondary stage of an eruption when the force of the eruption diminishes and the eruptive column collapses. The cooled and consolidated debris becomes the rock known as 'tufo' or 'tuff'.

**stenopoi** The narrow, 'vertical' streets of a Greek city, corresponding to the Latin *cardines*.

**styles of decoration.** Traditionally, Pompeian decoration is categorized as belonging to four, chronologically sequenced, styles. The First Style, typical of the second century BC, imitates coloured marble panels. The Second Style, typical of the middle two quarters of the first century BC, imitates architectural structures articulated by columns. The Third Style, typical of the last quarter of the first century BC and the first quarter of the first century AD, reduces columnar divisions to delicate decorations, sometimes as candelabra or plants, while elaborate scenes dominate the central panels. The Fourth Style, of the middle two quarters of the first century AD, develops more complex architectural vistas as dividing elements, and surrounds panels with 'tapestry' borders. Only the last two styles are commonly met in Herculaneum, and often they appear to overlap.

**tablinum** *see* atrium.

**tribune** *see* magistrates.

**tufo (tuff)** The soft, volcanic stone formed by the precipitation of ash and pumice in an eruption. Of various degrees of hardness, it was much used as a building material in antiquity.

**villa** In Latin, any residential building in the country, including a farmhouse, as opposed to the *domus* in the city. Modern scholars, influenced by the modern meaning of villa, tend to apply it only to luxurious residences. Some city buildings resembled villas because of their size and open space, but these should be called *domus*.

# CHRONOLOGY

## BC

**20,000–6,000** A series of major eruptions transforms the landscape of the Bay of Naples

*c.***1700** Major eruption of Vesuvius ('pumice of Avellino') destroys Bronze Age villages

*c.***750** First Greek colonists arrive on Bay of Naples

*c.***700** First traces of continuous settlement of Pompeii

*c.***650–474** Etruscans dominate much of Campania

*c.***470** Greek colony of Neapolis (Naples) founded

**338** Cities of Campania become subject allies of Rome

*c.***300** Earliest traces of regular settlement at Herculaneum

**211** Romans recover Capua from Hannibal, take over Campanian plain

**194** Roman colony founded at Puteoli (Pozzuoli), becomes major port

**91–89** The Social War: many of Rome's Italian allies, including Pompeii and Herculaneum, rebel

**89** Pompeii and Herculaneum besieged and captured by Roman armies. Latin replaces Oscan as official language of the cities.

**80** Pompeii becomes a Roman colony; Herculaneum remains a municipium

**43–31** Civil Wars follow assassination of Caesar

**32** Mark Antony denounces old ally Octavian (the future Augustus). Marcus Nonius Balbus as tribune defends Octavian in the Senate

**31** Battle of Actium. Octavian (Augustus) defeats Antony and Cleopatra and starts sole rule of empire

## AD

**14** Death of Augustus, succeeded as emperor by:

**14–37** Tiberius

**37–41** Gaius (Caligula)

**41–54** Claudius

**54–68** Nero

**62 or 63\*** Earthquake causes major damage to Pompeii and Herculaneum

**68–9** Civil War: Galba, Otho and Vitellius emperors in quick succession

**69–79** Vespasian establishes a new dynasty, with his sons Titus and Domitian

**79–81** Titus emperor

**79\*** Eruption of Vesuvius (traditional date 24 August, but maybe in autumn)

**472** Minor eruption of Vesuvius

**1596** Architect Domenico Fontana digs canal through Pompeii, discovery not reported

**1631** Minor eruption of Vesuvius

**1709** The Prince d'Elbeuf builds a palace at Portici and starts excavations in the theatre of Herculaneum

**1734** Charles Bourbon becomes King of the Two Sicilies

**1736** Work starts on the Royal Palace at Portici

**1738** Official start of excavations at Herculaneum by Alcubierre

**1741–5** Major public buildings excavated by Bardet

**1750** Excavation starts of the Villa of the Papyri by Weber

**1759** Charles becomes king of Spain, succeeded by his son Ferdinand

**1762** J.J. Winckelmann publishes letter attacking Bourbon excavations

**1764–1800** Sir William Hamilton envoy plenipotentiary to the court of Naples

**1801–15** French occupation of Naples

**1815–60** Naples restored to the Bourbons

**1828–37** First open-air excavations of Herculaneum

**1860** Garibaldi takes Naples from Francis II

**1861–75** Giuseppe Fiorelli directs excavations in Pompeii

**1869–75** Fiorelli reopens excavations in Herculaneum

**1907** Sir Charles Waldstein's appeal for an international excavation of Herculaneum is blocked

**1921–43** Fascist government of Mussolini

**1924–61** Amedeo Maiuri Superintendent of archaeology in the Naples area

**1927** Maiuri relaunches excavation of Herculaneum

**1980–2** Excavations by Giuseppe Maggi of the ancient shore of Herculaneum

**1995–2009** Piero Guzzo Superintendent of Pompeii, latterly also Naples

**1996–9** Excavation by Antonio de Simone of the strip leading to the Villa of the Papyri

**2001** The Packard Humanities Institute launches project to conserve Herculaneum

\*These are two chronological puzzles. Both the eruption of Vesuvius and the great earthquake that preceded it are normally dated to the day: 5 February 62 for the earthquake and 24 August 79 for the eruption. Both seemingly precise dates are, alas, much disputed. The earthquake is dated by the surviving text of Seneca to 63; the later historian Tacitus dates it instead to 62. There are arguments for and against both dates, and certainty is impossible. Similarly, the current editions of Pliny's letter gives the date of 24 August for the eruption. But that is the version of only some manuscripts, while others give alternatives, and the later historian Cassius Dio says it took place in the late autumn. Some botanical evidence, including a pile of ripe pomegranates, is said to support the later date; again, certainty is impossible.

# INDEX

Illustrations indicated in *italics*
Main entries indicated in **bold**

# ACKNOWLEDGMENTS

The Italian State, through the Soprintendenza Speciale per i Beni Archeologici di Napoli e Pompei (SANP), exercises copyright over all images generated on site in Herculaneum or in its collections at Herculaneum and Naples. All such photographic images are published with the kind permission of SANP. The majority of the images in this book were generated in the course of the Herculaneum Conservation Project, a joint Initiative of the Packard Humanities Institute, SANP, and the British School at Rome (BSR), under the terms of the sponsorship agreement between SANP and BSR. The individual authorship of these images is as follows:

**Massimo Brizzi/Akhet** 21, 39, 46, 253, 257 and foldout plan at back

**Domenico Camardo-Sosandra Srl** 19 right, above and below, 20 left, 34 left top & middle, 45, 46, 53 top, 66 above, 105 below, 144, 169 above, 194, 195 below, 275, 282, 283 below right, 284 left below

**Aldo Cinque,** 24, 105 above

**Kate Cook–Firefly Productions** 50, 112–13, 150

**Sarah Court** 196

**Brian Donovan** 2–3, 4–5, 6, 11, 12–13, 27–30, 42–3, 67–70, 82, 83, 90–1, 94–5, 96–7, 98–9, 100–1, 102 below, 107–10, 116–17, 120–1, 122, 147–50, 160–1, 180 above, 181, 187–90, 200, 201, 204, 205, 206–7, 214 above, 215, 217 above, 227, 228–31, 234–5, 238–9, 241, 250–1, 252, 260–1, 262, 263, 264 below, 265 above, 266 below, 267–70. 271, 286, 289–90, 307–10, 312, 316, 320, 321, 334–5, 336–7, 338–9; and in addition the house plans on 202, 204 below, 206, 211, 216, 218, 224, 226, 237, 240, 244, 262, 263, and 345

**Domenico Esposito-Sosandra Srl,** 118, 119, 165

**Riccardo Giordano** 195 above, 197

**Linda Irollo-Sosandra Srl** 104

**Monica Martelli Castaldi** 311 below right, 312 top, middle left and below, 313 left above and below, 326 top, middle and bottom left

**Paola Pesaresi** 195 below

**Amy Richardson** (drawings) 15, 31 below, 93, 128, 129, 157

**Gionata Rizzi** 319, 74 (drawing)

**Mark Robinson** 284 below, 285 top left and right

**Jane Thompson** 44, 87, 232, 323

**Andrew Wallace-Hadrill** 8, 14, 19 all, 21 above right, 22, 23, 26, 31 above, 32–3, 34 below, 36–7, 40, 53 below, 54, 66 below, 86, 87 above and below left, 88, 92, 102 above, 103, 106, 111, 131, 132 above, 138, 140–1, 152, 153, 154, 155 above, 162–3, 164–5, 166, 167, 168, 169 below, 170–1, 172, 174–5, 175, 176–7, 178–9, 186, 193, 198, 203, 208–9, 212 below, 217 below, 220–1, 222, 224 below, 225, 232, 237 left, 240 below, 245, 246, 247, 248, 249, 254–5, 256, 258–9, 261 below, 266 above, 272 below, 274 above, 277 top right, 281, 283 left and top right, 284 above left, 285 right middle and below, 287, 293 below, 294 right middle and below, 298, 305, 306, 310, 311 below left, 313 right, 324, 325, 326 right, 328, 333, 344, 352

The following images were generated outside the scope of the Herculaneum Conservation Project and are reproduced with the permission of SANP:

**SANP Photo Archive at Pompeii** 1, 35, 60–1, 64, 73, 75, 76, 77, 80 above, 81, 84 above, 119 above, 126, 127, 132 below, 177 left, 180 below, 211, 216 below, 219, 243, 272 right above, 277 middle right and below left, 278 below, 279, 314–15, 315, 330, 331, 332

**Museo Nazionale di Napoli** 137, 145, 173, 182, 184, 192, 296

**Studio Fotografico Foglia** 158–9, 233, 236 left, 237 below right, 242, 291, 294 above left, 299, 300, 301

**O. Louis Mazzatenta /National Geographic Stock** 123, 124

**Luciano Pedicini fotografo/archivio dell'arte** 78–9, 114, 134, 135, 136, 177 right, 183, 185, 212 above left and right, 213, 218 right, 244 below, 265 below, 284 right, 293 above left and right, 295, 303, 348

The following drawings are reproduced from Amedeo Maiuri, Ercolano. I nuovi scavi (1927–58) with the permission of the Istituto Poligrafico dello Stato: 58, 80, 85, 156, 187, 264, 272, 273, 274, 276, 277, 280

All remaining images are believed to be outside copyright and every effort has been made to trace their authors.